The Crisis
of Capitalism i
Contemporary

CW01623519

The Crisis of Capitalism in the Contemporary Novel

ANDREW ROWCROFT

McFarland & Company, Inc., Publishers
Jefferson, North Carolina

This book has undergone peer review.

Permissions: Some parts of this work have appeared previously in different publications. Parts of the introduction are taken from my editorship of a special issue journal with the Open Library of the Humanities. A version of Chapter 2, on China Miéville, has appeared in *Gothic Studies*. Chapter 4, on Thomas Pynchon, is partly derived from an article published in *Textual Practice*. My thanks to the editors and peer reviewers for their generous feedback.

ISBN (print) 978-1-4766-9226-5
ISBN (ebook) 978-1-4766-5217-7

LIBRARY OF CONGRESS AND BRITISH LIBRARY
CATALOGUING DATA ARE AVAILABLE

© 2024 Andrew Rowcroft. All rights reserved

No part of this book may be reproduced or transmitted in any form or by any means, electronic or mechanical, including photocopying or recording, or by any information storage and retrieval system, without permission in writing from the publisher.

Front cover image: © fran_kie/Shutterstock

Printed in the United States of America

McFarland & Company, Inc., Publishers
Box 611, Jefferson, North Carolina 28640
www.mcfarlandpub.com

Abstract

The book explores the role of radical ideas in contemporary fiction. It reads the selected works of nine critically acclaimed authors—Jonathan Lethem, Dana Spiotta, China Miéville, Thomas Pynchon, Rachel Kushner, Teddy Wayne, Colson Whitehead, Jacqueline Woodson, and Kim Stanley Robinson—all of whom share interests in left politics, the problems of protracted economic crisis, and the potentiality of post-capitalist ideas. Novels by these authors, this book argues, are defined by an imperative to confront current anxieties in left thought, while, at the same time, evidencing a nuanced degree of self-consciousness about the legacy of political radicalisms, the costs they accrue, and where they have led. *The Crisis of Capitalism in the Contemporary Novel* explores the entanglement of fictional form and political commitment, revealing the left tradition to be of immense importance in contemporary literary culture.

Acknowledgments

This book began as a doctoral dissertation in English Literature, under the supervision of Siân Adiseshiah, Ruth Charnock, and Martin Eve, at the University of Lincoln in the United Kingdom. I thank them all for their patience, guidance, and kind words. I am grateful to my colleagues in the English department at Lincoln, who have given their time, that most precious of resources, to assist me in diverse ways. My thanks to Lucie Armitt, Scott Brewster, Owen Clayton, Christopher Marlow, and Jason Whittaker. The following bodies generously provided grants, bursaries, and research awards: Santander Universities; University of Lincoln Doctoral School; Institute of Advanced Study, Lincoln; Lincoln Research Resource Allocation Fund; Amiel & Melburn Trust; British Association of American Studies; British Association of Contemporary Literary Studies. All the participants of the Reading Capital seminars, held at Lincoln from 2014 to 2016, offered perspectives crucial to my doctoral work as it was intensely revised. The University also assisted with funding for a conference, *What's Left? Marx, Literature, Culture*, in 2016, and I am grateful for the excellent keynotes given by Paul Crosthwaite and Stuart Sim. Parts of this work were presented at various conferences and my thanks to those who attended and asked questions.

Eastgate Tennis Club has afforded many pleasures over the years. My thanks to Simon, Julia, Maurice, Diletta, Nick, Matt, Jono, Paul, Henry, Ben, and Dom. *Infinite Jest* instilled this addiction (for tennis!), and I have no wish for a cure. For conversation, country walks, snooker, chess, badminton, and beer, my thanks to David.

John F. Davies is a close friend and critic. My conversations on literature and criticism with John, at Cambridge, Oxford, and Lincoln, are among the most pleasurable and rewarding discussions of the craft I have ever had.

Finally, my thanks to McFarland for working on the manuscript and the peer reviewers for taking the time to read it and offering suggestions and feedback.

Table of Contents

Preface

In 2008 I was studying English Literature at Newcastle University. That same year marked the beginning of the Great Recession and the near annihilation of the world's financial system. The origins lay in a government backed effort to boost homeownership levels in the U.S. among low-income workers. But poor public regulation and near absent policy oversight allowed a crisis to develop. Banks had sought to secure subprime risk through securitization, a process that mixed mortgages into bundles which were then turned into tranches and dispersed across a vast global base of investors. Making mortgages cheap fueled demand and many of these loans were given to families unable to cope with the repayments. This combination of predatory lending to low-income homebuyers and fantasy valuations by securities' ratings agencies resulted in a housing bubble. In September 2007, the British bank Northern Rock failed, and others quickly followed. Along with others in the UK, I watched the most spectacular symbol of this unfolding: the bankruptcy of Lehman brothers. Employees filed out of the bank's London premises, clutching their cardboard boxes of possessions. Even then, it was clear this was a major moment in a newly formed global economic crisis.

Unsurprisingly, the relationships among literature, economics, and political protest took center stage. But this has long been true for Marxist critics, who argue we cannot discuss culture without capitalism. Such an approach resides in a resolute effort to situate literary production within a historical perspective driven by dynamics in the mode of production. I would not claim the contemporary to be more challenging than any other period, but there is a strong sense—purely by living in it—in which each singular event is rapidly overtaken by a more pressing concern. (In *A Sense of an Ending*, by the British author Julian Barnes, a schoolboy remarks to his history teacher that each age is one of great unrest.) The 2008 global financial crisis initiated mass bailouts of the banking system, which led to the selection of austerity measures in Europe and the UK. The cuts to public services generated resentments, privations, and hardships, resulting in the roaring return of the political right after some decades silence. This anger was channeled into ethno-populist hatreds which drove through Britain's departure from the EU, or Brexit, and allowed the election of Donald Trump in the U.S. These political developments were intensified by the Covid-19 pandemic, excess deaths, and national lockdown measures, whose consequences for education, health, and perceptions of government (in)efficiency are still unfolding. This was followed by a new geopolitical and security crisis, one that had been bubbling in the background for some time, with Russia's invasion of Ukraine, soaring inflation rates, soaring energy prices, and a "cost of living" crisis necessitating government support.

This book represents many years of research and reflection on these debates. The *What Happens Now* Conferences at Lincoln, in 2014 and 2016, and Loughborough in 2019, exposed the breadth and depth of contemporary literary studies. I was privileged to perform a small role in BACLS, as an elected member, while still a doctoral student. The work of Fredric Jameson has been instrumental in developing my research, while studies by Peter Boxall, Nancy Fraser, Nicholas Brown, Gregory Claey, Barbara Foley, and Paul Crosthwaite have proved immensely influential. My book departs from previous scholarly efforts in examining an array of authors in the left tradition who remain acutely conscious—even conflicted—about the nature of such political commitment. *The Crisis of Capitalism in the Contemporary Novel* charts a constellation of politically committed texts that give a comprehensive coverage to the vast array of crisis formations in the present—political, financial, and ecological.

Introduction

From the perspective of the third decade, the twenty-first century has been marked by the emergence of a more menacing capitalism. In the West, governments and politicians continue to cling to a discredited free-market logic, promoting profit and rescinding the political gains of the twentieth century through the reduction of employee rights, assaults on pay, and the privatization of the welfare state.[1] The 2008 global financial crisis, which saw the collapse of banks, and the loss of hundreds of homes and jobs, necessitated the injection of billions of U.S. dollars into the world economy, a move that socialized costs and privatized profits.[2] Post-crash political mobilization saw the rollout of austerity measures by European governments, which cut welfare programs, public services, and sharpened class inequality.[3] The anger and violence of austerity was channeled into Britain's exit from the European Union, or Brexit, which, regardless of the validity of the departure, powerfully displaced class antagonism into ethno-populist hatreds which shattered the post-war promise of a common European sphere, bound together by reasoned deliberation and shared interest.[4] In the U.S., in particular, neoliberalism has intensified state violence with the expansion of the prison system, increased incarceration rates, aggressive state policing against non-white citizens, the continued waging of the war on drugs, and a prolonged housing crisis where homes are an unattainable asset class rather than a social good.[5] The troubling impact of digital technologies has been all too apparent in their influence operations, which have outsourced the labor of data extraction to users while affecting electoral turnout and damaging public trust in politics.[6] Rising global temperatures and ecological issues have been met with largely stalled political responses, with the U.S. only recently returning to international accords, at a moment when the next few decades will decide whether humans will continue to survive on Earth.[7] In 2019, the outbreak of the Coronavirus shut down daily life in China, India, Europe, and the U.S. Despite the immense contributions of public sector workers, the pandemic exposed the fragility of underfunded healthcare systems, crashed economies reliant on precarious work, and is on course to create another recession.

The "return" of capitalism in the contemporary has recalibrated the cultural visibility of economic, ecological, and political crisis. As Nancy Fraser argues, this moment can be welcomed, only insofar as after many "decades in which [capitalism] could scarcely be found outside the writings of Marxian thinkers, commentators of varying stripes now worry openly about its sustainability" and scholars "scramble to systematize criticisms of it" while "activists throughout the world mobilize in opposition to its practices."[8] For Fraser, current talk marks a "growing intuition that the heterogeneous ills" that surround us "can be traced to a common root," meaning political "reforms which fail to engage with the deep structural underpinnings of these ills are doomed to fail."[9] As Fraser argues, what has emerged in recent years is a renewed form of crisis critique that takes seriously questions about the relationship between the structures of our capitalist system and the requirement to secure more equitable forms of social and political organization. It is increasingly clear that without radical reforms in our economic infrastructure, crisis remains inevitable.[10]

If the contemporary is distinguished by a political and economic transparency, this has led many thinkers to call for more moderate, anti–Marxist practices which favor surface, symmetry, and restraint, the implication being that a hermeneutics of suspicion is superfluous when political figures take no pains to veil their statements or the consequences of their actions. As Bruno Latour queries, in a popular essay: "While we spent years trying to detect the real prejudices hidden behind the appearance of objective statements, do we now have to reveal the real objective and incontrovertible facts hidden behind the illusion of prejudices?"[11] For critics including Stephen Best and Sharon Marcus, we can dispense with the shared inheritance of our critical armature (that is, qua Fredric Jameson, an insistence on a "repressed, mystified, latent meaning behind a manifest one") because truth "appears there for the taking."[12] We might read these operations as a kind of interpretation in advance, in which the ingenuity of dialectical thinking is substituted for schematizations which mistake ethical virtues (the humbleness, self-effacement, and restraint of the critic) for critical positions on literary texts. Most importantly, surface reading cannot comment on the conditions of its own existence or its conceptual instruments; indeed, the guiding premise for these thinkers is that texts provide the most accurate description of their own operations; as one critic remarked: to venture depth would compromise its credentials.[13] Fredric Jameson, an important presence in this book, offers a corrective to such approaches, arguing that the "conviction that there are areas of life, areas of activity as well as of thought, which are nonideological" is "an illusion most easily entertained in moments of historical stasis, or at least in places in which ideological or class struggle seems to have been contained or reduced to manageable proportions."[14] In contrast to anti-theoretical thinkers, Jameson suggests that it is precisely at such moments that Marxism is most required.[15]

I will examine the questioning of ideology critique and suspicious reading practices in a moment, but it is my conviction that despite the negative externalities of capitalism sketched at this book's outset, and the emergence of anti-theoretical approaches that are interesting and insufficient, criticism and critique are in a healthy state: alive, vibrant, and driven. In her survey of theory, past and present, Anna Kornbluh writes about the rich "intellectual affinities of then and now": the "past churning with those numerous terrors offered in its present passionate, systematic, outrageous mediations, and synthetic, projective elaborations of alternatives. Utopia. Socialism [...] Communism. Theory itself."[16] Ranging across this historical array of potential futures, she singles out Marx's break with philosophy, which since Althusser, has been commonly situated with the moment of *Capital*:

> Theory materializes from philosophy presented to itself, its relational connections avowed, its social position charted. Reflections on these environments and situations allow theory to encompass the social fact that "the ideas of the ruling class are in every epoch the ruling ideas: i.e., the class which is the ruling material force of society is at the same time its ruling intellectual force." [...] taking present social situatedness as the ultimate condition, theory looks around at the present of thought, shows the investments and limits of ruling ideas, and at the same time it shows that better ideas (and their attendant better rules) are attainable.[17]

Marx's inventiveness, his probing of the gaps and omissions of economic thought, the turning of such thought against itself, and his ability to construct critical insights, makes his analysis of capital indispensable in the present.

Marx's work transcends the partial approaches of other efforts, such as *laissez-faire* liberalism, to grasp capitalism as a social relation, grounded in a mode of production, with dynamics, tendencies, contradictions, and conflicts.[18] In *Capital*, volume 1 (1867), Marx embarks on a critique of political economy, exposing the limitations of bourgeois economics which deal in sectional analysis and individual phenomena in isolation.[19] In the *Grundrisse* (1857–58, [1939]), a series of notebooks he never published, Marx argues that such approaches belonged "among the unimaginative conceits of the eighteenth-century Robinsonades" who could not see that each "individual's production is dependent on the production [and consumption] of all others."[20] Political economists liked to begin with the supposedly "natural" state of humanity, which they strangely imagined to be Robinson Crusoe, the central character of Daniel Defoe's novel, who is shipwrecked on an island.[21] But, as an isolated individual, Crusoe does not represent the real condition of society.[22] For Marx, it is by thinking in terms of fundamental processes, rather than isolated fragments, that we see not "the chaotic conception of a whole, but a rich totality of many determinations and relations."[23] Drawing upon concepts and categories developed by G.F.W. Hegel, Marx grasped the primacy of the economic and set out to give a picture of capitalist totality, to represent a system of relationships ever in dynamic expansion and perpetual breakdown.[24] Marx offers not only the tools to comprehend the contemporary, but actively seeks to work through the contradictions of capitalism to create more equitable forms of social organization: the society of associated producers. In the twenty first century, a Marx freed from the travesties of political orthodoxy is being discovered.

The Marx Revival[25]

This book consciously situates itself within the current scholarly revival of Marx and Marxist intellectual culture in the twenty-first century. As I have intimated, the reversal of Marx's theoretical fortunes is due, in part, to a renewed interest in capitalist economy emerging in the 2008 crisis. A travestied subject during the Cold War, in 2009 *Time* magazine published a front-page article on Marx in the February edition, asking what the philosopher would say about our economic predicament.[26] In Europe and the U.S., *Capital* once again became a focus of attention, forcing many commentators to contend that, while Marx "was perhaps wrong on communism, he was perhaps right about capitalism."[27] While much of this media attention was "predictably trite," the sudden interest in Marx was useful for drawing attention to capitalism's tendency towards crisis and overproduction.[28] Alongside this interest, a number of important anniversaries occurred, in rapid succession: *Capital* reached its 150th year in September 2017; the *Communist Manifesto* attained its 170th anniversary in February 2018, and May 2018 was Marx's 200th birthday. Further celebrations came with the 100th year anniversary of the "October 1917" Russian Revolution, captured in a narrative history by the British novelist China Miéville, while 2018 marked fifty years since the Paris événements of May 1968.[29] Such convergences offered a unique critical opportunity to discuss the developments and demands of Marxist critique in the twenty-first century. Scholarly engagements with Marx's work came in the form of new companions to *Capital* by Jameson, David Harvey,

Alex Callinicos, Ben Fine and Alfredo Saad-Filho, and Slavoj Žižek, Frank Ruda, and Agon Hamza.[30] In addition, new intellectual biographies of Marx written by Jonathan Sperber, Gareth Steadman Jones, and Sven-Eric Liedman provided fresh and exciting encounters with the philosopher's life and works.[31] Overdue assessments of neglected figures in the Marx household, such as his daughter, the writer, radical, and feminist Eleanor Marx, came in the form of examinations by Rachel Holmes, Mary Gabriel, and a new single volume edition of Yvonne Kapp's monumental study.[32] Terry Eagleton has provided a powerful defense of Marx by showing the most common objections are grounded in woeful readings of his work, while Gregory Claeys has pulled Marx back from "metaphysical schemas" to reveal his achievements, mistakes, and oversights.[33] David Harvey has completed a free online course to *Capital* and the *Grundrisse*, a podcast called the "Anti-capitalist Chronicles," and a companion to Marx's most important text.[34] In Europe and the U.S., Marx@200 events reflected on his relevance for the present. An accompanying website features a blog, a media library containing interviews with key figures, and a variety of useful articles.[35] The success of popular guides and graphic novels, such as Rupert Woodfin's *Marxism: A Graphic Guide* (2018), Martin Rowson's *The Communist Manifesto* (2018), David N. Smith's *Marx's Capital: An Illustrated Introduction* (2014), and Kate Evans' *Red Rosa* (2015), suggest struggles against economic domination, gender inequality, and ecological devastation are all part of a common horizon.[36] Raoul Peck's 2018 film, *The Young Karl Marx*, first screened at the Berlin Film Festival and starring August Diehl and Stefan Konarske, depicted the early efforts of the philosophers and revolutionaries to end the oppression of workers and create a new political movement. The contributions of these nineteenth-century thinkers and this intellectual tradition are increasingly discussed in podcasts across multiple languages, ranging from the University of Oxford's *In Our Time* series to *Red Library: A Political Education Podcast for Today's Left*. Such convergences reveal that Marx's work is not an obsolete remnant of the past, but a true contemporary of the present.

Marx never proposed a single, universal route for capitalism to develop, nor was he teleological or Eurocentric. As Kevin B. Anderson argues, if Marx's response to the failure of European revolutions "narrowed his horizons somewhat, his relocation to London widened them in other ways. It placed Marx at the center of the world's only truly industrial capitalist economy [and] the center of the world's largest empire, which led him to take greater account of non–Western societies and colonialism."[37] I will examine this more carefully in Chapter 6, but Marx's descriptions of capitalism make clear, as Jameson has himself argued, that "each national trajectory—including the central illustration, and the oldest one, of British capitalism as such—is uniquely overdetermined by the empirical specificities of the national cultural and historical situation [...] although in the abstraction there exists an inescapable and irreversible dynamic of the development of capitalism [...] there is no basic historical paradigm, all the paths of capitalist development are unique and unrepeatable."[38] As a thinker, Marx was acutely aware of the many paths upon which capital could develop, and his manuscripts and workbooks demonstrate a restless figure always looking to incorporate the latest intellectual insights.

In recent years, critics have attended to the representational dilemmas posed in *Capital* as much as the political arguments that the book makes.[39] As one of the signature "achievements of the realist impulse" Marx's *Capital* was made possible by extensive research in the Reading Room of the British Library, the *Blue Books*, and the "existence of a set of bureaucratic institutions devoted to the production and dissemination of knowledge."[40] The collection, classification, and cataloguing of modernity by those working in new national and corporate bureaucracies formed the "raw material"—an "epistemo-politcal" basis—upon which was built the work of nineteenth-century writers.[41] "I desire it to be understood," wrote the novelist, Elizabeth Stuart Phelps:

> that every alarming sign and painful statement which I have given in these pages concerning the condition of the manufacturing districts could be matched with far more pungent perplexities from the pages of the Reports of the Massachusetts Bureau of Statistics of Labor.[42]

Phelps borrows prestige here, showing how fictional form was reliant upon economic fact.[43] But the empirical, official descriptions of workers lacked moral urgency, forcing Phelps and others to forge a "new, social instrumentality" to comprehend class difference and confront the newly emerging threat to social order posed by the labor politics of the working class, as she did in her novel, *The Silent Partner* (1871).[44]

But beware, thought Marx, the seemingly disinterested nature of professional expertise. Economic reports and labor statistics reify the worker in the same manner as industrial capitalism, treating them as an ostensible object of study. At the same time, literary figurations can reflect and represent dominant ideological positions and class interests, as the Christian pieties of Phelp's novel are thought to ameliorate the material conditions of factory operatives. In her account of nineteenth-century literature and literary form, Kornbluh rejects the staples of referentially, social documentation, and Auerbachian mimesis, to argue for realism as a critical exercise in modelling, where "form [is] the construction of possible relations" affording "liberation from the actual."[45] Modelling, not representation or referential capture, is key here; realism, she argues "queries the possible, and thus incites thinking and building more utopically than utopian fiction's normativity."[46] Realism, as *Capital* shows, was not the recording of arid facts, but the mobilization of multiple vocabularies (spectral, gothic, fantastic) to account for those realities "inaccessible to realist representation."[47] Not only does *Capital* move through multiple registers and genres, it passes through prohibited boundaries, with its narrator beckoning the reader to leave "this noisy sphere, where everything takes place on the surface and in full view of everyone, and follow them [the capitalist] into the hidden abode [...] on whose threshold there hangs the notice 'No admittance, except on business.'"[48] Marx's critique operates in defiance of prescribed spatial, temporal, and linguistic boundaries.

As numerous critics have observed, the novel is the literary form most closely tied to the rise and development of capitalism, and is, in Jameson's words "as much a component of modernization as the importation of automobiles."[49] Nicholas Brown complicates this dual emergence (of capital and novel) by adding a third: the dialectic; "literature in the modern sense and the dialectic were born in the same place, at the same time with the Jena school romantics."[50] For Brown, this triptych makes the "forms of attention required by literary analysis [...] particularly congenial to Marxism," which frames urgent questions for the study of form and confronts contradictions internal to capitalism.[51] While narrative fiction continues to capture the transformations of capital, in turns registering, probing, and challenging new global realities, the last forty years have witnessed the emergence of structural developments that have produced a new economic rationality based on finance, governance, and the changing role of labor. These socio-economic realities have necessitated new reading and interpretative practices sensitive to the structures of imbrication between neoliberal capital and novel form, and indeed the questioning of literature's once privileged role.[52]

American Studies, Neoliberalism, and the World System

Clear boundaries between American studies and world literature are difficult to sustain. Many efforts place literature within a singular, varied, global capitalism, establishing methodological norms and interdisciplinary practices sensitive to the emergence of "a radically uneven world-system; a singular modernity, combined and uneven."[53] Yet if recent scholarship has challenged the exceptionalism of the nation as a viable optic or model for understanding world literature, it has also continued to insist on the ways in which national localisms must be read alongside structural globalisms. As Alison Shonkwiler argues, "even the most locally focused text, however bound up in the particularities of [specific] cultures and subjects, presses the novel in outward, less nationally definable directions."[54] Understanding American cultural production as embedded in new global networks of reciprocity and exchange, complicating the ideologies of isolation or exceptionalism that have sustained the discipline since its formation, is no longer an optional extra but a core component of the parameters and possibilities of textual criticism. Wai-chee Dimmock has sought new global mappings for American literature through a richly termed exoticism, proposing "a larger, looser set of coordinates, populated by laboring bodies, migrating faiths, generational sagas, [...] the accents of unforgotten tongues, the tastes and smells of beloved foods and spices."[55] Liam Kennedy and Stephen Shapiro argue that American literature "must always be understood constitutively with a world-system framework," while Mitchum Huehls has explored the efforts of U.S. fiction writers to reconfigure politics under a distinctly global neoliberalism.[56]

The consequences of this shift are elegantly exposed by Jeffrey T. Nealon, who writes that while, under postmodernism, literature was king:

> this new historical shift of focus or orientation inverts (and maybe destroys) literatures' privileged syndochic role. In short, in our critical work throughout the humanities we no longer tend to go to the revelatory "part" in hopes of grasping the larger "whole" (arguing for example, that reading *Gravity's Rainbow* gives us a window into the workings of the world at large, the contradictory logic of everyday life); rather, we now tend to start with the larger post-postmodern whole (e.g., globalisation), of which any particular part (say, postmodern literature) is a functioning piece.[57]

Synecdoche, as a literary trope, insists on the dialectical dependence of the text to social and historical realities. We can take the current state of such criticism, with its intent focus on the novel under neoliberalism, as so many productive anti-formalist practices which refract the earlier notions of literature as whole rather than fragment, and affirming that literary language no longer holds such a privileged place in the contemporary moment, as it did in modernism. As Leigh Claire La Berge and Alison Shonkwiler have argued, current criticism reveals the substantially of economic crisis, and a "desire for the most thorough possible indexing of capitalism."[58] One can speculate (as the activity *du jour*) that future generations may consider the intense reading of such economic shifts and patterns, within their own internal rhythms of contraction and expansion, as a new formalism in which neoliberal capitalism constitutes so many texts whose terms of reference one cannot escape. Joseph North speaks for many when he observes "that the discipline's future shape will depend most of all on the character of whatever new period of capital emerges in the wake of the current crisis."[59]

* * *

One "cannot not periodize," remarks Jameson, writing of both the necessity and arbitrariness of dividing history into periods.[60] I take the contemporary as emerging with the events of the new century. Nothing shapes historical consciousness like a surprise attack, and those on the World Trade Centre and Pentagon, occurring in September 2001, provide a conceptual frame for the emergence of new crisis formations, tied in the first instance to global security and governance, and then propelling conflicts and occupations in the Middle East, before being "overtaken" by international economic crisis and the political response. Most critics come a little later in their designation. Kennedy and Shapiro define the contemporary as post-financial crash, "the period roughly from 2011 onwards" with the Arab Spring, Occupy Wall Street, and the return of Vladimir Putin to the Russian Presidency.[61] Huehls and Rachel Greenwald Smith contend four phases of neoliberalism, the last of which they call ontological, a neutral post-political and post-ideological market moment where corporations are committed to "whatever proves best for business" and have the "sheen of social justice activism."[62] Despite the many conceptual difficulties, there is still something compelling about efforts to punctually date the emergence, inauguration, or coalescence of the contemporary. In time, consensus will form, with standard readings and settled, accepted histories, full of liveliness and limitation. Theodore Martin's *Contemporary Drift* (2019) provides a satisfactory take on the issue. In a manner reminiscent of Robert B. Pippin's *Modernism as a Philosophical Problem* (1991), Martin is less concerned with historical parameters than conceptual consequences. The "accretive history of genre" feels like the measure of both "change and continuity, diachrony and synchrony, pastness and presentness."[63] For Martin, the "drift" of the contemporary is offset by the "drag" of genre.

This book argues that the most pressing forms of literary engagement are to be found in a range of novels written by a coterie of writers who actively seek to challenge the present conjuncture. Writers from the 1980s onward can be read as translating theoretical challenges into fictional-narrative terms, resulting in the emergence of the "theory novel."[64] In the following chapters, I read complex forms of anti-capitalist sentiment in novels by Jonathan Lethem, Dana Spiotta, China Miéville, Thomas Pynchon, Rachel Kushner, Teddy Wayne, Jacqueline Woodson, and Kim Stanley Robinson, all of whom share interests in left politics, the problems of protracted economic crisis, and the potentiality of post-capitalist ideas. Engaging closely with their work, this book reveals the ways in which contemporary fiction evidences a profound preoccupation with the left tradition.

A word on legacy. It is not something bequeathed in the manner of a gift but puzzled out by each new generation. Derrida understands this, writing that if "the readability of a legacy [was] given, natural, transparent, univocal, if it did not call for and at the same time defy interpretation, we would never have anything to inherit from it."[65] The exact status of this "Marxist" component is complex and loose and will be mapped out in the chapters that follow. While all the authors are interested in left politics, each work challenges any strict adherence to any interpretation or reading. There are rather multiple Marxisms, whose "formulations are always in movement and in historical rearrangement and reconstruction, along with their object of study, capitalism itself."[66] This book ranges across diverse forms of political commitment, whether in the case of Miéville's iconoclastic gothic Marxism, Kushner's leftist opposition to multinational corporations, or Robinson's utopian literature, while challenging the reduction of left politics to any single coordinate.[67] As such, the fictions here do not exhaust the potential or present range of left critical concerns but raise and represent what are increasingly among the most pressing preoccupations of the contemporary moment. Rather than treating this area of study as defined and delimited, this project insists on the ways in which this grouping of texts emerges in a dialectic that remains unfinished. This selection is exactly that, and by no means comprehensive. Methodologically, this book seeks to broaden and enrich contemporary literary studies by bringing the field's most prominent theoretical influences closer to Marxist modes of critical enquiry, by recognizing in texts themselves strong left political components. More traditional forms of Marxist criticism have often sought to impose rigid taxonomical features on texts, privileging reflection, typicality, and a narrow vision of class. Focusing on the self-reflexivity of literature, the book argues such thought can develop in and through narrative, as well as simply being applied to it. Calling on a selection of influential novels in contemporary British and American fiction, the book will argue these works revaluate left political thought in the context of new political, economic, and ecological challenges.

More importantly, this book argues the present moment affords an opportunity for the development of a critical Marxist knowledge that exists in and through a series of complex engagements with contemporary fictional narrative. This is achieved by considering Marxism in the novel (that is, texts that directly engage with Marxist ideas, politics, and critical contexts, and therefore offer specific forms of ideological commitment) and Marxism and the novel (an examination of how Marxist frames of reading illuminate political and ideological tendencies in contemporary fiction). These chapters turn on discussions of form and content and aim to offer astute analyses of what selected narratives do with Marxism.[68] As will become clear, the aim of reading texts through specific forms of political and ideological commitment in no way seeks to reduce the narrative's status as a carefully constructed aesthetic artefact. In a situation in which conventional literary criticism induces a reliance on the private, personal, and non-historical, it is my argument here that the Marxist critical framework becomes greatly enriched by considering works written by writers versed in such literary-critical approaches.

A dialectical transformation is in operation here: just when contemporary writers are drawing upon forms of left political commitment, many readers of this book will be aware that the status of critique has, in recent years, been challenged by a host of literary critics who have taken an adversarial relationship to deep reading practices, of which Marxism remains a central expression. Rita Felski probably speaks for many scholars when she takes issue with "a style of interpretation driven by a spirit of disenchantment" and a mood of "critical detachment [...] tied to the cultivation of an intellectual persona that is highly prized in literary studies and beyond: suspicious, knowing, self-conscious, hard-headed and tirelessly vigilant."[69] Instead, she proposes that we need to locate within literary studies a "theory of attachment."[70] Scholars have been quick to challenge such positions; as Nico Baumbach, Damon Young, and Genevieve Yue have argued, it never feels like there is a correct time to abandon such readerly protocols: it seems "that at the very moment we need a political critique of culture, we are busy disavowing the tools that might deliver one."[71] We should, they remark, not be reluctant to value suspicion under "historical conditions that call for nothing less."[72] The success of the recent "groundswell of support for new ways of reading," as Elizabeth Weed has defined it, prompted Marxist practitioners to respond in a special issue of *Mediations*, the journal of the Marxist Literary Group.[73] Marxist critics used the opportunity to sharpen materialist practices, suggesting that "surface readings will pay only when positioned against equally adept critique working at various 'depths.'"[74] These positions fell into polarized camps, but a compelling contradiction arises when we consider, as I do here, the ways in which works of contemporary fiction move profitably between these binaries of critique and post-critique. In conversations on the limits of critique, and the seeming exhaustion of "suspicious" forms of analysis, it is increasingly clear that more work needs to be done on the ways in which writers, pressured by historical and economic forces, bring to bear specific forms of commitment that are worked out in the situation of the literary text itself.

My approach largely focuses on twenty-first-century fiction, and is concerned with literary interrogations of what, I will argue, has been the ongoing recuperation and regeneration of left politics in British and American fiction after many years absence. My discussions cover a selected number of novels taken from the rapidly expanding corpus of twenty-first-century fiction. It is my hope that what a close reading of texts may sacrifice in comprehensiveness will be more than made up for in critical insight. This study sets out then, for the first time, to argue that these narratives consciously explore, engage, and develop the contours of left critical commitments, orientating Marx, and Marxism to take on new relevance, scope, and value, in the contemporary moment. To dispel any misconceptions from the outset, it is worth stating up front that in none of these texts does the figure of Marx appear as a character (the only literary novel where he does, that I am aware of, is Thomas Pynchon's *Gravity's Rainbow* [1973], which I discuss in Chapter Four).[75] While this novel is outside my temporal frame, it demands consideration for its unique engagement (and depiction) of Marx. Marx is occasionally invoked in texts, often in passing, as in the case of Ben Lerner's *10:04* (2014), when the narrator notes that Marx died "at his desk" in 1883 (a mistake: Marx died in an armchair).[76] Neither do all these fictions feature long disquisitions on Marx's work (again the exception is Pynchon, but we may add Robinson here, which I consider in Chapter 8). But if Marx and Marxism are seemingly absent, as in Jacqueline Woodson's *Red at the Bone* (2019) or Teddy Wayne's *Apartment* (2020), there are strong traces of left politics, political movements, and intellectual currents, where the fantasies of capital are on full display. Rather, it is the familiarity with radical politics, the revolutionary tradition of left thought, and the formal resources and tools of the novel that constitute a new foundational epistemology.

The novel remains a particularly effective site through which to examine the central problem of capitalism: namely, representation. To state representation as a central problem is not to endorse a whole series of post-structuralist positions which take flight from real, tangible, material facticity towards the concerns of language, discourse, and the signifier. Nor it to forget that capitalism is both capable of momentous changes, which Marx eloquently describes in the opening of the *Manifesto* (1848), and exploitative, unsustainable, and unequal. Rather it is, as recent studies have shown, to consider formal capacities, challenges, and the limits of specific representational approaches.[77] The world resides beyond representation but only representation can make it meaningful.

In literary studies, the gaps, absences, inconsistencies, divisions, and contradictions of a text have consistently proved to be among the most profitable and rewarding aspects for critical enquiry, and it is the perception of external unity that has attracted major Marxist thinkers of the last fifty years, including Jameson, Eagleton, and Pierre Macherey. While I will depart from these thinkers in provocative ways, I do here, following Jameson, and others, consider capitalism as a narrative category. Writing on *Capital*, volume 1, Jameson remarks he is less concerned "with Marx's facts as he presents them" than with the "representation of capitalism as a totality, as an infernal machine which can only be described dialectically."[78] The formal problem of *Capital* is the problem of representation, a condition mitigated by the "peculiar powers of dialectical thought, [...] a new type of thinking invented specifically to overcome the dilemmas of representation posed by this unique and peculiar totality called capital."[79] To examine *Capital* as a conceptual narrative is to consider the specific logic of the text, which has "its own categories of completeness and its own rules for introducing new material and problems."[80] It is this approach—to consider novelistic forms as particular dynamics and innovations—that concerns me here. As Marxist critics are aware, the novel's ongoing effort to develop modes of representation that are adequate to globalized capitalism may come down to a projected coherence. For Jameson, is "the privilege of aesthetic theory, however—maybe it's the only one!—[which] lies in the fact that there, in art, beginnings and endings are demonstratable: and that art alone seems to offer a laboratory in which these otherwise imponderables can be observed if not regulated."[81] Despite the heterogeneity of these literary works, they can, I argue, be productively considered within a formal project that considers literature a realm of relative freedom while turning to examine whether capital's processes have subsumed narrative altogether, and articulate structural ambivalences about the status of writing and political critique.[82]

This movement away from traditional modes of Marxist criticism is aptly captured by Ben Lerner. For Lerner, a host of approaches are concerned with reading texts, following Althusser's pronouncements on ideology, as imaginary solutions to real problems: "and that's the traditional Marxist understanding of art; but there's also this idea that you can attempt to [...] present and bring into the domain of experience and criticism the contradictions of your moment. And contradictions can be really moving and beautiful in addition to [...] hilarious and disturbing, you know? I think that's the space of the book for me."[83] Lerner mentions Althusser but targets Jameson's project of dialectical criticism, specifically his reading of cinema in *Signatures of the Visible* (1990), as establishing a strict divide between theory and narrative. Jameson's path-breaking work makes him an interesting target of critique to many of the novelists under consideration here. Rachel Kushner has invoked Jameson in interview, drawing a distinction between his work on the historical novel, which she reads as "providing a conception of what shapes people's lives among the larger forces of history" and her own methods of composition, which Treasa De Loughry has termed "condensation."[84] Many of the novelists under consideration here take exception with Jameson's approaches, while signaling him out as an iconoclastic theorist and critic. Perhaps the most interesting of these dissents is Kim Stanley Robinson, a former doctoral student of Jameson, and a close friend, whose fiction challenges Jameson's readings of utopia and science fiction in ways I will elucidate later.

For this writer, Jameson remains the most important Marxist critic, and his injunction, first articulated in *Marxism and Form* (1971) to "come to terms with the shape of the individual sentences themselves, to give an account of their origin and formation" remains as necessary today as when he first proposed it.[85] While we rush to identify Jameson as a Hegelian Marxist, his work is also loyal to the tradition of rhetoric, philology, and comparative criticism of the German critic Eric Auerbach, Jameson's doctoral supervisor. I would, then, be pleased if the pages that follow are useful as an explication and engagement with Jameson's books, from the publication of his first work, his doctoral thesis, *Sartre: Origins of a Style* (1961), to the pathbreaking *Marxism and Form* mentioned above, to his recent examination of allegory, and his book on Benjamin, to the forthcoming and final part of his monumental project, *The Poetics of Social Forms*. I fully admit to thinking through Jameson as much as Marx and consider the work of the former to be among the most important contributions to literary studies today.

As a study Anglo-American fiction, the novels under consideration here are produced in global hegemonic areas and focus their content on the world-system's metropolitan centers. For instance, five of the novels situate their action in some fictional version of New York City (whether completely recognizable, as in Wayne, or largely underwater, as in Robinson). But they also reveal the logics of unevenness and differentiation, whether, as with Miéville and Kushner, they explore the peripheries and semi-peripheries of the world system, or, in the case of Woodson, examine the hierarchical oppressions of race and class so often elided in popular culture. As such, they maintain a commitment to expanded geopolitical horizons while revealing this global consciousness as rooted in the relationship between rural populations and technologically advanced societies, without necessarily covering huge geographic scales and transhistorical scope in the manner of the traditional historical novel.

These texts are all written by commercially successful and critically acclaimed authors. That such literary radicalism has commercial appeal is itself encouraging, regardless of whether the publishers themselves are concerned with sales. As Paul Crosthwaite has demonstrated, contemporary authors exhibit "signature tensions," as consequence of the neoliberal structuring of the literary field, in which "writers face barely resistible pleasures to tailor their work to the market, even where they are deeply skeptical—aesthetically, intellectually, and politically—about the market approved styles."[86] Sally Rooney's *Normal People* (2018), shows such tensions about writing and commitment, with Connell attending a literary reading and thinking: "It was culture as class performance, literature fetishized for its ability to take educated people on false emotional journeys, so that they might feel superior to the uneducated people."[87] Connell's stance, part frustration, part longing of literary ambition, questions the arenas of complicity and critique. Interestingly, Rooney has described herself as a Marxist. In an interview, she gives an articulate reading of her novel in relation to the social and economic pressures of global capitalism. "In my own life," Rooney says, "the way that I think about the world that we live in is [...] mostly through a sort of Marxist framework."[88] In Chapter 2, I turn to Walter Benjamin's writings on art, autonomy, and hack writers, to consider the inventive and resourceful ways in which authors, still mindful of these pressures, create narratives driven by political influence. That these texts are widely read and frequently discussed lends confidence to the undertaking, even if they routinely question the value of their own contribution.

Chapter Structure

The argument of this book is divided across eight chapters. It is my hope that the shorter sections—Chapters 4, 5, and 7—are refreshing interventions in themselves but also complement the more sustained chapters through a tonality and rhythm. The book argues that the novels under discussion set out to examine left radical politics, seek to understand the problems of protracted economic crisis, and explore the potentiality of post-capitalist ideas, while, at the same time, evidencing a nuanced degree of self-consciousness about the legacy of left political radicalisms, the costs they accrue, and where they have led. All the authors I consider here—albeit, in different ways, and to varying extents—are concerned with left politics and committed to examining the suitability of the novel to demystify capitalist social relations and chart a course of cultural and political renewal. Chapter 1 is a theory chapter exploring Marx, the dialectic, and literary form. Using the work of Jameson, Kornbluh, Caroline Levine, and Caroline Lesjak, the chapter argues for the dialectic as a series of ever widening critical climaxes rather than complete conceptual solutions.

Chapter 2 turns to the vexed question of U.S. radicalism. Historians have tended to frame this subject as a story of missed opportunities, taking their lead from Werner Sombart's classic study, *Why is There No Socialism Here?* (1906), but books by Paul Buhle, Richard Flacks, Christopher Phelps, and Rhodri Jeffrey-Jones, have all challenged this "reputation for failure," arguing the left has helped extend rights to previously excluded populations, reshaped the nature of democratic practice, and fostered a culture of political activism.[89] This chapter reconsiders the melancholic dimension of left politics. It turns to narratives, written in the wake of postmodernism, that interrogate the Kondratiev-like waves of radical U.S. progressivism, which found its high point in the organizational activities of post-depression U.S. communism, but radiate across the century, into the successes of 1960s civil rights activism, before waning under the Reaganite pressures of deregulation, deindustrialization, and union busting, only to see a new upsurge of political dissent entangled with capitalist regeneration in the 2008 financial crisis and Occupy movement. Lethem's *Dissident Gardens* (2013) and Spiotta's *Eat the Document* (2006) set out to engage with a legacy of radical action, dwelling on the failures, and missed opportunities, while attempting to retain the optimism inherent in key decades of U.S. progressivism. Exhibiting a suggestive dialectical relation, these fictions are remarkable for the extent to which they demonstrate, and self-reflexively dwell upon, the successive waves of loss that have animated the last half-century, and specifically the historical loss of Marxism as a "privileged object, intellectual investment, and emotional cathexis."[90] Asking whether black writers mourn 1960s movements in analogous fashion, the end of the chapter turns to an indicative text, Colson Whitehead's *The Nickel Boys* (2019), which examines the death of Civil Rights activism through the wrongful incarceration of black activist, Elwood Curtis. In all these fictions, left loss is brutal and redemptive, pointing the way to future change.

Chapter 3 continues this interest in the defeated revolutions of the past, but turns to more speculative literary engagements in the work of the British Marxist China Miéville, who remains one of the most intellectually interesting writers of fiction to emerge in the last twenty years.[91] Initial approaches have focused on Miéville's politics as a kind of "taxonomic playfulness" and a "surrender to the [new] weird" aesthetic, following the unintelligible cosmic terrors found in the work of the twentieth-century American writer, H.P. Lovecraft.[92] In part, building upon the work of Carl Freedman, who argues Miéville's fictions are not only socialist generally, but Marxist precisely, this chapter reads Miéville's *The City & The City* (2009) as a Gothic Marxist fiction that articulates new modalities of communist expression which "haunt" the more mainstream work of the "Idea of Communism" conferences.[93] The chapter engages with key passages drawn from Miéville's novel set against the contributions of Alain Badiou. Miéville's novel is a powerful engagement with twenty-first-century communism, unearthing new and productive relations with left thought while refusing to banish or conquer the history of the twentieth-century effort.

Chapter 4 reads Rachel Kushner's *The Flamethrowers* as a narrative which details a precise path of political education. The chapter begins by focusing on the novel's cinematic features, world systems and slave labor in Brazil, before turning to Kushner's depiction of the Red Brigades, Autonomist movements in Italy during the Years of Lead (the period of bombs, blood, and bullets from late 60s to the early 80s), and UAW/MF and Black Mask in New York, to better understand the forms of violence, insurrection, and protest contained in the novel. It begins with the story of Valera, an Italian industrialist who develops a rubber business in Brazil. Valera fought in the First World War, mixed with Italian futurists and fascists, and had a son, Sandro, who lives in New York and becomes the partner of the protagonist, Reno. The chapter reads Kushner's exposure of Brazilian plantation workers, alongside the strikes and revolutions of the 1970s.

Chapter 5 examines narratives concerned with housing crisis. Housing is at the root of social inequality and drives all kinds of disparities in health, wealth, education, and exposure to the criminal justice system. Rent and housing are central themes for black writers, due to a legally enforced decades-long denial of homeownership opportunities. These racial restrictive covenants were enabled by state and federal law, municipal ordinances, assessment practices, private deed restrictions, racial steering, redlining (the denial of financial services like mortgages, insurance, and loans), disinvestment, blockbusting, and violence.[94] Matthew Desmond's *Evicted* (2016), Eva Rosen's *The Voucher Promise* (2020), and Meredith Grief's *Collateral Damages* (2022) have explored the horrors of federal housing policy, while Britain's broken housing market has been carefully catalogued in Chloe Timperley's *Generation Rent* (2020), Hashi Mohamed's *A Home of One's Own* (2022), and Mel Nowicki's *Bringing Home the Housing Crisis* (2023). The chapter reads Teddy Wayne's *Apartment* (2020) and Matthew Desmond's *Evicted* (2016). Despite the asymmetries of perspective—Desmond is an American sociologist, and Wayne a novelist—the texts share narratological features. In her account of the 1980s realist novel, which she terms "Reagonomic Realism," Shonkwiler shows how even when "the contemporary economic novel appears to seek a landscape-orientated mode of reading rather than a portrait one, it exposes how powerfully attached to portrait modes we remain."[95] *Apartment* is such a portrait mode, in which the struggles of housing and property play out in the background of the novel, secondary to the concerns of the creating writing program and a frustrated relationship between Billy and the unnamed male narrator.

Chapter 6 turns to the work of Thomas Pynchon. Pynchon has produced innovative fiction across the twentieth and twenty-first century and is typically regarded as paradigmatic of U.S. literary postmodernism.[96] Scholarship on Pynchon is substantial, leading one group of critics to contend that Pynchon's work demand a "collective enterprise of reading wherein none of us could succeed without the help of the others."[97] While scholars have, historically, tended to favor Pynchon's postmodernism, his millennial fiction offers up new legible left political commitments, posing fresh and exciting challenges for those interested in the political dimension of his works. This engagement with the more expansive global and political networks underpinning recent readings of American Literature is captured in *The New Pynchon Studies* (2019), which situates Pynchon's post-millennial fiction in relation to new materialism, digital ecologies, and post-postmodernism.[98] Still, scholars continue to draw upon other Marxist models of scholarship, such as the Frankfurt School and post–Althusserian critique. In focusing upon *Against the Day* (2006), *Bleeding Edge* (2013), and *Gravity's Rainbow* (1973), this chapter challenges critical works which take an adversarial relation to Marx. Instead, the chapter proposes Pynchon's fiction is closely connected to Marx's concern with historical development, dialectics, and class struggle.[99] My approach will situate Pynchon's narratives as more interventionist than has been considered within postmodern coolness and apathy.

Chapter 7 explores new constructions of race and class in the work of Jacqueline Woodson. More readily established as a writer of YA fiction, with a litany of conferred honors and awards including "Young People's Poet Laureate" and "National Ambassador for Young People's Literature." Woodson's *Another Brooklyn* (2016), *Red at the Bone* (2019), and *Brown Girl Dreaming* (2014) address memory, race, class, sex, and female friendship through radical formal experimentation. *Red at the Bone* unfolds through the voices of five characters over three generations, extending from the 1921 Tulsa race massacre (when white residents attacked black residents and businesses) to 9/11. Focusing on the largely overlooked class solidarity of Black Americans, the narrative establishes new critical and political intersections.

Nowhere are the concerns with climate, ecology, and environmental struggle more powerfully addressed in a single literary figure than in the work of Kim Stanley Robinson.[100] Robinson is generally regarded as a hard science-fiction writer, meaning his novels are less interested in sensational plots than practical solutions to political problems. His fiction remains one of the most progressive, yet understudied, bodies of literary work in its critique of neoliberal capitalism. His novels and short-story collections have relentlessly mapped the turbulent historical cycles of material despoliation, violence, and expropriation of capitalist networks, in turn proposing radical visions of social and economic justice through science, worker-ownership, and stewardship. Robinson's *New York: 2140* (2017) concerns a partially submerged Manhattan operating in the wake of ecological disaster. The city continues as a hub of financial industry, with Robinson having created an economic situation in which "capital having considerably more liquidity than water, slid."[101] However, in the wake of this liquid (and liquidity) disaster, a common is created through the formation of "cooperatives [...], communes, squats, barter, alternative currencies" which are important because they conjure a kind of utopian chaos: "a ferment, a tumult, a mess."[102]

The epilogue opens the study to fresh engagements in Marxist cultural studies, looking beyond the novels considered here to other contemporary authors, while the appendix surveys current work in Marxist literary criticism over the last two decades.

1

A Search for Method

The appearance of a whole host of books in recent years has confirmed that form continues to dominate debate.[1] Traditionally, form refers to the unique compositional qualities of a literary text—qualities which distinguish it from the formlessness of reality. Set apart from history, form was the hermetic sealing of literary language within itself, so that questions of shape and structure came to the fore. But these impasses began to gnaw, as critics wanted to connect the internal resources of texts to political and historical realities once ostensibly outside. Recently, literary studies has sought a more dynamic, rather than reflective notion, considering form as a nexus of speculative possibilities.[2] Caroline Levine favors the interactions and collisions of overlapping forms, which open up "aleatory possibilities" that make the world more chaotic and "contingent" than previously imagined.[3] Form, for Levine, is defined as "all the shapes and configurations, all ordering principles, all patterns of repetition and difference," which have the "potential to unsettle conventional, rigid social" structures.[4] Anna Kornbluh is fascinated by a formalist mathematics, which "values the force of structural interrelationships over any putative outside of structure."[5] With Marxian materialism, the nineteenth-century novel becomes "the construction of possible relations" and realism an "exercise in social modelling" rather than reflection or mimesis.[6] Finally, Tom Eyers proposes a theory of form in which literary texts "embody a formal speculative capacity that prevents their final absorption or neutralization by those prior conditions, even as the result may well be stasis or immobility rather than, say, contestation or critique."[7] In a review essay, later adapted for the same book, Eyers calls the current moment the "revenge of form," a suggestive point given that revenge is all about surpassing structural limits in the pursuit of a logic of symmetry.[8]

In this chapter, I want to range over the work of Fredric Jameson, a figure who has done more than most to sketch bold, signature, visions of form. Contributions by others, such as Caroline Lesjak are broached, but the readings here furnish a scaffold of enquiry rather than an object of discursive history, as I try to think *with* Jameson rather than *about*. Jameson, Lesjak, and Kornbluh, mentioned above, are all Marxist thinkers, acutely aware of the part played by social, political and, above all, historical, pressures, in the constitution of literary texts, but without ever seeing these forces or structures as anything other than multiple and complex. In the case of Jameson, my approach has always been to consider his work in relation to perception, in which he pursues a microscopic attention to the formal features and pleasures of an individual text—sentences!—before suddenly stepping back to survey an astonishing landscape of veritable contexts, conditioned by capital, and the text's unique position within it.[9] It is such an approach that helps us confront the central charge against his work: that the text is lost in Jameson, buried beneath the scaffolding of theory and political commitments. In Jameson, the text is pressed outwards, a strategy that results in the "expansion of the meaning of cultural texts and not their reduction, and of an enlargement of their resonance, an increase of their complexity and the number of their symbolic levels, an enrichment in the contexts in which a given act or symbolic gesture or expression is situated and understood."[10] But, at the same time, the chapter will consider the relationship of this interest in form with the work of Marx, and the dialectic, and it is fitting I begin with Jameson, who combines all three interests.

"Is the dialectic wicked or just incomprehensible?" asks Jameson.[11] A playful question given that the dialectic is all about the suspension of judgments and the halting of conclusions, which Jameson argues appear so readily—and readily formed—in the work of Anglo-American positivist, pragmatist, and empiricist philosophers.[12] "The dialectical method," he writes, is "precisely this preference for the concrete totality over the separate, abstract parts" resulting in a situation whereby the dialectic becomes visible only when it tries to take on everything.[13] The "peculiar difficulty of dialectical writing" writes Jameson, "lies indeed in its holistic, 'totalizing' character: as though you could not say one thing until you had first said everything; as though with each new idea you were bound to recapitulate the entire system."[14] Jameson, of course, takes his position from Marx and Hegel; the former of whom writes in *Capital* of the dialectic's ability to generate a series of ever widening critical climaxes, of "not simply a vicious circle of problems, where the solution of one problem presupposes the solution of the other, but a whole complex of contradictory premises, since the fulfilment of one condition depends directly on the fulfilment of its opposite."[15] Tortuous, yes; incomprehensible, maybe. Dialectics is undoubtedly difficult, and Jameson makes this density, this abstraction, appealing, and indeed even necessary. We are not here, he writes, "to salute a readymade idea effortlessly, in passing" in the manner of tabloid journalism, but recognize "real thought demands a descent into the materiality of language and a consent to time itself in the form of the sentence."[16] One of the central contributions of Jameson's work is to demonstrate the formal pleasures of such sentences, an experience forgotten or unremarked on in dialectical criticism.[17] We can recall Marx's intense fascination with the intricacies of capital and pleasurable horror evoked in confronting capitalism itself. I will consider these energies more carefully in the final chapter on Robinson, who similarly constructs a kind of Marxist *jouissance* in overcoming problems.

Jameson's question about the status of the dialectic however, and his invocation of wickedness recalls a gothic sensibility, a mode uniquely qualified to describe the properties of dialectical thought. Rather than density and abstraction, the dialectic can be a phantasmagorical staging of an ideal cross-section in history. Jameson himself has not been attentive to the powers of the gothic—strange, given Marx's use of an extensive gothic repertoire to frame the horrors of capital—referring to it in his book on postmodernism as "class fantasy (or nightmare) in which the dialectic of privilege or shelter is exercised."[18] Like any imagined terror or gothic creature, it is difficult to face the dialectic fully; it more comfortably resides at the edges of our vision, threatening to vanish if examined too closely, ready to take another form when called forth again. The idea of a gothic dialectic will be more carefully considered in Chapter 3.

Despite the range of critical commitments, Marxism still offers the most intellectually coherent historical and economic explanation for our moment.[19] As the major proponent of such a position, Jameson's Marxism does not suggest other philosophical positions should be jettisoned, but rather that they can be completed or enlarged with some dialectical synthesis which accounts for the historicity of their application and reveals their cognitive operations. Such a position would entail grasping distinct methods as sets of critical impositions that impose limits and boundaries on the interpretative process and are considered complete only in an arbitrary sense.[20] Working through such positions involves a prolonging of their critical inferences and observations until we reach history itself, an act that has the distinct advantage of both resetting past approaches and paying homage to the energy of non–Marxist traditions in their pursuit of aestheticism, formalism, anti-historicism and apoliticism. As the dialectic itself demonstrates, little is to be gained in relying on value judgments: in time, such approaches become objects of scrutiny and are indispensable insofar as they are placed in productive tension with one another. This does not stop us taking pleasure in such dialectical processes, which is tied up with the intricacies of genuine thought, and I for one certainly share the "excitement of a vast range of post–New Critical developments [which] arose from a perceived potential to reorient critical practices toward a more radical politics or at least an alternative ensemble of counterhegemonic consequences."[21] For Jameson, we grasp such interventions as events or even conflicts rather than theories per se, a realization that returns us to the moment of the intervention itself and a reawakening of the productive processes by which theorists attempted whole new ways of conceptual thinking that could only have appeared at that time.[22]

In a collection of interviews, Jameson argues for Marxism as a "critical rather than a systematic philosophy" that always arrives as "a correction of other positions," meaning we cannot "understand Marx's materialism until we understand that which it is directed *against*, that which it is designed to *correct*."[23] Marx's work developed the structural and historical specificities of the production of value in capitalist societies. After Marx, this problematic was translated into problems and investigations which required greater specialization and technical skill. As Jameson notes of Marx's concept of surplus value, for example, it can be traced through commodity production, which would lead on to a discussion of the social psychology of commodities and consumerism, arriving at money theory in banks, speculation, inflation, and the stock market before descending into considerations of class structures, legal forms, judicial categories, and property relationships, until grappling with the dilemmas of modern historiography itself. For Jameson, while "innumerable introductions to the dialectic have been written" the "tempo seems to be slowing down today."[24] This does not mean the dialectic is no longer essential in the present moment, but that there has occurred a dwindling of "traditional" presentations, many tainted by Engels, orthodoxy, and the codification of Marx in the twentieth century. Jameson's efforts capture the striking heterogeneity of dialectical processes, in which conceptual antagonisms move in multiple directions and pathways, ensuring "the inclusion of many indispensable" concepts a "Marxism unschooled in Hegel left out or [...] censored."[25]

Marx, Hegel, Dialectics

Dialectics contests traditional modes of thought, and has taken a number of different, even contradictory, forms over time.[26] In Hegel, dialectics was a metaphysical system that constructed a sequential or teleological series of concepts whose movement and dynamism came to organize the world under the Idea.[27] As such, *The Phenomenology of Spirit* (1807) is not philosophy but a preparation for philosophy, a sequential series of concepts and categories (but never the only sequence) that the individual must work through to attain knowledge.[28]

For Marx, the emergence of industrial capital forced a radical reappraisal of Hegel, and the dialectic was inverted to become a tool for materialist historical analysis. Only in the most general sense, dialectics is a process of social or conceptual discord in which the staging of the conflict of oppositions leads to a fuller, or more adequate, mode of perception.[29] As Robert Albritton argues, dialectical thought, at least in the Marxist tradition, "radically opens thinking to consider relations between the economic and non-economic, between the quantitative and qualitative, between the empirical and normative, between more abstract levels of theory and history, and between theories of political economy and theories of subjectivity."[30]

Marx's dialectic endeavored to respond to the representational dilemmas instigated by the recognition of capital as a totality. Marx never completed his treaty on dialectics, although he left behind, as Ernest Mandel notes, the "striking application of [the] dialectical method" in *Capital.*[31] For Marx:

> The method of presentation must differ in form from that of enquiry. The latter has to appropriate the material in detail, to analyze its different forms of development, to trace out their inner connection. Only after this work has been done, can the real movement be appropriately presented. If this is done successfully, if the life of the subject matter is reflected in the ideas, then it may appear as if we had before us *a priori* construction.[32]

The characteristic move, in the face of such oppositions, is to enact a dialectical reversal, in which, as Jameson argues, "the drawbacks of a given historical situation turn out in reality to be its secret advantages."[33] For Marx, this meant the construction of a framework in which capital was perceived through several expanding interconnected categories, rather than a linear historical sequence. In the afterword to *Capital*, Marx demonstrates just such an inversion, and the creation of a dialectical criticism with "no pre-established categories of analysis."[34] For Marx:

> My dialectic method is, in its foundations, not only different from the Hegelian, but exactly opposite to it. For Hegel, the process of thinking, which he even transforms into an independent subject, under the name of "the Idea," is the creator of the real world, and the real world is only the external appearance of the idea. With me the reverse is true: the ideal is nothing but the material world reflected in the mind of man, and translated into forms of thought.[35]

However, while Marx breaks from Hegel's concept of the Idea, he conceals his debt to Hegel. As David MacGregor writes on this issue, Marx acknowledges the Hegelian dialectic "is what separates his work from [...]

mainstream bourgeois thought" but Marx is complicit in constructing "the myth of Hegel the idealist who had everything upside down."[36] Such a position has created the doctrine of a closed system, hence recent efforts to stress the vitality of "an open-ended Hegel."[37] Marx practices determinate negation, enabling him to observe the process by which categories arise from Hegel to form more inclusive totalities, which he makes the starting point of his own research.

Marx's inversion of Hegel rests on the notion of a dialectics of the contradictory forces of capital, a critique of political economy, and a careful identification of the anomalies and absences in previous research efforts. Marx's claims his approach "does not allow itself to be impressed with anything, being in its very essence critical and revolutionary."[38] Faced with Hegel's *Geist* (Spirit) as the animating force of historical development, Marx converts Hegel's idealism into a solution at a higher conceptual level. For Jameson, such a moment is the most sensitive in the whole process:

> that in which an entire complex of thought is hoisted through a kind of inner leverage one floor higher, in which the mind, in a kind of shifting of gears, now finds itself willing to take what had been a question for an answer, standing outside its previous exertions in such a way that it reckons itself into the problem.[39]

This transformational moments constitutes the dialectic.[40] It resides in the "purely formal pleasure" of the sentences themselves, "in which the shifting of the world's gears and the unexpected contact between apparently unrelated and distant categories and objects find sudden and dramatic formulation."[41] Marx himself observed this in his reflections on Hegel, arguing "this positive becomes the medium through which the absolute light shines, the absolute breaks into a fabulous play of colors" and "points to something other than itself."[42] The dialectic is not simply a device for unmasking presuppositions; it is the enumeration of formal pleasures generated by the skillful arrangement of sentences which nurture an alertness to new directions, possibilities and pathways. It is Marx's attention to the formal powers, and pleasures, of reading Hegel that leads to him comprehend capital as a system of contradictions ever in dynamic movement.

Marxism and the "New" Dialectic

Recently, several approaches in dialectical criticism have sought to distinguish between the Hegelian-Marxism and what Christopher Arthur, Jim Kincaid, and Fred Moseley have called "New Dialectic."[43] At the core of this project lies a renewed emphasis on Hegel's *Logic*, which Marx returned to in the winter of 1858. This moment proved pivotal in the composition of *Capital*.[44] Emphasizing the importance of method in the construction of dialectical arguments, scholars of New Dialectic argue that "Marx's use of elements drawn from Hegel's two books on *Logic* should be a central focus of attention."[45] For these critics, Hegel's *Logic* forced Marx to restructure *Capital* through the motions of dialectical necessity. Marx sought to penetrate the abstract categories of political economy to arrive at the reality underlining them and exhibit the meaning of these categories in terms of human activity.

Chris Arthur's *The New Dialectic and Marx's Capital* (2002) has remained at the center of recent debates regarding the Hegelian-inspired re-appropriation of dialectics. This has taken the form of a "systematic" dialectic that articulates capitalist totality over that of a "historical" dialectic which simply outlines fluctuations in the rise and fall of economic systems.[46] For Arthur, "because capital as a totality given to us cannot be known by a linear logic, only a systematic development of categories can demonstrate [the] *inner* structure of capital as a *system*."[47] Rather than a set of abstract schemas or conceptual exercises, such a dialectic proposes a totality structured by relations that are conditioned by "the interchanges of its inner moments."[48] For Marx, Hegel was much more than a series of stylistic reference points, as prescribed by Althusser. Hegel offered a dialectic concerned with the articulation of categories that was designed to conceptualize a changing concrete whole. As Arthur maintains, Hegel's authorship of the modern dialectic is essential: "without it, our critique [...] would be utopian in the scientific sense of unallocated or dislocated."[49]

Hegel provided a philosophy that sought to reveal the underlying wholeness of society. Marx's discovery of the "rational kernel" in the "mystical shell" of Hegel implies a dialectical critique best characterized as a form of developmental consistency: consistency shown by connected theories in an ongoing research program in science, or the development of an acorn into an oak as in Hegel's famous example.[50] This kind of consistency is redeemable only in the course of its completion, however: "only in the course of, and at the end of, the day."[51] As the new dialecticians argue, this backward-looking project smooths over any fissures in the original research process. This "licensed constellationality" results in an "ideological plasticity" which implies a limit or closure to the whole process, reducing the dialectic to the status of a general structural principle.[52] The imposition of strict limits threatens the emergence of a doctrine, in which the most dangerous kind of thinking (the reduction of oppositions and the cancelling of possibilities, of ignoring inverse spirals and spreads) can dominate.

An attention to method challenges this cut-and-dried formalism, restaging Marx's dialectics as a multidimensional approach which is holistic, integrative, and developmental. In January 1858, while working on the *Grundrisse*, Marx wrote a letter to Engels in which he stated a recent return to Hegel had been of "great service" in his own theory.[53] Marx mentioned he was "getting some nice developments":

> For instance, I have thrown over the whole doctrine of profit as it has existed up to now. In the method of treatment the fact that by mere accident I have again glanced through Hegel's *Logic* has been of great service to me [...] I should greatly like to make accessible to the ordinary human intelligence, in two or three printer's sheets, what is rational in the method which Hegel discovered but at the same time enveloped in mysticism.[54]

As Stuart Hall argues, these cryptic remarks reveal a methodological procedure.[55] Marx takes up points of departure within political economy, such as production, and through critique shows their ideological presupposition. Concomitantly, political economy is shown to begin from determinations which have not been considered fully; it is a space of arrival rather than a departure, substituting the study of real material relations for ideological distortions. Marx's method remains striking in this regard, revealing how common-sense beginnings are really the sum of many prior determinations.

Marx's method is suggestive and provides a solution to current debates about ways of reading in the academy. Recently, several literary critics have sought to challenge the efficacy of critical models that, in their own words, take an adversarial relation to texts, where meaning is considered "hidden, repressed, deep, and in need of detection and closure" by the critic, in turn proposing a variety of new critical formalisms.[56] These are disparate practices, which Jeffrey J. Williams has nevertheless productively grouped under the rubric of a "new modesty" in criticism which involve "less grand speculation, more empirical study."[57] While Williams grants such approaches are refreshing and required, not least in their attention to traditional formalist elements long overlooked, they evidence more than simple "generational turnover" and augur a change in "the basic assumptions of literary studies." They "express the shrunken expectations of academe, particularly of the humanities, and a decline in the social prestige of literary criticism."[58]

Most famous among them is surface reading, argued for by Stephen Best and Sharon Marcus, and which turns to "what is evident, perceptible, apprehensible in texts; what is neither hidden or hiding; what, in geometrical sense, has length and breadth but no thickness, and therefore covers no depth."[59] While Best and Marcus stress the essays included in the volume constitute "neither a polemic against nor a postmortem of symptomatic reading" this has not stopped the emergence of a triumphalist strain within the responses. For Emily Apter and Elaine Freedgood, this new allegiance is to be celebrated, as "thirty years of plumbing textual depths has returned us to the surface" meaning that the "recalcitrant, mystified, out-of-control, and conflicted text of Marxist-psychoanalytic reading has been replaced by texts that are friendly, frank, generous, self-conscious, auto-critiquing, and unguarded."[60]

Surface reading is considered politically efficacious because it is *not* deep reading. This is because surface reading is symptomatic of a moment in which ideological statements can be identified for the purportedly obvious political content they elicit:

> The assumption that domination can only do its work when veiled, which may once have sounded almost paranoid, now has a nostalgic, almost utopian ring to it [...] these demystifying protocols appear superfluous when images of torture at Abu Ghraib and elsewhere were immediately circulated on the internet; the real-time coverage of Hurricane Katrina showed in ways that required little explication the state's abandonment of its African American citizens; and many people instantly recognized as lies political statements such as "mission accomplished."[61]

Surface reading is analogous to the methodological situation in Edgar Allan Poe's short story "The Purloined Letter" (1844), which Best and Marcus mention, but, importantly, do not pursue. In Poe's narrative, the detective Auguste Dupin is asked to solve a mystery concerning the theft of a letter from a high-ranking official.[62] An exhaustive search of the apartment by the local police fails to locate the letter because it is not hidden in conventional places, such as "secret drawer[s]," hollow tables, and false chair legs.[63] As such, these critics use this narrative to deduce that the letter of a text can exist in plain sight, hidden from literary "detectives who look past the surface in order to root out what is underneath it."[64] As Best and Marcus stress, surface reading is "not antithetical to critique" but the operation is clear: surface is privileged, while depth is mere background.[65]

Best and Marcus present an interesting critical practice, but they provide a mere surface reading of surface reading. As Jason Baskin argues, perception is much more than the presentation of a discrete object to an isolated subject.[66] Perception "opens the subject to a whole social and historical world—a totality—on which subject, object, and the act of perception all depend."[67] For Baskin, depth marks the presence of a social totality as the medium through which subject and object, reader and text, are actively constituted.[68] Surface reading thus ignores this constitutive dimension of reading because surface is taken as a natural, obvious, and seemingly objective model of perception.

Poe's text offers a synthesis of these two positions. The search is forestalled not simply because the letter is hidden in plain sight, but because its appearance differs from the original, having been "turned out, as a glove, inside out, redirected and resealed."[69] The conclusion reached by Poe's detective—analogous, for our purposes here, to the literary critic—is not merely to note the failure of attentiveness in others, but to realize that being able to read carefully relies on being "strongly corroborative of suspicion in one who came with the intention to suspect."[70] Part of the project of surface reading is to challenge the presumption of rigor attached to suspicious reading practices. Such an effort is welcome, but this effort, in its commitment to remain on the surface, poses further challenges which have yet to be fully addressed. Principally then, surface reading conflates the cultural conservatism of the Bush era with forms of political legibility where "truth appears there for the taking."[71] As Carolyn Lesjak argues, such approaches are part of a larger project of "disciplinary conservatism," where "theory is out and reading is (back) in."[72] Lesjak argues abandoning deep reading and Marxist models of critique is tantamount to accommodating "to the given, to common sense [...] a kind of Blairite Third-Way of reading, which is neither new criticism nor Marxism but a nice compromise midway between them."[73] Remaining on the surface, she remarks, "is simply not an option, if reading is about something other than the performance of reading."[74] Such approaches remain incapable of critiquing Marxist reading practices. To venture beyond, behind, or through surface to what is hidden beneath would compromise their credentials.[75] Marxism can perform deep reading and account for the current turn to surface reading by locating this practice within the ensemble of historical social relations and practices. Marxism can analyze this identification and repudiation historically, with a view to understanding why it is that so many intellectuals feel committed to this style of critique. Surface reading, as a passionate repudiation of depth, must be grasped as both anxiety and symptom of contemporary crisis conditions.

This, then, is the movement of the dialectic itself, which proceeds by marking a moment of closure which in turn requires a new solution. Jacques Derrida attempted just this, in *Specters of Marx* (1993), which shifted debate about Marxism towards debt, mourning, and hauntology. Yet, for Warren Breckman, in his consideration of the affective dimensions of the text, *Specters* "is anything but a sad book."[76] In conjuring Marx as a ghost, able to disrupt the chronological present through haunting, Derrida claimed to retain a "certain spirit of Marxism" absolved of the "letter" of totalitarianism.[77] Žižek's response, given some years later, goes further, arguing for a redefinition in the foundation of melancholic thought:

> the mistake of the melancholic is not simply to assert that something resists the symbolic sublation but rather to locate this resistance in a positively existing, although lost, object. [...] melancholy interprets this lack as a loss, as if

> the lacking object was once possessed and then lost. *In short, what melancholy obfuscates is that the object is lacking from the very beginning,* that its emergence coincides with its lack, that this object is nothing but the positivization of a void or lack, a purely anamorphic entity that does not exist in itself.[78]

For Žižek, the political effects of melancholy are clear: "to legitimize the actuality of its opposite, of the full and unconstrained participation in the global system."[79] This makes it even more important to pursue the ethical dimension of melancholy as "this deceitful translation of lack into loss enables us to assert our possession of the object [that] we never possessed."[80] Through a fixation on the lost object, the melancholic can, albeit fictionally, seize it in a manner they could not previously.[81]

The next chapter shows how contemporary fiction offers a renewed challenge to an otherwise remorselessly bleak view of left political defeat and the power to help "reignite the dialectic of revolutionary thought."[82] If, for the twentieth-century political left, "History itself appears as a landscape of ruins, a living legacy of pain" it is necessary to ask what critical work such fragments provide for the future.[83] The next chapter turns to Jonathan Lethem's *Dissident Gardens*, Dana Spiotta's *Eat the Document*, and Colson Whitehead's *The Nickel Boys*.

2

Reading the New Ruins

Mourning, Melancholy, and Loss in Dissident Gardens *and* Eat the Document

> "Do not think that one has to be sad in order to be militant, even though the thing one is fighting is abominable. It is the connection of desire to reality (and not its retreat into the forms of representation) that possesses revolutionary force."—Michel Foucault, 1977[1]

> "The whole road of socialism—so far as revolutionary struggles are concerned—is paved with nothing but thunderous defeats. Yet, at the same time, history marches inexorably, step by step, toward final victory! Where would we be without those 'defeats,' from which we draw historical experience, understanding, power and idealism? [...] we stand on the foundation of those very defeats; and we cannot do without any of them."—Rosa Luxemburg, 1919[2]

For the left, the collapse of communism in the closing decades of the twentieth century marked an intensification of a melancholic vision of history which Walter Benjamin first called "Left-Wing Melancholy."[3] Understanding struggle as a series of losses, left melancholy is an affective state which manifests as a feeling of guilt for not challenging authority, in a mourning for the human costs of political resistance, and in a sense of despair and failure for not realizing utopian aspirations.[4] The study of melancholy is among the most emphasized of Benjamin's preoccupations, a situation Jameson laments, and blames himself for, in his most recent book.[5] But if Benjamin is considered a thinker of melancholy, he is also a melancholic thinker. All too frequently, Benjamin is identified with the very shortcomings he sought to critique in that essay on left melancholy. Benjamin abhorred left-wing radicalism without a "corresponding political action" and bemoaned the "metamorphosis of political struggle" into "an object of pleasure" for bad writers and poets.[6]

But Benjamin understood melancholy could be related to history in productive ways. In its "tenacious self-absorption," writes Benjamin, melancholy "embraces dead objects in its contemplation, in order to redeem them."[7] His original essay targeted poetry: he never turned these reflections upon the novel form. Indeed, Benjamin's position as a collector and a writer of mosaics (reviews, essays, articles, his book of quotations) forbid any sustained examination of "novelistic psychology," a position almost unthinkable today.[8] And yet given the moments of crisis and transformation through which Benjamin lived, we can acknowledge that twentieth-century literary works which actively intervene in the past risk either commemorating political failure and defeat or mourning the trauma of a collective agony repeatedly experienced. Such approaches are "locked in the past, but in active and passive registers respectively; the one brooding over the failures of praxis, the other immobilized by intense and vivid physical suffering relived repeatedly."[9]

My position here is that selected twenty-first-century narrative fiction displays a critical apprehension of loss set against the commemorative strictures of mourning, bereavement, and despair. Produced at a cultural, geographical, and historical remove from the centers of state-socialism and communist atrocity, recent fiction has an ability to trace the political, psychological, and aesthetic contours of left loss in more reparative ways. This chapter is concerned with the ways in which fictional narratives work through left loss, disappointment, injury, and despair. It sets out to juxtapose, and place into dialogue, key thematic strands from Jonathan Lethem's *Dissident Gardens* (2013), Dana Spiotta's *Eat the Document* (2006), and Colson Whitehead's *The Nickel Boys* (2019) with critical accounts of mourning, memory, and loss by Freud, Benjamin, and Jodi Dean. Exhibiting a suggestive dialectical relation, these fictions are remarkable for the sheer extent to which they demonstrate, and self-reflexively dwell upon, the successive waves of loss that have animated left political thought across the last sixty years.

While left radical currents take on a plurality of influences and diverse aesthetic forms, Marxism remains the dominant expression of twentieth-century revolutionary movements. In the twenty-first century, this relation is far more ambiguous, with left political parties and protest groups invoking the spirit of Marx while seeking to avert revolutionary upheaval and the overturn of private property. As Warren Breckman has remarked of Occupy for instance, "a Marxist call for revolution could not be counted even as a minor key in the chorus of protests."[10] Occupy was "against a certain kind of capitalism, not against capitalism *as such*."[11] As

Dean has argued, Occupy is symptomatic of the emergence of a spontaneous, leaderless, and sporadic social protest movements which spurn traditional political groupings and Marxist ideologies, and sets itself against the politics of class and party which irrevocably shaped and defined the array of twentieth-century movements. Both *Dissident Gardens* and *Eat the Document* attempt to come to terms with these complex legacies, ultimately reflecting this movement away from the vanguard party towards open, inclusive, and non-hierarchical forms of protest. The first section of this chapter unpacks meta-fictional commentaries on loss in Lethem's novel, before situating the text as an engaging extension of Freud's famous 1917 essay "Mourning and Melancholia." I argue that Rose Zimmer's disruption of the normal-psychopathological binary of loss articulated by Freud offers a sensitivity to communist praxis. As Maria Melgar has argued, Freud's text does "not answer the question of how the psychic pain produced by the loss of a person or an ideal, of something concrete or abstract, can trigger creativity."[12] Rose's working through of the "intimate wounds" of twentieth-century U.S. communism offers a symbolic efficacy that stages more plural relations with Marxism and communism.[13] *Dissident Gardens* staging of left political struggle through genealogy, family discord, and crisis resists a normative historical operation, one that seeks to reduce communism to the synonym, Stalinism.[14] The second section situates *Eat the Document* in relation to the work of Benjamin. Benjamin's writing seeks to discern a way in which the lost fragments of the past, rather than mourning the "single catastrophe" of history, can be put to rethinking an emancipatory relationship between past and present in the context of a ruptured narrative of progress.[15] Benjamin is not opposed to dwelling on ones' losses and his study of Charles Baudelaire treats melancholia as a creative disposition.[16] His investigations into the melancholic dimension of left-wing culture are powerfully articulated in his review of a volume of Erich Kästner's poetry, published in 1931. For Benjamin, left melancholy was the work of a "hack writer" who had renounced revolution and turned "the struggle against poverty [into] an object of consumption."[17] Such writers desired market prestige over Marxist politics, and had, for Benjamin, given up, sold-out, and moved on.

Eat the Document extends Benjamin's initial work in conceiving left melancholy as a critical product which turns melancholic fatalism into a new vector of political intention. This is not to say that all hack-writing is revolutionary. Rather Spiotta's novel warns against the more damaging elements of left melancholy by revealing the operative strategies of capitalist depoliticization which seek to neutralize, repackage, and "sell-off" left loss. As the novel reveals in striking detail, capital seeks to turn the sentiments of left loss against itself, manipulating left political figures, movements, and political ideologies into "objects of distraction, of amusement, which can be supplied for consumption."[18] Revealing this critical function forms the revolutionary content of the novel.

It is important to outline how this chapter approaches scholarship on these two novels and twenty-first-century U.S. fiction. *Dissident Gardens* and *Eat the Document* both deploy a range of narrative devices familiar to postmodern theory. Nevertheless, both texts rethink left loss outside the prison-house of postmodern apathy, coolness, and cynicism. The problem here, as Amy J. Elias notes, is that the prevailing consensus on postmodern fiction still orbits theoretical perspectives developed by Fredric Jameson, Linda Hutcheon, and Patricia Waugh as far back as the 1980s.[19] A challenge to the efficacy of postmodern frameworks has been mounted by Adam Kelly. In an essay on the fiction of Dana Spiotta, Kelly argues for selected narratives to be located within a subset of new "literary novels about the events of the radical years [...] published by American writers too young to have participated in the activities of those years, and in many cases, too young to remember the period at all."[20] For Kelly, as writers like Spiotta (and Lethem) reached maturity under the developing doctrines of American neoliberal hegemony, their fiction concomitantly:

> displays a deep nostalgia for the radical years, for an era widely perceived to be prior to total corporate conglomeration and hegemony, an era when political agency still seemed possible, when individual acts of protest could make a difference in the public sphere, and when notions of responsibility, while difficult and pressing, seemed comparatively well-defined.[21]

In Kelly's reading, the future history of conservative entrenchment offers a powerful pull on fiction writers to repackage the prior decade as an unfulfilled moment of political idealism that has returned to haunt the present. Labelled as a "New Sincerity," Kelly's highlights the existence of a political impulse that compels a new generation of novelists to return to key incidents in the left political heritage and retroactively inscribe these moments as possessing affective qualities which challenge the more cynical tendencies of postmodern writing.

Contemporary authors engaging with sincerity do not necessarily seek to reject all aspects of postmodern theory. The move away from irony still brings with it serious doubts about the existence of an authentic self. Nicoline Trimmer has sought to clarify these debates, claiming that a "turn to the human" in fiction and theory does not necessarily "amount to a naïve return to the more traditional view of the self as centered and autonomous meaning-maker."[22] For Trimmer, the fiction of David Foster Wallace, Dave Eggers, and Mark Z. Danielewski suggests that system and self are "*inter-personally* constructed" where the self resurfaces as a "vague presence" and "systems and structures [...] are no longer conceived as impersonal."[23] Moving from the taxonomy of postmodern experience, the self that emerges in twenty-first-century fiction is relational, geared towards an "emphatic expression of feelings and new sentiments" which envisage "possible reconfigurations of subjectivity that can no longer be framed as postmodern."[24] Sincerity marks a shift from the disinterested gaze of postmodern narration towards an affective desire for free, action-orientated subjects.

There are problems with sincerity as an epistemological framework. Sincerity remains locked in a legitimation struggle with objectivity and truth. Lionel Trilling sees sincerity as connected to authenticity, a term designating an exact correlation between one's hidden inner "self" and one's outer assertion and behavior: a mode in which "there is no within and without."[25] Authenticity is the removal of any separation between an individual inner essence and outer self-expression. Freud's discovery of the motivating power of the unconscious and the existence of self-regulating mechanisms challenges Trilling's argument that the subject can know themselves sufficiently to collapse distinctions between manifest and latent content.

Debates about sincerity, authenticity, intention can be bracketed within ethics. Ethical reflections and dilemmas often attempt to exclude historical originality for a flattening out of situations in a kind of perpetual present:

> That a more sophisticated philosophical ethics knows as much and seeks to draw the historical situation itself back into the ethical decision (should I not resist the norms of my own society?) is not a solution but the very diagnosis and symptom, less of the dilemma itself than of the very framework of the philosophical subfield in question: for by the time ethics has subsumed historical content, it has already become something else, namely politics.[26]

Marxism has remained sensitive to the ways in which the situational content of specific historical conjectures "will later cool off and sediment into the various systems of ethics."[27] Paul Blackledge likewise affirms Marx's rejection of moralism.[28] Discussing the declaration of principles for the Workingmen's International Association in 1864, Marx argued the first draft was "a fearfully cliché-ridden, badly written and totally unpolished preamble."[29] His fellow revolutionaries, he wrote in a letter to Engels, quickly adopted his proposals but he was obliged to insert two sentences about duty and right, morality and justice.[30] For Marx, these concepts are acknowledged for the sake of form, but must be deployed where they "can do no harm."[31] Marx's resistance to specific forms of moral and ethical judgment is clear.

Questions of sincerity often seek to reject representations of a common world for measuring statements against a notion of being true to their own determinate nature. This has led Elizabeth Markovits to argue that the search for sincerity in politics is a false problem, a distraction from being able to measure the truth of individual statements in relation to collective interest.[32] As the philosopher Harry Frankfurt argues, the idea of being true to oneself rather than true to the facts is particularly perplexing, given "there is nothing in theory, and certainly nothing in experience, to support the extraordinary judgment that it is the truth about [oneself] that is the easiest for a person to know."[33] Our natures are elusively insubstantial, "notoriously less stable and less inherent than the natures of other things."[34] Defined this way, Frankfurt argues, "sincerity is bullshit."[35]

What Remains? Mourning Marxist-Communism in Dissident Gardens

Jonathan Lethem is an American novelist, essayist, and short story writer. He has published twelve novels and five collections of stories. Lethem has a longstanding interest in legacies and communities, and his works give voice to the damaging and destructive effects of American capitalism on generations and families. Both *Motherless Brooklyn* (1999) and *The Fortress of Solitude* (2003) fit in legible left frameworks, while Lethem credits his involvement in Occupy, two years before the publication of *Dissident Gardens*, as a life-changing experience: "I had displaced my own left thinking into the past," writes Lethem, "and it made me realize that was lazy and indulgent. [Occupy] gave capitalism back its name, so you could be an anti-capitalist in America again."[36] Here, as across his fiction, Lethem remains attentive to how a focus on the past can depoliticize left political struggle in the present. As James N. Gregory argues, the key feature of the U.S. left is discontinuity:

> The organizations of the American Left come and go, flourishing for a time, sometimes making important impacts on policy, public discourse, and cultural production, then withering, only to be replaced at some later point by a new Left based in different organizations, with potentially different demography, geography, and ideological agendas.[37]

Many labor histories ignore the richest source material, which is in a range of recent novels that grapple with the history of American radicalism. Such as Philip Roth's *I Married a Communist* (1998), Jonathan Franzen's *Freedom* (2010), and Paul Auster's *4321* (2017).[38] As Gregory argues, the exceptional character of the American Left is to be found in the shifting constellations of left social movements without the anchoring presence of a competitive left-wing political party, resulting in a unique series of regenerative efforts, operating on the fringes of electoral politics.[39] *Dissident Gardens* is Lethem's most avowedly left political novel. The fiction chronicles a history of the American left, following the lives of left political cadres Rose Zimmer; Rose's daughter, Miriam, and husband Tommy; chess prodigy and numismatist, Lenny; and academic, Cicero Lookins. Divided into four parts, each section of the novel is subdivided into four chapters. Section one details Rose's expulsion from the American Communist party, and an extended oratory given by Rose on memory, mourning, and left loss which is my central concern here. Section two follows Miriam's affiliation with the student protest movements of the 1960s and her murder in the revolutionary seizure of power in Nicaragua in 1979. In the third section, with the two-fold circumstance of Miriam's death and Ronald Reagan's ascent to the White House, Rose experiences a psychological-breakdown and is interned in a nursing home, albeit with visits from Cicero.[40] The fourth and final section closes with Miriam's son Sergius being detained for boarding a flight, his speculations on the ambiguity of the term "*American communist*" (an affiliation he wishes to proclaim but cannot utter), and the realization that communism makes him a "cell of one, beating like a heart."[41]

Largely confining my analysis to the opening of the novel, I want to remain with Rose's reflections on her "living room trial," conducted by members of the U.S. communist party. As Rose observes:

> *There were* five, *including [Sol] Eaglin*. They'd overdressed, overcompensated with vests and jackets, now arraying themselves on her chairs like some Soviet oil, postured as if on some *intellectual* assignment. In pursuit of that chimera, the Dialectical Whosis, when really there was no dialectic here. Only dictatorship. And the taking of dictation [...] the respectable lynch mob that availed themselves of your hospitability while dropping some grenade of party policy on your commitment, lifting a butter knife to slather a piece of toast and using it in passing to sever you from that which you've given your life.[42]

For Rose, as for Marx, historical repetition as rhetorical device cancels the performative power of the ruling ideology.[43] Towards the close of this passage, Rose intimates that the very banality of the living room inquisition serves to compound the emotional trauma of the committee "severing the affiliation."[44] And yet, what Rose terms the "executioners' errand" appears in a chapter titled "Two Trials."[45] In making coffee for the guests shortly after they have arrived, Rose candidly remarks that "this second one, really, [was] only a lousy parody of the first. The first one *that* had been something. Then Rose was important in American Communism."[46] Rose reflects here that the "first trial [...] the one that mattered, that changed everything," actually occurred in the "spring of '47."[47] In a form of "classic party perversity" Rose's husband Albert, "wrongly accused of spying when he was only an incompetent blabbermouth [is] made a spy" and shipped "into service overseas" to become "an East German citizen and spy."[48] As a "lousy parody" Rose's exile from the party—the loss of that to "which you've given your life"—no longer effectively functions as the fundamental "real and final expulsion."[49] In returning to the past, Rose is able to re-inscribe the former trial as the true moment of "Kafkaesque penalty" enabling her to mitigate the effects of the recent expulsion.[50]

Freud's theory of *Nachträglichkeit* is useful.[51] Receiving its most extended elaboration in the case history of the "Wolf Man," Freud argued the neuroses experienced by this individual were a product of a delayed response to a traumatic "impression to which he is unable to react adequately."[52] Seeing the "primal scene" of his parents engaged in sexual intercourse, it is "only twenty years later, during the analysis, [that he] is he able to grasp with his conscious mental processes what was then going on in him."[53] As Peter Nicholls argues, *Nachträglichkeit* is "not simply a matter of recovering a lost memory, but rather of the restructuring which forms the past in retrospect as the original site [...] comes to be reworked."[54] *Nachträglichkeit* demonstrates a complex temporality in which the subjective impact of the encounter is shown to be marked by dimensions beyond the particulars of the event itself.[55] For Freud, past and present become malleable; more specifically, the past can be reactivated in the present and produce life-changing effects.

Nachträglichkeit illuminates Rose's response to the loss of her party membership. Rose's "deferred action" can be positioned as an attempt to mitigate her "incomprehensible loss" by appealing to the prior trial in an effort to underscore what for her, is the arbitrary nature of the latter.[56] The "lousy parody" currently unfolding in the living room is not so much chronologically revised—whereby Rose would come to realize the true importance of the first trial—as it is retroacted, wherein the first trial is suddenly endowed with a new force, visibility, and intensity.[57] To complicate this further, Rose's current trial is ameliorated, albeit partly, by the emergence of a deeper historical awareness in which her liberatory efforts are seen to be too far ahead of their time: "bringing revolution to Negroes, fine. To have one [...] black cop in her sheets, not so fine."[58] Through the injunction of a historical apprehension unavailable during the moment the text purports to represent, Rose slips into the meta-fictional, recalling that: "none among them knew American communism wouldn't wake from this particular winter. Oh the beauty of it! After all Rose had seen and done, to be kicked out bare months before Khrushchev, at the Soviet Congress, aired fact of Stalin's purges."[59] In keeping with the Freudian concept of *Nachträglichkeit*, the text stages, as Peter Nicholls writes, the necessity of a "second event to release [the] traumatic force" of the former.[60] However, it is more complex: the narrative evidences a trauma (the first trial) that awaits revivification with a similar encounter (the second), while simultaneously leaping forward in time to take refuge in the very processes of historical linearity it seeks to decry. While the novel would register highly on the spectrum of metafictional practice, Rose's refusal to surrender to the more fixed empirical distinctions posited by Freud can be read as a legitimation strategy for registering loss as a more open, active, and creative politics.[61] Rose is excommunicated from the American communist party twice and suffers two losses, but she uses the first loss to ameliorate the second.

Dissident Gardens is a not merely a novel that challenges the critical judgements of Freudian psychoanalysis, just as it is not simply a re-working of psychoanalytic theory that is at stake. Rather, the narrative articulates a challenge to the affective political dimensions of left loss. To elucidate this, I will now turn to Freud's identification of mourning [*Trauer*] and melancholia [*Melancholie*] as distinct responses to loss.[62] This diagnosis, synonymous with the understanding of normal versus pathological responses to loss, is predicated on the patient having lost a loved person, object, or ideal. Thus, for Freud, mourning is:

> the reaction to the loss of a loved person, or [...] some abstraction [...] such as one's country, liberty, an ideal and so on. [...] although mourning involves grave departures from the normal attitude to life, it never occurs to us to regard it as a pathological condition and to refer it to medical treatment. We rely on its being overcome after a certain lapse of time, and we look upon any interference with it as useless or even harmful.[63]

Central to Freud's conception of mourning is the notion of a progressive, even healthy, slow psychic detachment from the object of loss, where the "mourner is able to declare the object dead and to move on to invest in new objects."[64] While mourning is considered a type of closure, a location where the past is declared resolved, even finished, melancholia is constituent of an enduring devotion, one characterized by an inability or unwillingness to disengage from the loved object, place, or ideal. As such melancholia is:

> the loss of a more ideal kind. The object has not perhaps actually died but has been lost as an object of love [...] a loss of this kind has occurred, but one cannot see clearly what it is that has been lost, and it is all the more reasonable to suppose that the patient cannot consciously perceive what has been lost either.[65]

Manifesting itself as "an extraordinary reduction in self-esteem [and] a great impoverishment of the ego," Freud argues for the emergence of a voice or critical conscience that splits from the subject and renders harsh judgment upon it.[66] Melancholia, then, creates a "lowering of the self-regarding feelings to a degree that finds utterance in self-reproaches and self-reviling and culminates in a delusional expectation of punishment."[67] As Freud's clinical experience shows, these failings are not really directed to the object of lost love: "the self-reproaches are reproaches against a loved object which has been shifted away [...] to the patient's own ego."[68] For Freud, mourning is temporary; melancholy, a durable disposition. The melancholic cannot abandon their sadness and can even find gratification in their pain.

Understanding melancholia's devotion to the lost object as antithetical to the ego's well-being, Freud casts some doubt upon the inevitability of these distinctions, implying, as David Lang has argued, that to "understand melancholia better [...] one would no longer insist on its pathological nature."[69] Rose's response to loss is an extension of Freud's terminological apparatus, forming a richer reservoir of experience in which loss can contain untapped sources of hope.[70] To demonstrate this, we must consider what Freud's observations ignore. As Vamik Volkan argues, Freud fails to account for the existence of "perennial mourners: individuals [who] become stuck for years—or even for a lifetime—unable to let the lost person or thing go."[71] Distinct from Freud's melancholic, such an individual "cannot identify with the enriching aspects of the mental representation of the lost person or thing [or locate] 'suitable reservoirs' for externalizing the representation."[72] While the mourner engages in "project identification" (the act of depositing the images of the lost object or person within "a suitable reservoir" before moving on), the "perennial mourner" cannot assimilate the object-image or "introject."[73] For Volkan:

> an introject is an object representation or a special object image with which the individual who has it wishes to identify. But the identification does not take place, and the object representation or the special object image, with its own "boundaries," remains in the individual's self-representation as an unassimilated mental construct.[74]

The "perennial mourner" is unique for the adoption of constantly shifting ego mechanisms which try and assimilate the introject, and is "torn between a strong yearning for the restored presence of the lost person or thing and an equally deep dread that the lost item might be confronted."[75] The severity of this varies between individuals, but all perennial mourners "daily expend energy to 'kill' or 'bring back to life' the lost person or object."[76]

Clinical reports show perennial mourners construct innovative engagements with loss, which can often make daily life extremely difficult.

The presence of the introject—the object image with which the mourner cannot identity—offers the illusion of choice but never a solution to their loss. A perennial mourner may compulsively consult newspaper obituaries, evidencing a clear concern with their own death, but also a denial of the death of a loved person because that person's name does not appear in the list. Others are well-aware of the death of a loved person but routinely see that individual walking in a crowded street. In one final clinical example, the perennial mourner is forced to repeat certain procedures, such as finding and losing a loved one or object. Volkan cites one patient who repeatedly dreams of trying to rescue the lost person from a burning car, only to wake up each time before learning the result of their efforts. If the lost item was an object, the perennial mourner will repeatedly act out this moment by losing an item, only to later discover it in a coat pocket, or another safe space.[77]

Rose is a powerful example of a perennial mourner. Unable to deposit the objects of left loss within a suitable reservoir, Rose's response to the collective failures of global communism is to try and absorb these defeats within herself. In one key passage, Lethem references Rose's seemingly inexhaustible ability to store-up left loss in a description that triangulates twentieth-century left political commitment with the female body and the slow-time of geological tectonics:

> Dying inside was for Rose a way of life. Within her mother was a volcano of death. Rose had spent her life stoking it, trying to keep the mess inside contained but fuming. In Rose's lava of disappointment the ideals of American communism had gone to die their slow death eternally. Rose would never die precisely because she needed to live forever, a flesh monument, commemorating socialism's failure as an intimate wound.[78]

The metaphor for Rose's harboring of left loss is the inactive volcano, where the ideals of Marx, communism, and revolution are kept "contained but fuming."[79] Strictly speaking this is neither the transitory phase of mourning nor the more durable state of melancholy, but the deep-time of geology where ideas "die their slow death eternally."[80] In the image of the volcano, Lethem turns away from the crisis of utopian imagination to relocate communism as a geological fixture within an impermanent landscape. Communism no longer exists as an ensemble of events put on a plane of measurable time but serves to establish political truths as geological features.

As a "flesh monument" to these defeats, Rose spends the remainder of the novel staging a series of suggestive ego actions. In one key moment, Rose plays out a mock murder-suicide which bears striking allegorical reference to the Holocaust:

> From her knees she tackled Miriam to the floor. For one instant Miriam found herself swept into her mother's incoherent embrace, arms of iron, bosom of cloying depths, corkscrewed face corroding her own with its bleachy tears. Then, as if she was and had always been only a child, her body to be handled, limbs shoved through sleeves, hoisted bruisingly here and there, a terrifying slackness came over her, feeling Rose's next intention. Every strength unavailable to Miriam had apparently flowed into her mother's monstrous wrists and shoulders, her wrestler's grip. Rose shoved Miriam's head into the oven. Miriam only slackened. Perhaps it didn't matter, so much gas filled the room already [...] that was how you earned the right to inflict murder: by showing a willingness to murder yourself first.[81]

Rose's act intersects with Volkan's arguments on the perennial mourner expending energy to kill (or revive) the lost person. Miriam is not lost as such, but the mock murder is approached as a kind of test, "Rose was testing Miriam" for the "absence of struggle," while Miriam "wanted to believe she'd been defiant rather than suicidally helpless."[82]

Unable to distinguish between a loss in an external object and a loss inside oneself, Rose attempts to weave aspects of signification around an event which poses profound challenges to comprehension. In James Berger's phrase, the Nazi Genocide remains an "absent referent" in which only an outline is possible within the contours of Lethem's prose.[83] A detailed reflection on the representational challenges this event evokes is offered by the continental philosopher Maurice Blanchot. For Blanchot, the holocaust remains:

> *the absolute event of history—which is a date in history—that utter-burn where all history took fire, where the movement of Meaning was so swallowed up, where the gift, which nothing of forgiveness or of consent, shattered, without giving place to anything that can be affirmed, that can be denied [...] How can thought be made the keeper of the holocaust where all was lost, including guardian thought?*[84]

Blanchot transforms the impact of the Nazi-perpetrated genocide into a critical philosophical strategy. As he notes the "absolute" occurrence of the event in historical time, he also gestures to the possibility that such profound challenges—to meaning, comprehension, knowledge—may be deferred to some future moment. Elie Wiesel has argued that such a moment is an epistemological absolute, writing that only those who lived through the Holocaust can "transform their experiences into knowledge."[85] Wiesel's requirement for direct experience forbids any kind of written comparison. The Holocaust cannot be re-composed into knowledge; analogies cannot become a substitute for lived experience.

On the face of it, this is a position with which Lethem, even as a post-war Jewish author, does not seem to agree. In a recent conversation with Sarah Anne Johnson, Lethem has noted the centrality of the Holocaust to his childhood, stating he was "raised in a family that commemorated and mourned" the event outside its traditional referential status.[86] Lethem's novel challenges a historical methodology which insists that the events of this period can only be inscribed within personal factual narratives. Theodore Adorno famously proposed that this "working though the past" was a highly suspect formulation. It did not mean "seriously working upon the past, that is, through a lucid consciousness breaking its power to fascinate" but, on the contrary, it meant rather "to close the books on the past and, if possible, even remove it from memory."[87] Lethem's allegory proposes the sentiments of left loss can be captured under radically new regimes of knowledge distinct from the "closed" and "buried" official rhetoric of national collective memory.

Reading each political failure as an "intimate wound," Rose's staging of the genocide demonstrates an attempt, however limited, to weave aspects of signification around a moment of profound loss. Rose's parody offers strategies that attempt to work through this moment in ways that chime with Adorno's warning on official memory. Rose's melancholia avoids representations of commemoration prevalent in Western memory discourse, but the scene, in its clear allegorical reference to the Auschwitz crematorium, represents a servitude to the lost object that enacts "a hallucinatory wishful psychosis [...] on to the patient's own ego."[88] Her act thus calls for a revision of the past through reinvention, opening up, as Jameson remarks, a "vulnerable space and entry-point through which ghosts might make their appearance."[89] The narrative refuses to settle within an epistemological framework that sees left loss as an immutable constellation of historical defeats that can never be fully broached. *Dissident Gardens* can also speak to the importance of left loss in public ceremony. Following her staged Shoah, Rose retreats into the bedroom, "aligned sepulchral on its high narrow bed like a figure in a marble crypt, Grant or Lenin."[90] In "playing to some invisible distant gallery," Rose's performance of left loss through excess—overplayed gestures and exaggerated acts—is marked by a servitude that inaugurates new forms of political desire. Historically, as Susan Buck-Morss argues, the spectacle of Lenin's death was manipulated to ensure obedience to the party, thus marking the termination of the emancipatory project of communism. "Lenin's mausoleum" she writes, remains "the ultimate ideological sign" where the project of political modernization turns to totalitarian mummification.[91] Revolution is no longer a moment of becoming, but a closure that marks the omnipotence of the Party.

Wolfgang Becker's film *Goodbye Lenin!* (2003) offers an illustrative example of the relationship between Lenin and left loss which is useful for my reading of Lethem's novel. In the film an East Berlin woman, Christine, enters a coma at the precise moment of the fall of the Berlin Wall and subsequent German unification. Her son, Alex, stage-manages a transfigured version of the past, involving faking newsreels and searching out foodstuffs no longer available in post–Wall food chains, and creating a disjunction between Christine's consciousness of the world around her and the post–Wall reality. This illusion is torn apart when she wakes up and walks out onto the street. In the ending of the film, Christine, now outside her home, is puzzled to watch the airborne statue of Lenin go past her.[92] As the statue swings through the city it momentarily aligns with Christine's position, the outstretched hand of Lenin beckoning directly towards her. The image is absurdly comic but conceals layers of depth. For Žižek, the film is less an expression of nostalgia for communism than an attempt to come to terms with its collapse; "an exercise in distantiation, detraumatisation, a farewell to a now-vanished form of life."[93] For Žižek, the film "sustains an ethics of protecting one's illusions" with communism to be "staged and sustained for naïve believers."[94] More importantly, the passing statue gestures to the immanence of revolutionary time, recalling Rose's communism as "contained but fuming."[95] Lenin, figured in the statue, is leaving the city, but the departure is hardly elegiac. The outstretched arm of Lenin is framed as kindly, welcoming; an invitation to Christine to remember the emancipatory potential of communism, distorted though it was under state socialism. Falsifying the past as Alex does stimulates debate about history and the more flexible ways of apprehending the past. As Roger Hillman has argued, the film is "history in the subjunctive" or "socialism in surreal mode."[96] The mismatch between a belated rewrite of history, only possible in the frozen time of Christine's amnesia, and the historical interim between the dismantling of the GDR and the reconstruction of German national identity, opens forays into the past as it never was, flashbacks to a non-existent world. The film is not about the recreation of an illusion, but rather socialism as it should have been. For Rose, then, the importance of her figurative death—"aligned [like] Lenin"—offers a symbolic return to the historical moment when revolution became political dictatorship.[97] The gesture is thus one of frustrated potential, offering a proximity to the vanguard party she worships before the emergence of a reality of dictatorship and oppression, and the "complete hopelessness of the situation."[98]

Rose's performance of left loss becomes particularly acute towards the end of the novel, when she becomes romantically attached to local tavern owner Archie Bunker.[99] After a catalogue of bereavements that include the death of her daughter Miriam, son-in-law Tommy, cousin Lenny, and former lover Douglas Lookins, Rose "went looking for a proper funeral, which turned out [...] to mean a proper *Jewish* funeral."[100] Rose attempts to mitigate the effects of melancholy through overexposure: as her "perambulations grew increasingly random [...] she began attending the funerals of strangers."[101] As Rose reflects, in a moment of self-analysis:

> Maybe she'd become meshuggah ahf toit [Yiddish], loon crazy with bereavement. One of those who, losing everyone in cataclysm, begins seeking situations both anonymous and which exemplify grief. Possibly this wasn't crazy at all, or crazy not like a loon but like a fox. The trick might be to diffuse and depersonalize the act of mourning, and also to freeze it, to entrench it as a permanent occupation. *We Jews mourn, there's nothing to it, also nothing new to it.* Let me attend six million funerals, maybe then I'll be done. By that time my personal dead will be raindrops in the sea. I'll forget the names.[102]

Rose's attempt to "entrench" and "freeze" her mourning, ideas which we will return to later in *Eat the Document*, accords with Freud's melancholic and Volkan's perennial mourner. As with Freud's original distinction between mourning and melancholia, Rose's desire to attend funerals lies with her sense of mortality, alloyed to her status in revolutionary history: "the difficulty with omitting the fire of your gaze to melt the humans down to ghosts was this: if Rose then glanced down at her hands gripping the teacup, they'd gone invisible too."[103] Motivated by the loss of others, and the loss of herself, Rose desires to render her mourning a "permanent occupation" evidencing a wish for stability, continuity, and persistence.

It is here Rose meets Bunker, who is asked to give a eulogy for his deceased friend, Stretch Cunningham. Nervous, Bunker delivers a rambling yet humorous address. It emerges that Bunker, an anti–Semite, did not know his friend was Jewish, and the address unfolds with Bunker "plunging ever deeper into the maze of his charismatic stupidity."[104] The scene of the novel is taken from an episode of *All the Family* aired in January 1977. Bizarrely, Rose is present at the funeral and cognizant that she has watched a television episode about these events, thus collapsing distinctions between the two narrative forms.

Choosing to spend time with Bunker in his bar, Rose notes that these daytime drinking-sessions represent similar forms of "Camraderism" that are absolved of the street pounding duties of communist affiliation. Realizing that her years as an "unrepentant communist" have "frozen [her] into oppositional postures" Rose's loss dissolves as she understands communism is beyond party affiliation:

> [Communism] existed as the space between one person and another, secret sympathies of the body. Alliances among those enduring in the world. You found this where you found it, suddenly and without warning, at a certain meeting or protest. You'd then seek a similar sensation, at the next hundred such meetings [...] it might be found in a pickle factory, in the pleasures

of actual solidarity in labor. You found it at the counter of the White castle, lunching on boiled eggs [...] And now, at a boor's tavern on Northern Boulevard.[105]

For Rose, to "talk and laugh at inanities and drink" offers up an activity that is "outside of capitalist exchange" of which "socialists can only dream."[106] Offering a powerful extension of Freud's work, Rose's performance of left loss widens psychoanalytical terms to encompass the emotionally demanding and historically varied processes by which individuals respond to injury, injustice, despair, and loss. In the end, Rose's communism is about forms of solidarity that "weren't ideological nor even really ideals" but connections.[107] Communism is more than party discipline; it is intimacy, feelings, and passions.

The Promise of the Object: Benjamin, Kitsch, and "Suburban Guerrilla"

The fiction of Dana Spiotta is an extended meditation on memory, mourning, and loss. Her first novel *Lightning Field* (2001), orbiting postmodern territory staked by Don DeLillo, traces consumerist fetishes of middle-class LA residents, leading to a discussion of "Rancid America" and "the longing, [the] sadness that leaks through."[108] In *Stone Arabia* (2011), a narrative exploring memory, fabricated history, and familial loss, Denise reflects that in the Amish settlement near her home, they: "protect their undistracted life [...] are suspicious of progress, improvement, new things [and] consider such things with deep skepticism. It wasn't hard to see how much better that might work."[109] *Innocents and Others* (2016) explores changes in human intimacy in the shift from analogue devices to digital technologies while *Wayward* (2021) follows Samantha Raymond's rehabilitation through the restoration of a ruined house.

Concerns with left politics and loss are most forcefully registered in *Eat the Document*, with *Wayward* a close second. Beginning with a bomb plot targeted against the empty summer homes of corporate executives, Bobby Desoto and Mary Whittaker are forced into hiding after the death of a housekeeper. Spiotta has acknowledged in interview that the novel draws on the activities of the Weather Underground, a militant organization started at Ann Arbor Campus, University of Michigan, and active during the Vietnam years.[110] Committed to the end of war, the success of liberation struggles, and the overthrow of the federal government, the group organized numerous protests, arson attacks, and bombing campaigns.

Like *Dissident Gardens*, *Eat the Document*'s discussion of the

American radical left is conducted through temporally dispersed fragmentary sections. The novel works through left loss in two ways: first, Jason's journal entries stage challenges against the fixed empirical distinctions of loss and mourning that are the subject of traditional case-histories; secondly, in one key narrative episode, the novel stages two contrasting readings of left loss by focusing, with remarkable clarity, on the melancholic properties of left political objects. Warning against the sublimation of left political ideals for what can be bought and sold within the marketplace, the narrative reveals the ideological strategies by which the more revolutionary sentiments of left loss can be neutralized.

Structured through fragmentary sections, it is worth mapping some of the key narrative developments and characters. Nash is a joint owner of a left-wing bookshop, "Prairie Fire" (a book by The Weather Underground) with retired alcoholic Henry Quinn. Quinn's suffers from PTSD, even though he never participated in combat and was absolved from the draft on a faked 4F status.[111] Quinn was not in Vietnam, but his night terrors demonstrate the psychological implications of the war's legacy. Alongside managing the bookshop full-time, Nash chairs acronym protest groups, in attendance at which are Miranda and Josh. Miranda exemplifies a longing for more direct forms of political activism (regularly admonishing members for drinking Coca-Cola, for instance) and offers a counterpoint to Nash's proclivity for ironic, disparaging, and witty demonstrations that privilege meaning over outcome.[112] Josh, while beginning the novel as a hacktivist, ends it by working for a multi-national corporation called Allegecom (the same company that made Agent Orange and Henry's PTSD medication). Finally, there is Mary's teenage son Jason, who discovers her disavowed past (he knows her only as Louise) and reunites her with Nash, who is revealed to be Bobby Desoto. Outside most of the important occurrences within the novel (temporally, and spatially, as Jason rarely leaves his room), Jason's journal nevertheless contains extraordinarily rich readings of 1960s music culture, in particular his obsession with The Beach Boys. In love with the unfolding of a cultural moment he has never witnessed, and therefore not properly lost, Jason's attachment to the period is intimately tied to his developing sense of identity and selfhood.

Jason's journal has largely been ignored in scholarship. Most treat the journal as a plot device to further the unfolding of Louise's revolutionary past, rather than a valuable account.[113] Comprising seven sections, the journal entries vary in length from a few lines to slightly fewer than twenty pages. Jason's final confrontation with Louise is not recorded in the journal but occurs in a section entitled "Contrapasso," a stipulation of Dante's *Inferno* in which the punishment of souls is conducted by a "process either resembling or contrasting with the sin itself."[114] As Dorothy Sayers argues, fraud for instance is depicted as an "image of the City in corruption: the progressive disintegration of every social relationship, personal and public [...] all the media of the community's interchange are perverted and falsified."[115] In *Eat the Document*, the allusion to Dante references the consequences of Louise's crime, accentuating the image of her suburban life as tedious, even hellish, in contrast to her militant past. Jason adds to this notion of suburbia as a form of carnivalesque punishment, noting that suburban existence is "a freak's dream world."[116] In not recording this incident in the journal, the text can grant the confrontation between Jason and Louise an immediacy that could only exist in the narrative present, rather than the retrospective and more elegiac tone of the journal itself.

Jason's devotion to 1960s culture is not simply a case of nostalgia. Jason is objective about his fixation, making a clear distinction between his appreciation and VH1 (replaced by MTV and MTV Classic before downloadable music) which he considers sentimental. As Jason writes, "naturally, I find this nostalgia embarrassing."[117] Jason's fixation forms a richness termed by Benjamin as the "enchantment [of] the collector."[118] Jason's fixation on the "extended-box-set-bootleg" which features "exclusively alternative takes" allows him to "jump [...] to a new level in [his] obsession" where "even the most arcane details become fascinating."[119] For Jason, "listening deeply" is "mesmerizing" allowing "you to follow a course of minutia and repetition" which keeps you "utterly enthralled."[120] As Lauren Berlant argues, such attachments are "the operation of optimism in an affective form."[121] As "objects of desire" they articulate a cluster of promises "we want someone or something to make to us and make possible for us."[122] Read through Berlant, Jason's love of The Beach Boys is intimately tied to what the object promises to give to him.

In this instance, the promise of the object is clear. Much like Rose, Jason wishes to mitigate the effects of his loss by attempting to freeze the moment in perpetuity. "I never want to get sick of it," Jason writes "and I never, ever, want to outgrow this or anything."[123] For Berlant, objects contain promises which furnish "an explanation for our sense of endurance in the object."[124] In this sense "all attachments are optimistic" although they do not all "*feel* optimistic."[125] It is our surrender to these objects of promise that is important, regardless of whether we love or dread them. Jason's devotion to the object fractures when he learns his mother is a former radical militant and revolutionary and has therefore been lying about her past. Over the course of the journal, Jason registers "something is definitely up" which is annoying because it is an intrusion into his "privilege of total absorption."[126] Acknowledging that "something has changed" Jason's suspicions develop into the knowledge that his mother is a revolutionary, fugitive, liar, and killer.[127]

Jason is first alerted to this by the story told by Louise, in which she claims she had a relationship with the co-founder of The Beach Boys, Dennis Wilson, before Jason was born. As a melancholic, Jason has already identified the lost experience or object with the ego's continuity. The realization that his mother had a relationship with the lost object of his love—no matter how brief or inconsequential—spurs Jason into the series of investigations which eventually lead to uncovering his mother's disavowed past. The gradual withdrawing of his investment in the object of his love is intimately connected to developing a deeper emotional connection with his mother. It is his love of the lost object that ultimately leads Jason to the real identity of his mother.

The loss of his "deep-felt desire" for The Beach Boys does not result in abandonment, however. Rather Jason wishes to preserve these objects because he may wish to "listen again and it might sound fresh and new."[128] More importantly however, he retains the records because of something he is "quite certain will transpire."[129] For Jason: I need these records because [...] years from now, I will listen to the music and I will remember exactly what is was like to be me [...] totally inhabited by this work, in this very specific place and time.[130] This marks an important shift in his approach to the object. Jason moves from investing in the object in the hope of securing fixity and permanence—"I never want to get sick of it. [...] outgrow this or anything"—to holding onto the object as a hallmark of his own youth. Jason now considers The Beach Boys as an "aural time capsule" that will recall "what I felt, all of what I longed for, all of who I used to be."[131] Having come to process the loss—now regarded as a historical moment rather than a fixation—Jason can move on to invest in new objects and experiences, and, we assume, develop a more stable relationship with his mother.

Alongside revealing object investment to be a creative process, *Eat the Document* powerfully registers the ideological mechanisms by which capitalism attempts to profit from left loss. To make this case, I want to consider *Eat the Document* in relation to Benjamin's work in detail.[132] In the *Trauerspiel*, Benjamin's dissertation later published as *The Origin of German Tragic Drama* (1928), mourning and melancholy are philosophical dispositions rather than discrete pathological conditions.[133] Benjamin's use of the term "Left-Wing Melancholy," first used in a review of Kästner's poetry, offers a more malleable categorization than Freud's clinical symptomatology.[134] Decrying a "left-wing radicalism" that inheres in an "attitude to which there is no longer in general any corresponding political action," Benjamin reads Kästner as synecdoche for a literary movement that "has made the struggle against poverty an object of consumption."[135] For Benjamin, artists like Kästner have sold the failure of revolutionary struggle to a bourgeoisie eager to savor its passing:

> Left radical publicists of the stamp of Kästner, [...] are the decayed bourgeoisie's mimicry of the proletariat. Their function is to give rise, politically speaking, not to parties but to cliques, literarily speaking, not to schools but to fashions, economically speaking, not to producers but to agents [Marxism's] political significance was exhausted by the transposition of revolutionary reflexes, insofar as they arose in the bourgeoisie, into objects of distraction, of amusement, which can be supplied for consumption.[136]

Kästner's writing is for Benjamin "the metamorphosis of political struggle from a compulsory decision into an object of pleasure, from a means of production into an article of consumption."[137] Characterized by a false or hypocritical sadness, left-wing melancholy offers a "curious variety of despair [even a] tortured stupidity" that seeks out profit and acclaim for the artist rather than radical social and political change.[138]

One of the most significant aspects of Benjamin's critique concerns the so-called selling-out of writers or poets, a charge exclusively reserved for those who seek legitimation by financial gain. *Eat the Document* extends these arguments further, demonstrating how loss can warn against market legitimation. Near the close of the novel, Josh and Miranda pay a visit to a trendy clothing store named "Suburban Guerilla" where includes a "totally appalling" section selling revolutionary kitsch—"coffee table anthologies [...] on anarchy and radical environmentalism [...] May 68 calendars, revolutionary scarves and posters."[139] In response to Miranda's disgust at the appropriation of left political figures—receiving its most vulgar expression, she thinks, in a printed pack of themed playing cards[140]—Josh responds with an argument on the inescapable logic of the capitalist world system:

> But you're looking at it all wrong. See, Capitalism can exploit your desire and exploit your need to subvert its exploitation of your desire. It revives—reinforces—itself on the blood of its critics and their critique. It embraces contradictions. It revels in irony.[141]

For Josh, capitalism's successful appropriation of irony—"the favorite mode of the new corporate generation"—leaves only the "tedious, shrill, and feminine [...] earnest stance you love to use."[142] Despite Josh's troubling equation of sincerity with femininity, the forms of political resistance are, for Josh, inconsequential: they "can never touch the perfect, all-powerful, underlying system."[143] Legitimizing capital's appropriation of left-wing political dissent, Josh later goes on to recapitulate this act, acknowledging that while multinational capitalism creates devastating implications for the environment, it can nevertheless provide contentment for him:

> What it comes down to is I just don't want to look at other people's garbage my whole life. There is always garbage blowing around the street outside our

> apartment. Life is too short. All I want is a clean, quiet place. Beauty and order and peace. If Allegecom contributes—as it most certainly does—to the world's degradation, undermining, at least in the global sense, order and peace, as well as multiplying garbage, and—let's face it—suffering, then it also mitigates, quite directly, my own contact with garbage and suffering.[144]

While Josh's capitulation to market forces would earn Benjamin's ire—he has abandoned authentic revolutionary efforts to become the leader of Allegecom's "franchised alternative community"—Josh masquerades these abandonments by attempting to justify his new position as a form of truly liberated thinking in keeping with his argument about "the perfect, all powerful underlying system":

> "You're wrong, you know," Josh said, taking out the playing cards and waving them at her.
> "What?"
> "When you said a confused context causes alienation. But altering the context—appropriation—is subversive. Even Liberating. Walter Benjamin said that about a thousand years ago."[145]

"As Benjamin would argue, however revolutionary irony and reflexivity might initially appear, they function [...] in a counterrevolutionary manner as long as the [the individual] experiences his solidarity with the proletariat ideologically rather than as producer."[146] The cards Josh considers to be potentially "subversive" and "liberating" render left politics into amusing content for bourgeois consumption, turning revolutionary ideals into tacky consumer products.

Over the course of the novel, Josh has become accommodated to a seemingly inevitable global capitalism, which despite its destructive practices, can nevertheless mitigate his contact with human suffering. He has sublimated revolutionary desire for what the political theorist Jodi Dean has termed "democratic drive."[147] Concerning himself with smaller local projects that offer partial reprieve, his enjoyment now "comes from [the] withdrawal from responsibility, [the] sublimation of goals and responsibilities into the branching, fragmented practices of micro-politics, self-care, and issue awareness."[148] Josh initially sought to contest the ownership of private property, but in working for Allegecom he will now seek to protect many of these rights: "no elimination of private property for God's sake [and no] shared lawn mowers or water heaters."[149] Josh no longer feels guilty about private ownership; indeed, the protection of these arrangements furnishes him with activities that feel "productive, important, and radical."[150] Josh's use of Benjamin is an interesting appropriation. It is an attempt, like the playing cards, to turn the practices of left radicalism upon itself, and neutralize its revolutionary content. As Miranda corrects Josh in the closing pages of the chapter, the use of subversive context applies to ideas and images: Benjamin, she notes, "was talking about art, not people. She gestured at the playing cards. Those are human beings. Human beings don't need to be appropriated."[151] Indicative of "confused context," Josh's refusal to see distinctions between cultural and human appropriation highlights the foreclosing of critique under his brand of postmodern irony. The most damning critique is that he himself has been appropriated by the corporation Allegecom.

Left Loss in The Nickel Boys

As Anna Hartnell argues in her survey of the African American literary tradition, Black Lives Matter "inherits the unresolved ghosts of the civil rights past."[152] But this movement has styled itself as both a continuation of and corrective to the race struggles of previous generations. The core activists of Black Lives Matter, notes Fredrick C. Harris, "have been quick to remind us that this is not your grandmamma's civil rights movement."[153] Desegregation of the South was the principal aim of civil rights, meaning many economic and social issues were left untouched by the Civil Rights Act and Voting Rights Act. Attempting a more capacious movement, Black Lives Matter has focused on feminism and LGBTQ issues alongside a critique of state and police violence, and mass incarceration. BLM has also deployed a decentralized leadership structure, in contrast to the largely male-led model of civil rights and black nationalism.[154] These various ghosts of slavery haunt literary fiction by Toni Morrison, Jesmyn Ward, Percival Everett, and Colson Whitehead.

Whitehead is a premier American novelist, accomplished non-fiction writer, and two-time winner of the Pulitzer Prize. He works includes eight novels, a collection of essays about New York, and a memoir about poker. Christopher Lloyd refers to his "extremely varied writing" and "uncategorisable novels" which feature "diverse protagonists" such as an elevator inspector, a nomenclature consultant, an escaped slave, an apocalypse survivor, and a furniture salesman.[155] Whitehead blends elements of genre fiction in his novels, notably in *Zone One* (2011), *The Underground Railroad* (2016), *Harlem Shuffle* (2021) and *Crook Manifesto* (2023). But *The Nickel Boys* eschews the speculative and fantastical elements of other works. As Ron Charles writes, the narrative feels "restrained and transparent" and this stylistic strategy may have everything to do with the violence of racial discrimination. That "groundedness in the soil of natural life is, perhaps, an implicit admission that the treatment of African Americans has been so bizarre and grotesque that fantastical enhancements are unnecessary."[156] Electing realism, the novel also weaves in selections from Dr. Martin Luther King, Jr.'s, radical pacifism and subtle references to Ralph Ellison's *Invisible Man* (1952), a novel I consider in Chapter 5. Critical consensus largely places Whitehead's narrative as concerned with the character's experiences of confinement. For Sean McCann, *The Nickel Boys* is a prison novel which "describes correctional officers who have inherited a tradition of violence from fathers and grandfathers who bossed Southern work gangs and served as slave overseers" while Paula Martín-Salván has explored the novel's complex rhetoric of secrecy and unveiling.[157]

This novel follows Elwood Curtis, a promising African American school student living in 1960s Tallahassee. Elwood holds down a part-time job at a tobacco store, participates in Civil Rights marches, and is selected to attend free college classes. On the day of the first class, he hitchhikes to campus with another black man, only to discover the car is stolen. As noted by Aminatta Forna, the novel notoriously eludes the narrating of legal process, showing that the racism of the period renders Elwood's predicament a foregone conclusion.[158] Elwood is sent to Nickel Academy, a brutal fictional Florida reform school inspired by the real-life Dozier School for Boys. The novel's prologue narrates an archaeological investigation unearthing unmarked graves, unrecorded deaths, and a history of beatings, rape, and torture. As the boys wryly observe at the time, their lives are not worth five cents. Students are taken "out back" to the "White House" and struck with a strap called "Black Beauty" until they cannot walk.[159]

The narrative alternates between the 1960s and 2010s, in which Curtis is a successful business owner of Ace Moving (at Nickel, Ace was the top tier required to "graduate" from the school). But it becomes clear in the final section of the novel that Elwood Curtis does not exist. This is because Curtis was shot in an attempted escape from Nickel, after the other boys hear he will be killed by the administration. In a decision of real courage, one he will never recognize as such, Curtis is freed and rescued by his friend Turner, and the two boys attempt an escape. Turner survives, takes Curtis' name, and tries, despite his cynicism, to live his friend's ideals. The reasons for this are as follows: Curtis manages to secure lighter duties called community services which involve trips out of Nickel with Turner, and a white worker, Harper. Curtis keeps a detailed account of all the illegal activities undertaken under the auspices of community service. The administration is involved in selling off black students' supplies, making a profit on food, medicine, and even stationary. Arriving at "JOHN DINER," an establishment Elwood observes, lacking a letter and apostrophe, the boys must unload the van's cargo: "cartons and crates of Nickel's kitchen stores. Cans of peas, industrial tins of peaches, applesauce, baked beans, gravy. A selection of this week's shipment from the state of Florida."[160] White residents and business owners—even the local doctor is involved—purchase these goods at low prices. These illicit networks underscore the operation of the political economy of segregation, a form of profit maximation in which food and staples are denied the boys to be sold to local business. Curtis and Turner must assist with this criminal distribution, while doing chores off campus for townspeople, such as gardening, painting, and rubbish removal. Curtis includes all this information in a letter which he tries to give to a school inspector but fails. Turner takes the letter and deliveries it on his behalf, thus inaugurating a sense of guilt for Curtis' death. The novel closes with Turner taking a meal in a restaurant and being told by the young waitress to sit anywhere he wants, both a mild and momentous gesture in the context of the novel's focus on Jim Crow. In a moment of dramatic irony, Turner is too tired to see the significance of the name of the restaurant. It is the Richmond, the same one that Elwood worked in when he was twelve, at the beginning of the novel, when his life was one of pure potential. This recognition is imparted alone to the reader.[161] Despite this misrecognition, Turner has returned to Florida to speak about Elwood's story, to find his friend's grave, and confront the lingering remnants of the Nickel administration. But, at least in this moment, he feels oddly at peace with the post-segregation situation: he is hungry, and the restaurant will serve him.

Dissident Garden, *Eat the Document*, and *The Nickel Boys* all concern acts of violence, political resistance, and a skepticism of law enforcement. But Whitehead's novel more carefully crafts the arena of absence, potential, and promise. Curtis is denied a role in the accelerating civil rights struggle, the youth mobilization of Black high school students, and the slowly emerging educational opportunities for Black Americans.[162] The function of the novel is primarily ethical as it engages in a counterfactual speculation of an unlived life in response to the racial violence of the twentieth century. Curtis is subject to a disciplinary logic that punished Black students through mass incarceration and shaped a school-to-prion nexus. There is a sense throughout the narrative of Curtis as a future leader, one who could forcibly attack the inequalities that accompanied racial discrimination and exclusion. If, as King believed, civil rights would be assured by civic participation and peaceful protest, Curtis would likely have become an influential and prominent activist. The novel suspends this narrative of promise and potential for others, first Turner, the reader, to take it up.

This chapter has explored the ways in which three twenty-first-century novels stage engagements with left political defeats, demonstrating how this rich legacy of left loss can be orientated towards new expressive possibilities. As I discussed in the introduction, in recent years several writers have moved from left loss and melancholy towards an embrace of revolutionary communism. More than any other living writer, China Miéville's fictions articulate a precise engagement with Marxism and communism, albeit in less critically established modes. The *City & The City* (2009) blends genres, communist historiography, psychoanalysis, and radical politics to produce a Gothic Marxism. In the following chapter I will argue that this specific strain develops new modalities of expression that challenge critical interest in communist thought.

3

The Return of the Spectre

Gothic Marxism in The City *&* The City

> "The realization of the world as a global market, the undivided reign of great financial conglomerates, etc., all this is an indisputable reality and one that conforms, essentially, to Marx's analysis. The question is, where does politics fit in with all this? What kind of politics is really heterogeneous to what capital demands?"—Alain Badiou, (2000)[1]

This chapter argues for China Miéville's *The City & The City* (2009) as a gothic Marxist fiction that articulates new modalities of communist expression which productively haunt the work of the "Idea of Communism" conferences.[2] To achieve this I set out to juxtapose, and place into dialogue, key passages and thematic strands drawn from Miéville's novel with communist intellectual Alain Badiou. In staging a close and intimate relation between theory and text, the chapter continues the book's interest in dialectics, in which a comparative presentation allows for the development of other possible dispositions that transcend the initial binary.[3] Through this process, Miéville's novel becomes a powerful symbolic engagement with selected aspects of twenty-first-century communism, unearthing new and productive relations with left thought while refusing to banish, conquer, or forget the history of the twentieth-century effort.

The City & The City is a gothic police-procedural narrated by Inspector Tyador Borlú of the Beszél Extreme Crime Squad. Borlú and his team investigate the murder of Mahalia Geary, an international research student found dead and disfigured in a Beszél street. Borlú soon learns Geary had been involved in a scandal involving Beszél and its alter-city, Ul Qoma. His investigations begin in his home city of Beszél, but later lead him to assisting the Ul Qoman police. Eventually the investigation results in an examination of the legend of Orciny, a mythical third city existing between Beszél and Ul Qoma. Orciny is revealed to be symptomatic of the state-induced paranoia that links the two cities together, its purpose to mask the commercial exploitation of the cities by U.S. capitalist enterprise. As becomes clear across the novel, the cities are an uncanny construct as they occupy the same geographical space but are thought to be legally, culturally, and politically distinct. This makes strange occurrences: drivers must "unsee" oncoming traffic, adjacent cafés serve different "local" drinks, and citizens occupy apartments in buildings in different cities.[4] Citizens must repress the traces of the alter city and move "grosstopologically": Miéville's term for how the cities inhabit identical topological space but different cognitive geography.[5] A secret police punish any breach of national, linguistic, or ontological boundaries.

This chapter is divided into three parts. The first establishes a relationship between Marx, capital, and the gothic literary tradition. In Marx, the gothic is much more than a rhetorical flourish, but an essential representational strategy for expressing the capitalist social relation. The gothic illustrates capital's use of fear, manipulation, and dread, alongside an attention to the strangeness of the market, marginal or peripheral places, and transitional time periods. As David McNally argues, Marx shows capital's ability to be "both monstrous and magical"—its ability to conceal the true nature of political economy and blind us to the horrifying transactions between human bodies and work.[6] For McNally, "enhanced by this sorcery, the equivalent of magic-caps pulled over our eyes and ears, bourgeois common-sense vigorously denies the monsters in our midst [...] as with all anxious denials, what has disappeared performs a return of the repressed."[7]An attention to the gothic not only clarifies Marx's analysis of capital, but also his ambition to create a society based on the living of full and free lives.

The second section argues gothic Marxism is the central problematic of Miéville's novel. Warning against a Marxism constructed in narrowly Enlightenment terms, Miéville's narrative sets out to capture the sensual, irrational, and seemingly trivial aspects of life under capitalism, remaining, "in the tradition of a gothic Marxism on this issue," an alternative tradition of Marxism centered on "surrealism and other fantastic currents" that exists "in opposition to the leaden literalism of other Marxist approaches."[8] Miéville challenges the world of progressive bourgeois rationality by way of an attention to the revolutionary energies contained within the arcane and the everyday. Miéville's invocation of surrealism is intended to reference the work of André Breton and Walter Benjamin, whose gothic Marxism entailed an attempt to deploy Freud's exploration of the irrational to modify Marxist notions of praxis, subjectivity, and causality with psychoanalytic concepts and dream-content.[9] But while Breton and Benjamin sought to externalize a dreamworld of unconscious interiority, Miéville's gothic Marxism is centered in materialist mediations on socialist revolution, combining Marxist politics with an aesthetically defamiliarized (gothic) narrative form.

For Jameson, in a genuinely conceived dialectical criticism, there can be no pre-established categories of analysis: each work is the result of a kind of inner logic that evolves its own categories and dictates the terms of its own interpretation.[10] Dialectical thought exists in the "form of the differential perception" and must be comparative in character.[11] To situate the novel as a gothic Marxist fiction that haunts the more mainstream communist accounts, the third section offers a critique of Badiou. While radical left thought contains a plurality of approaches, Badiou has perhaps done more than most to return critical thought to communism. As such, he remains one of the most interesting and problematic figures here. As I will argue in the third and final section, Badiou's communism is idealist and not Marxist *Kapitalkritik*.

Marx, Capital & the Gothic

There are multiple Marxisms, each one dedicated to a specific complex of problems whose "formulations are always in movement and in historical rearrangement and reconstruction, along with their object of study, capitalism itself."[12] Gothic Marxism is an undercurrent, when set against the more mainstream models of Marxist scholarship, although it has gained traction in recent years in relation to a "rising tide of fascination in the gothic which may not yet have reached its apex."[13] It is delineated from other Marxist approaches in its treatment of imagined terrors as a rich field of social production, rather than a form of mystification or, as Margaret Cohen notes, a "mirage to be dispelled."[14] For Cohen, gothic Marxism charts "the contours of a Marxist genealogy fascinated with the irrational aspects of social processes, a genealogy that investigates how the irrational pervades existing society and dreams of using it to effect social change."[15] This entails "not only reclaiming obscured texts for the Marxist repertoire but attending to the darker side of well-known Marxist topoi, starting with the writings of Marx himself."[16] Gothic Marxism suspends an account of the supposed rationality of capital and turns to Marx's monstrous metaphors, the ghostly objectivity of ideological processes, and the political economy of the dead.[17]

Marx was sensitive to the rhetorical powers of the gothic, and *Capital* itself can be considered a gothic text. Francis Wheen means this as invective, dismissing Marx's critique as a "Victorian melodrama or a gothic novel [...] a picaresque odyssey through the realms of higher nonsense

[...] a shaggy-dog story."[18] As Anna Kornbluh argues, Wheen's problematic conceptualization of Marx's work opens up registers attentive to how the book's insights materialize narratively, figuratively, and aesthetically.[19] For Kornbluh, reading *Capital* as a gothic text means pursuing those insights, which were themselves unassimilable, within the discourse of nineteenth-century political economy[20]: The gothic symbolism of *Capital* indexes Marx's ability to think capitalism historically, scientifically, politically, and poetically; as Kornbluh argues, "some of the text's most pressing insights find their most intense formulation performatively: *Capital* means what it means not simply through denotative reference, but through the connotative ways the language *works*."[21]

The move to the interior, the privileging of transgression, and lure of the meaning that lies beyond rational quantification is not exclusive to *Capital* and can be located, albeit to a lesser extent, in Marx's earlier work. *The Communist Manifesto* announces a "spectre is haunting Europe," a spectre capable of transforming the present, rather than a remnant of an outmoded past.[22] Bourgeois society "is like the sorcerer, who is no longer able to control the powers of the nether world whom he has called up by his spells" while the bourgeois subject becomes his own "gravedigger."[23] Capital itself, Marx claims, "is dead labour which, vampire-like, lives only by sucking living labour, and lives the more, the more labour it sucks."[24] The prolongation of the working day into the night "only slightly quenches the vampire thirst for the living blood of labour" and the "vampire will not let go while there remains a single muscle, sinew or drop of blood to be exploited."[25] For Marx, capitalism's capacity to ceaselessly resurrect itself requires a narrative mode able to encapsulate its horrors. For Scott Brewster, Marx's concern with tyranny and class draws on "an extensive Gothic repertoire" to represent capital's ghostly and uncanny aspects.[26]

Evident already then is a rich and rewarding relationship between Marx and the gothic, suggesting the initial contradictions that might traditionally separate the two, at least when approached through orthodox thought, can be absolved within some vaster dialectical synthesis. The gothic's emphasis on malevolent motives is no longer mystification but deeply historiographical, its recurring horrors staging conflicts between the values of a seemingly despotic past and an ostensibly enlightened present. Still in its early critical formation, the notion of a gothic Marxism—and a gothic dialectic, with certain stylistic, formal, and thematic patterns—has yet to be fully developed in the critical dialogue. Feminist, psychoanalytic, and cultural criticism has examined the ideological dimensions of the gothic, while work in historical materialism has remained far behind. Lukács confines the gothic to the eighteenth century, refusing to venture into discussions of the gothic in realist texts.[27]

Jameson considers the gothic a hopelessly "boring and exhausted paradigm" because it is mere "class fantasy (or nightmare) in which the dialectic of privilege and shelter is exercised."[28] Derrida's *Specters of Marx* (1993) remains a rare exception, with Derrida tracing Marx's use of ghosts and spirts.[29] Derrida's reading resists grand narratives, arguing for a gothic haunting—apparitions, conjuring, temporal disruption—as a transformative mode.

A gothic dialectic entails a differential perception attuned to the resonances among the irrational, the illicit, and the supernatural aspects of social topography.[30] Cohen does not share this ambition, writing that "attempts to theorize Gothic Marxism" have led to a critique that "moves beyond logical argument and binary position towards a process of thematic comparison regulated by overdetermination [rather] than dialectics" per se.[31] However, there is nothing undialectical here. Cohen assumes a mechanical, or vulgar, determinism, itself an "overdetermined and mythically hypostatized category" present in selected Marxist circles during the early twentieth century.[32] There is nothing in Cohen's approach or the gothic tradition more broadly to suggest that the gothic's sensitivity to trauma, haunting, and repression cannot be considered a narrative apparatus sensitive to dialectics, or indeed to registering determining relationships between a superstructure and the infrastructural shifts and modifications occurring in the economic sphere. As has been suggested by other critics, literary narratives are never simply a reflex or reflection of the economic plane; their determination is always a question of limits and pressures, of complex interacting elements within a totality of social relations.[33] The gothic enables one to grasp the subjective particularities of a given historical situation: to be contemporary with transformations which figure uncompleted historical developments as ghostly, uncanny, supernatural, or strange. Approached this way, the gothic is a crucial theoretical framework for advancing dialectical thought.

Miéville, Marxism & the Gothic

To proceed we first need an account of Miéville's political and intellectual mission. Miéville is an activist, writer, scholar of international law, and former member of the Socialist Worker Party.[34] He began his career by claiming, against the influential approaches of J.R.R. Tolkien and C.S. Lewis, that fantasy can be radical rather than conservative.[35] Additionally, Miéville contested the distinction between science-fiction and fantasy, the former held as possessing superior critical value for what Darko Suvin called "cognitive estrangement."[36] Miéville is in agreement with the tendency of the last few years to move towards the more inclusive category of "speculative fiction" which has slowly begun to replace certain strains of science-fiction and fantasy, but the genre distinction he prefers is the "New Weird."[37] Inextricable from the pulp fiction of H.P. Lovecraft, the "weird" is the subject of critical fascination, spawning speculative realism and "horror" philosophy.[38]

Gothic Marxism conceptualizes *The City & The City* in more intriguing political modes, as it is expertly suited to exploring the darker side of neoliberal enterprise.[39] Miéville first aligned himself with the term in a speech given for "Socialism 2013," an event hosted in London by the Socialist Party (formerly Militant). Exploring Halloween from a Marxist perspective, Miéville argued the existence of alternative spaces of fear are constitutive of our ability to conceptualize utopian futures. As the left have been made gothic creatures by global capitalism—Miéville cities the tabloid coverage of former Venezuelan President Hugo Chavez—he proposes a "socialist defense of monsters" that would recognize the institutional networks of discrimination and censorship levelled at left ideas and political figures.[40] In occupying these spaces—in coming to think politically about the monstrous—the left can articulate a fresh engagement with the "monstrous dialectic of modernity" and the capitalist grotesque.[41] As suggested in Miéville's account, what remains truly monstrous about the existential structures of capitalist existence is the manner in which such horrors are normalized. As McNally argues, "what is most striking about capitalist monstrosity [...] is its elusive everydayness, its apparently seamless integration into the banal and mundane rhythms of quotidian existence."[42] For Miéville, the most salient representations of capitalism occur in fictional environments which treat bourgeois social relations as profoundly othering, uncanny, and strange. The blurring of genres is a constituent feature of Miéville's fictional practice. Breaching arbitrarily rendered and punitively regulated boundaries produces unexpected conjunctions which are useful for thinking about the emergence of a communist politics. Attention to the material demarcation of *The City & The City*'s fictional world is required.

The parts of the cities fall into one of three locations (depending on your perspective, of course): being either total (firmly ensconced within that city), alter (within the other city), or crosshatched (citizens of both cities who "unsee" each other). At the center of the two vast metropolitan sprawls is Copula Hall, an architectural structure that exists in both cities under the same name. Functioning as a border, lawful passage through the Hall enacts an ideological, rather than geographical, displacement: individuals remain in the same physical space, but are considered to have crossed into the alter city:

> Then the vehicles with their stamped permissions-to-cross emerged at the opposite end from where they entered, and drove into a foreign city. Often they doubled back, on the crosshatched streets in the Old Town or the Old Town, to the same space they had minutes earlier occupied, though in a new juridic realm.[43]

Those who spend sustained periods in either city must first complete an acclimatization test. When Borlú is assigned to Ul Qoman he is given an "accelerated orientation" designed to help the citizen "through the potentially traumatic experience of *being in* Ul Qoma, unseeing all their familiar environs, where we lived the rest of our life, and seeing [buildings] we had spent decades making sure not to notice."[44] Borlú is placed in a simulator which contrasts his home city of Beszél with Ul Qoma, projecting "images and video of Beszél with the Besz buildings highlighted and their Ul Qoma neighbors minimized with lighting and focus."[45] Gradually the authorities "reverse the visual stress, so that for the same vista Beszél would recede and Ul Qoma shine."[46] This form of ideological totalism is known in the novel as a distinct branch of manipulative neurology termed "acclimatization pedagogy."[47] "We've got so much more sophisticated ways" of enforcing these ideological restrictions, remarks one official, "we work with neuroscientists, all sorts of stuff."[48] This form of indoctrination, experienced by Borlú as procedure for inter-city travel, posits numerous ethical quandaries. The acclimatization test resembles the Stasi practice of *Zersetzung* (decomposition, corrosion, undermining), whereby individuals are subjected to a complex array of disorientation tactics in a bid to discourage civil activism.[49] In *Zersetzung*, secret methods of control, manipulation, and repression replace the overt terror of political dictatorship.

As Mark Bould and Sheryl Vint suggest, such moments loosen the more stable definitional criteria as the "bizarre alternative geography is the product of *ideological* rather than *material* difference."[50] Conventional narrative strategies often fail to register the unseen forces of capital; they assume that what is invisible is not there. For Miéville this is to miss the essential: the hidden forces and invisible powers that are fantastically real, constituting horrifying aspects of a strange and bewildering world that represents itself as free from sentimental delusions and comforting mythologies. An attention to ideological difference is powerful, in this case producing a narrative which mimics the absurdity of capitalist rationality, the better to expose it.

Situated within a "curl of coastline" at the "edge of Europe," the novel registers a number of thematic affinities that constitute elements of twentieth-century communist regimes, and such features situate the text in relation to the lingering remnants of communism operating in capitalist geopolitical modernity.[51] It is tempting to read the novel as an allegory of "actually existing socialism" but the cities are a complex mediation, a series of reciprocal determinations closer to the theory of combined and uneven development.[52] As Miéville states:

> I didn't want to make it narrowly, allegorically reductive, in any kind of lumpen way. I didn't want to make one city heavy-handedly Eastern and one Western, or one capitalist and one communist, or any kind of nonsense like that. I wanted to make them both feel combined and uneven and real and full-blooded.[53]

The cities maintain seemingly normal international relations, connected through commercial trade, diplomatic embassies, and international air travel. Besźel and Ul Qoma occupy something of a cold peace, regarding each other with suspicion but acknowledging state sovereignty. Besźel is worn and disheveled, made up of "antique sites" and outdated technology. By comparison, Ul Qoma is advanced, integrated with the west, and more ethnically diverse. An emerging hub of infrastructural growth, Ul Qoma has international hotel chains, underground rail, and wireless technology. As Borlú notes of these divergent economic fortunes, "like all Besźel dwellers, I had become used to shopping in the [...] shadows of foreign success."[54] Breach presides over the cities, but Besźel and Ul Qoma differ markedly in their approach to governance, political repression, and censorship. Ul Qoma's police force is a "*militsya*" state security service rather than a "*policzai*" or civil law enforcement, and officers have stronger powers of prosecution, interrogation, and surveillance. Borlú's opposite in Ul Qoma, Senior Detective Qussim Dhatt, uses "robust interrogations" and intimidation, physically assaulting members of various political factions whenever leads run dry. Radical groups and political parties are illegal in Ul Qoma, but tolerated by the police if they display restraint. Alongside distinct judicial procedures, the cities possess different languages, customs, and traditions. For Carl Freedman, the names of citizens from Besźel (Corwi, Borlú, Briamiv) appear of Russian or Eastern European origin, while those of Ul Qoma (Aikam, Tsueh, Dhatt) are of the Far East.[55]

The revolution near the end of the novel is one of violence, a "bloody war between those dedicated to bringing the cities together and the forces charged with keeping them apart."[56] Borlú notes what he considers to be the failure of the uprising, but registers the danger of sparks:

> the streets we went through the last throes, the nerve twitches of a little revolution that had died before it was born and had not known it. Those dying flails remained dangerous, though, and we were in a soldiery way. No curfew could contain this panic.[57]

Borlú is escorted by his Breach sentinel, Ashil, and the mass panic of Besź and Illitian citizenry is evident, with "wall to wall spraying slogans" written in a dual-national typography.[58] For Ashil and the other members of Breach, the uprising constitutes a new spatial-geographic designation: "both cities are Breach now."[59] Breach now names forms of social and political organization as the residents of the cities challenge divides, censorship, and repression.

It is in this encounter with limits that a rift opens where communism is revealed as the dissolution of capitalist social relations. Breach becomes revolutionary, yoking together disparate and wholly incompatible entities within a new assemblage that cannot be reconciled to a predictive form or union. The graffiti sprayed across the walls during the revolution names but one aspect of Breach through the creation of new linguistic articulations.[60] Introducing a focus on language—the concern of his later novel *Embassytown* (2011)—Miéville hints at a shared spatial-ontological premise between the two cities:

> in its original or later written form, Illitian bears no resemblance to Besz. Nor does it sound familiar. But these distinctions are not as deep as they appear. Despite careful cultural differentiation [...] the languages are closely related—they share a common ancestry after all. It feels almost seditious to say so.[61]

Considering Besźel and Ul Qoma as possessing a common linguistic ancestor is, of course, an illegal act. While the separate languages provide distinct forms of order, the realization of a shared cultural premise results in a breach of these fragile relations. Borlú reports, that now:

> We are all philosophers here where I am, and we debate among many other things the question of where it is that we live. On that issue I am a liberal. I live in the interstice yes, but I live in both the city and the city.[62]

However, Borlú's "liberal" position—living comfortably in the interstice—is overshadowed by the separation of the cities and the power of multinational corporations. As Freedman notes, the American executive responsible for the murder of Geary escapes at the close of the narrative in a corporate helicopter, highlighting the unpursued criminal power of global capitalist exchange.[63] The ending is indicative of what Miéville calls "anguished optimism" in which the transcendental claims of Breach as an enforcer of political, legal, and linguistic controls have been forestalled rather than overturned. It is in the unclaimed space between the cities—what the novel calls "controversial *dissensi*"—that revolutionary action can exist. For Borlú, this "interstitiality [...] was not only possible but inevitable [...] life could thrive in that little gap."[64]

New Horizons: Marx, Badiou, Communism

In the same year *The City & The City* was published, the Birkbeck Institute for the Humanities hosted "The Idea of Communism," an event that attracted over one thousand spectators and featured left-wing luminaries Alain Badiou, Toni Negri, Judith Balso, Jodi Dean, and others.[65] The conferences were repeated in Paris, Berlin, New York, and Seoul, with proceedings appearing in edited collections.[66] Verso launched what it called the "pocket-communism" series featuring titles including Badiou's *The Communist Hypothesis* (2010), Boris Groy's *The Communist Postscript* (2010), Jodi Dean's *The Communist Horizon* (2012), and Bruno Bosteels' *The Actuality of Communism* (2014).[67] Despite this collective effort, Badiou remains a central figure within the collection.

As Nicholas Thoburn argues, Badiou's "Idea" comprises three distinct elements: "a truth procedure"—"a concrete time specific sequence in which a new thought and practice of collective emancipation arise, exist and eventually disappear"; a belonging to history—"a truth procedure inscribed in the general becoming of Humanity" and an individual subjectivation—"whereby an individual determines the place of a truth with respect to his or her own vital existence and to the world in which this existence is lived."[68] In his focus on the "Idea," Badiou seeks to uncouple communism from twentieth-century historical time, and situate it as a trans-historical imaginary operation "by which individuals, in pursuit of this idea, can become fully-fledged subjects engaged in a universal 'truth procedure.'"[69]

For Thoburn, Badiou's "Idea" is problematic for privileging an idealist and utopian impulse at odds with Marx's communism as a "real movement" rather than "a state of affairs" or "an ideal to be overcome."[70] Badiou's provides no critique of capitalist social relations, and his "Idea" exists in separation from the material conditions of life outside it. In the *Communist Manifesto*, Marx and Engels insist communism is existent only immanently to social relations as a whole.[71] Communism, then, does not designate a subjectivity or political faction, "but the antagonistic quality of capitalist social relations, the tendencies, forces, and acts that push toward their overcoming."[72] "For communism is not born of the past but leans into the future with a fragmented temporality engendered of its relation to the transforming limits of capital and the untimely shocks of the present."[73] Without this dimension, communism has no historical purchase, no way to live in the now. At its worst, Badiou's "Idea" of communism as a universal truth procedure "can nurture and extend *capitalist* social relations" because it provides no critical account of capital itself.[74]

Conversely, in the literary realm, Miéville approaches communism in much closer dialogue with Marx's writings. Indeed, one can note that the materialist strategy of Marxism grows stronger whenever ideology takes on a more spiritual, religious, or in this case, idealist character.[75] Like Marx, Miéville is interested in the irrational aspects of capitalist processes, and the ways in which capitalism can construct a gothic phantasmagorical landscape. Miéville's use of "Breach" is a prime example here, rendering a powerful attack on the ideology of capitalist social relations through a series of estrangement affects. Conceived by Miéville, "Breach" is dialectical, naming the clandestine force controlling the "existential protocol" of urban movement and elevating border contravention—physical or cognitive—above all crimes.[76] It also, however, names the potentially revolutionary act of crossing borders, and recurs throughout the narrative as a way of naming contact points between legal, ontological, or conceptual entities. Borlú signals the porosity of the border in his own act of (unwitnessed) transgression when canvassing the crime-scene at the very opening of the novel:

> An elderly woman was walking slowly away from me in a shambling sway. She turned her head and looked at me. I was struck by her motion, and I met her eyes. I wondered if she wanted to tell me something. In a glance I took in her clothes, her way of walking, of holding herself, and looking. With a hard start, I realised that she was not on GunterStráz at all, and that I should not have seen her.[77]

The moment of communion between Borlú and the elderly woman never transpires, or rather the articulation—the shock of difference—is registered through several non-linguistic means predicated on the woman's clothing and deportment. Drawing attention to the social production of space, Borlú's (criminal) glimpse highlights the importance of filtering; the process of "unseeing" and avoidance that occurs within capitalist environments, such as the way we might pretend not to notice a beggar on the street. The use of gothic terror and the irrational is clear here, albeit dependent on carefully delimited materialist practices. As once critic comments, the "reader's initial perception is that Borlú has seen a ghost; an absence made present" registered through repeated use of the negative.[78]

Capitalist existence is predicated on communal estrangement which is experienced in the narrative through the registration of a ghostly other who "I should not have seen."[79] Borlú's glimpse, however, is starkly opposed to the hauntological which traditionally implies that the figure of the ghost represents the return of the repressed and "a time out of joint."[80] Rather, this is a present stained with the residue of the ghostly, a "radicalized uncanny" in Miéville's own words, which estranges reality not through a strategy of reverence for the ghostly, but a radical gothic ontology constructed out of antagonistic capitalist social relations.

Such a position is distinct from Badiou's idealism, as the forms of estrangement in the novel construct a gothic Marxist materialism where uncanny expressions are the product of material relations. A further example occurs at the level of discourse itself. The ambiguity of the novel's language is supplemented by the gradual realization that English is unknown to most of the characters. Readers are therefore asked to imagine a process of transcoding, in which the clichés and colloquialisms of *Besź* are translated into corresponding images and meanings within our own. In Miéville's novel, one has a very real sense of language unfolding as a system, in which the selection of words is never simple or easy. The notion that the text is (albeit fictionally) translated and therefore actively unfolds within the present in the manner of speech gives the unsettling illusion of discourse. The most striking feature of the novel's language however is the tension between this kind of narrative description—always pushing at its own limits and capacities—and the pressures of the more dampened "official" tone of the police report which structures the entire dialogue, and which Borlú eventually signs off, as "the last case of Inspector Tyador Borlú."[81]

While the reader experiences Borlú's "seeing" of the alter-city citizen as a ghost or specter—a misrecognition paralleling Borlú's own mistake—this uncanniness receives its fullest expression in the novel's panorama of deindustrialization. As Borlú canvasses the surrounding area with his subordinate Corwi, he offers a uniquely gothic vision of capitalism, "a history of autonomies gained and lost, a future that alternatives between threats and promises, and the ever-precarious present."[82] Borlú's description of Beszél's cityscape records the uneven development of individual enterprises, and individual branches of industry, inevitable under the capitalist world system. As Borlú narrates:

> There were places of crosshatch in the larger streets and a few elsewhere, but that far out of the bulk of the area was total. Few antique Besź stylings, few steep roofs or many-paned windows: these were hobbled factories and warehouses. A handful of decades old, often broken-glassed, at half capacity if open. Boarded facades. Grocery shops fronted with wire. [Houses] burnt out and left as crude carbon renditions of themselves.[83]

While the human subject of the alter-city is half glimpsed and eventually "unseen" because of the novel's unique ideological restrictions, the effects of capital's creative destruction are more openly acknowledged here. The combined and uneven development of capitalist industrial development—with Trotsky's initiating formulation concerning the mixture "of archaic with more contemporary forms"—is powerfully rendered in the bridging of the temporally and spatially bounded power relations that exist between the crosshatched and total sections.[84] A "handful of decades old," the "hobbled factories" and "boarded facades" of industrial wreckage point to a gothic materialism, showing that modernity has exhausted its utopian potential. On this occasion, Borlú's crime of seeing the subject goes unpunished, and indeed Breach generally ignores minor transgressions: however, "Ul Qoman pickpockets or muggers at work" are to go unseen "from where you stand in Besźel, because Breach is a worse transgression than theirs."[85]

The absurdities of this situation—familiar from the cities of Belfast, Berlin, Jerusalem, Johannesburg, and the Israeli-occupied territories—is intensified when the archaeology student Yolanda Rodriguez is shot dead by a Besźel nationalist. This crime is not subject to the punishment of Breach because both subjects are in the same city when the murder is committed. Borlú pursues the subject from the alternative city, resulting in a remarkable chase where certain streets, rooftops, and alleyways are forbidden because they reside within the topography of the other city. Borlú eventually fires on the suspect (from Besźel) and is apprehended because his action inverts juridical precedent and constitutes Breach. Once activated Breach is supralegal, with sanctions that are "pretty limitless."[86] As the Besź councilor, Yorj Syedr, makes clear, attempts to resist the power of Breach are themselves treated as acts of defiance:

> "Breach is ... an alien power." Several of the Besź and some of the Ul Qoman members of the committee looked shocked. "We all know it's the case," Syedr said, "whether it is polite to acknowledge it or not. Breach is and I say it again an *alien power*, and we hand over our sovereignty to it at our peril. We've simply washed our hands of any difficult situations and handed them to a—apologies if I offend—but a shadow over which we have no control. Simply to make our lives easier."[87]

A focus on surveillance is pursued by Michele Foucault in *Discipline and Punish* (1975) and furnishes an analytical perspective from which to address Miéville's presentation. For Foucault, discipline in society aims to control the populace so completely that the agencies charged with its responsibility can effectively disappear. In the model of the Panopticon, borrowed from Jeremy Bentham, surveillance is no longer exceptional but runs throughout the entire social body:

> The ideal point of penality today would be an indefinite discipline: an interrogation without end, an investigation that would be extended without limit to a meticulous and ever more analytical observation, a judgement that would at the same time be the constitution of a file that was never closed.[88]

This "ideal" form of penality is referenced when Breach claims their power primarily through non-violent means: "we're only the last ditch: it's everyone in the cities who does most of the work."[89] Breach works through acquiescence "because you don't blink. That's why unseeing" is so vital.[90]

It is here that the undisclosed East European setting of the novel becomes significant, where the skill of disavowal—of a friend, neighbor, colleague—was a survival mechanism within a totalitarian power. While the narrative is set in the twenty-first century, the implication being the events of the novel take place at some ostensibly liberated moment, Miéville reveals how these repressive ideological strictures continue to exist within and alongside the flourishing of capitalist markets:

> President Ul Mak [...] had announced certainly not a repudiation but a development of the National Road, an end to restrictive thinking, a *glasnostroika*, as Ul Qoman intellectuals hideously neologized. With the CD-and-DVD shops, the software startups and galleries, the bullish Ul Qoman financial markets, the revalued dinar, came, they said, New Politics, a very vaunted openness to hitherto dangerous dissidence. Not to say radical groups were legalized, but their ideas were sometimes acknowledged [...] so one heard.[91]

The writing is conditioned by the ideological struggles it seeks to overcome, a kind of hesitancy in Borlú's account, for he is in clear violation of Breach by talking to us, and would, we assume, be immediately apprehended if this crime become known. Offering a mixture of frustration, of thwarted rationalization and hope, a reluctance to articulate the political dilemmas at stake can be clearly detected here. Borlú ends his discussion with the caveat that "so one heard," an attempt to extricate himself from any potential Breach. Disquisitions on city archeology, history, geopolitical secession, language, and the like are entwined with plot development, and yet these narrative asides routinely break off in what becomes a characteristic retreat and representational dilemma. It "would be far worse than illegal for me to pursue it," Borlú's notes in one aside.[92] When trying to explain Breach to non-residents, Borlú's produces a series of hesitant statements: "well, among other things, yes. It ... they aren't like the police":

> But it is ... it isn't like other powers. You have some sense of its ... capabilities? The Breach is ... it has unique powers. And, it's ah, extremely secretive. We, the embassy, have no contact with ... any representative of Breach. I do realize how strange that must sound, but.... I can assure you Breach's record [...] is ah, ferocious. Impressive.[93]

We have an intriguing texture of incomplete statements. It is as if some censorial presences were lurking in the background to Borlú's digressions, a kind of third interlocutor watching and conditioning the material of the novel itself. There is something about Breach that resists direct representation, in which a relatively straightforward progression from experience to textual inscription becomes undone. These moments of veiled representation are powerful techniques of figuration. They allow characters to turn from the destructive and devastating facts of history—what for Borlú is clearly a gesture of survival and denial—while rendering those facts with greater precision than direct representation could give.

Any content that insists on remaining unclear, unmastered, and unresolved is by its very nature more troubling than that which can be understood, assimilated, and explained. The suppression of history is subversive, propelling us forward in our search for answers.

Miéville's "Breach"—which clearly references twentieth-century communist ideology and exclusion—examines the period of penance that followed state socialism. In seeking to sweep aside the despair of the 1980s and 90s, the triumphalist "end of history," and the rise of U.S. hegemony, Costas Douzinas and Slavoj Žižek's have celebrated new antagonisms, the return of political participation, and the flowering of anti-austerity movements as marking a much-needed shift from post–Cold War complacency.[94] But for the gothic, the intellectual landscape is always one of ruins in which the present and future are grafted onto the wreckage of old systems, and where the breaks and fractures between these realms threaten at all points to open onto an abyss. And yet the gothic is a cultural code that seeks to address and accommodate these ruins, a language in which to speak to the ghosts of the past, present, and future. For David Punter, the gothic has "something quite specific to do with [new beginnings] as though the very attempt to turn over a new leaf unavoidably involves conjuring the shadow of the past, watching its curious shapes fall over the attempted purities of the future."[95]

The City & The City is a gothic Marxist narrative, sensitive to the intangible qualities of capitalist subjectivity, and committed to a more critical politics. Miéville's use of breach reveals the antagonistic character of capitalist relations, and potential methods of opposition. The novel does not seek to construct an outline for future change but highlights points of contestation and opposition—fissures and cracks—to contest capital.

4

From Reel to Real

Forming Radicalism in The Flamethrowers

In its representation of global economic crisis, left political movements, and modern art, Rachel Kushner's *The Flamethrowers* revels in the aesthetics of cinema. The death of the German soldier at the opening of the book is framed through a script or screenplay, establishing violent action, and the immediacy of the cinematic image "HE KILLED HIM WITH A MOTORBIKE HEADLAMP (WHAT HE HAD IN HIS HAND)" as central to its storytelling apparatus.[1] The opening sequence—if we may call it that—stages military action through the metaphor of professional sports, in which the two lone combatants, one German, the other Italian, without weapons or the ability to lay a hand on them, struggle for possession of the headlamp, "just about the size and shape of a rugby ball."[2] Combat as competition: with all the hallmarks of football, or in concession to the European reader, rugby: shoulder charges, dump tackles, grubber-kicks, the two men loose from the pack, and of course, in the theater of conflict, "no penalty here for foul play."[3] It is a terrible, dark, and ominous scene, in which the German soldier is killed—"brained"—with the headlamp taken from the bike of a deceased Italian comrade.[4] It is in this opening sequence that the First World War is confronted, dealt with, and will not be returned to until the close of the novel, a form of backstory and a method of exposition which will link the Italian Ardito or shock troops with Avant-Garde movements of the 1970s. The Italian soldier here is the father, T.P Valera, who will survive the war and build the Valera motorbike empire which is at the center of the strikes and protests which form the final third of the novel. But here, at the opening, in the dense woods near the Isonzo River, the "faint whoosh of a flamethrower" can be heard from across the valley, handled by a military figure that gives the narrative its title. Valera's children, Sandro, and Roberto will construct paper figures of this trooper, which they will burn in a restaging of their father's own military exploits.

This focus on incineration is indeed a staple of the text. To make it burn—"FACT UT ARDEAT"—is a phrase repeated throughout, establishing the revolutionary credentials of Kushner's novel through forms of violence and reprisal.

Other filmic features of the text deserve empathize. Reno's journey into Nevada which quickly follows is likewise told through various shots and camera angles. She herself is an art student, a photographer, and film maker, with an appreciation of movement and perspective: "the two things I loved," Reno confides, "were drawing and speed."[5] The set pieces of the novel are cinematic, with Kushner cutting between two visual images (the bike headlamp as weapon and later, the bike as a vehicle for speed, freedom, and liberation) or moving between two locations, such as the Italian Front, and U.S. West Coast.

But to what extent can we link a novelist's work to any fondness they may have for cinema? Sartre demonstrates the importance of such biographical facts when he confides that his first novel, *Nausea* (1938) was, in part, derived from the experience of watching films as a child. In *Words* (1963), Sartre writes of "picture-going" and cinematic spectatorship:

> I was witnessing the delirium of a wall; solids had been freed from a massiveness that weighed on me, that weighed even on my body, and my young idealism was delighted with that infinite contraction [...] I loved the cinema even in plane geometry. To me, black and white were the supercolors that contained all the others and revealed them only to the initiate; I was thrilled at seeing the invisible. Above all, I liked the incurable muteness of my heroes. But no, they were not mute since they knew how to make themselves understood.[6]

The big reveal comes when Sartre, still a child, leaves the cinema, blinking in the harsh light, only to notice the strangeness of the real world outside. It is not the illusion of the film, which is shattered, but a recognition of the unreality of life, lacking vision, color, and direction. We should add that cinema, for Sartre, was a mode of collectivity, in which one gropes through the dark towards one's seat, noting the lack of "social hierarchy" in the theater, into which one had inadvertently stumbled.[7] For Sartre, then, the experience of writing was itself is cinematic, the composing of sentences a kind of picture thinking. As a young boy, he tried "to pluck the pictures from my head and realize them outside of me, between real pieces of furniture and real walls as bright and visible as those that flashed on the screens."[8] In *Nausea*, the character Roquentin, based on Sartre himself, is a frequent visitor to the cinema and mentions a silent historical film, *Imperial Violets* (1924), directed by Henry Roussel.[9] But, at least for Sartre, cinema is necessity, not luxury. In his calculation of his monthly expenses, Roquentin must cover a "room for three hundred francs, fifteen francs a day for food: that leaves four hundred and fifty francs for laundry, incidentals and the cinema."[10] Sartre and de Beauvoir's journal, *Les Temps Modernes*, published in October 1945, took its title from Chaplain's masterpiece, *Modern Times* (1935), and Sartre had passion for American cinematic writers, like Fitzgerald, Faulkner, Dos Passos, Steinbeck, and Nathanael West.[11]

Kushner's fondness for cinema is also well known, a passion she shares with another contemporary writer considered in these pages: Dana Spiotta, whose fictions are filled with films and film-makers of many kinds; the avant-garde productions of Bobby Desoto and Mary Wainwright of *Eat the Document*; Hollywood cinema in *Lightning Fields*; the experiment of watching, some twenty times, Chaplain's *City Lights* (1931), the fictional affair with Orson Welles, the many student short films, and the destroyed, never-to-be-aired documentary of the arsonist Sarah Mills, contained in *Innocents and Others* (2016). Kushner has herself appeared in an avant-garde film, *Readers* (2017), which recorded writers and directors silently reading books. She has written film criticism, compiled a list of her favorite films for magazines, and was recently chosen by the Telluride Film Festival as a guest director to select a series of films to screen for Labor Day Weekend.

To read her novel as drawing upon cinematic devices, is to confer on it a scriptable status. Barthes proposed that scriptable—or "writerly"—sentences made you wish to write yourself.[12] They stimulated the imagination and "promised a pleasure in combining language," that was perhaps more visual than linguistic.[13] Barthes' other term, however, was no less visually inclined. What he called the "readerly" text seeks to "transform the transparent flow of language as much as possible into material images and objects we can consume."[14] But there are important distinctions here. Film can only register the inner action of the subject externally, deploying devices such as mood, gesture, and deportment most familiar from the silent period. It must partake of situating objects, creating affect through the arrangement of materials, where the action unfolds. As Jameson writes, in his book on cinema:

> [in film, effects] are the result of the pre-positioning of objects, the pre-arrangement of the object world, within the shot, rather than as auto-referential exhilaration of a medium taking its contents as some mere pretext for a display of itself and its own unique linguistic powers. The great moments here are those of the restitution of a world transformed into images rather than infected and fragmented by them: that of the secret blueness of the Parisian night sky, as in the famous Magritte evening cityscape, or that vision of the lighthouse refuge beyond the world, and the elegant and powerful white Citroen which moves across its causeway in the breathtaking openness of dawn.[15]

The references are to European cinema, no doubt different to American film with its more rigorous empathize on capital and commercialization. But if film has the primacy of the image, then its weakness is the interior, and interior monologue specifically (even detailed and lavish interiors are taken together as a single object of consumption for the camera lens). To be sure, other languages convey an interior because we cannot access them. But the representational tools of film, as attractive as they are, cannot properly account for the intimacy of the novel.

Is there a heightened visual quality to Kushner's sentences? I would suggest that her framing devices are uniquely cinematic: "I walked out of the sun, unfastening my chin strap. Sweat was pooling along my collarbone, trickling down my back" have all the visuals of American advertising. Reno's journey to Nevada takes place in a chapter titled, "Spiritual America," and the text here recalls all the staples of the American road narrative: freedom, mobility, becoming, and the incorporation of the outsider.[16] Jameson remarks that film is "*essentially* pornographic, which is to say that it has its end in rapt, mindless fascination."[17] This scandalous comment captures the hallmarks of cinema: heightened attention, captivation, film as a physical experience, the visual as an addiction, and the potential for moralizing alarm. But the invocation of the pornographic has one fault: such a comparison would mean the film is somehow consumed in the moment of its engagement, or more properly speaking, exhausted, requiring variations on a theme rather than revealing signature traces. To carry the comparison to its logical conclusion would mean the "film [would] destroy itself in the process, that it uses itself up without residue, that it be disposable."[18] Such a comment seems at odds with our need to return to cinema and to specific scenes.

The freeze-frame of film is the photograph, a form far closer to narrative fiction. Walter Benjamin used photography to measure the effects of technology on aesthetic perception. For this task, he adopted multiple methods, writing book reviews, a "Short History of Photography (1931), and giving public talks and radio addresses."[19] His most famous essay, "The Work of Art in the Era of Mechanical Production" (1936) turns on the question of "aura," a concept concerned with aesthetics and beauty, in part rendered through a unique spatial and temporal presence, "the place where it happens to be."[20] In this text, Benjamin explores efforts to neutralize or disarm older categories of aesthetic contemplation through reproducibility. The photograph is separated from other art objects by a unique temporal suspension. It has a simultaneous existence both in the past and the present, a matter complicated in Benjamin who often records when the act of looking takes place: we "see" Benjamin in the present examining a photograph taken in the past. Marxist criticism insists on the ways in which texts bear the traces of their historical moment, of the time in which they came into being, but the surface of the photograph visualizes these temporal dilemmas in direct terms.

The Flamethrowers, along with Ben Lerner's *10:04*, is suggestive among the novels considered in this study for incorporating images and photographs. Lerner engages in ekphrasis in his consideration of the Joan of Arc Painting, Challenger Mission photographs, a doctored *Back to the Future* (1985) film still, and a text, used as an epigraph, taken from Giorgio Agamben's *The Coming Community*, and typically attributed to Benjamin, read through the condition of "risk and [the] insecurity of millennial conditions in the novel."[21] Lerner's narrative some thirteen different illustrations, "ranging from paintings and photographs to film stills and postage stamps"; each "serves to supplement or to develop an idea made in the novel," while many of these texts "are described objects in the narrative."[22] If *10:04* has a profound interest in visual culture, it uses artworks to engage in constantly unfolding interpretative acts. Kushner, however, at least in the novel itself, does not follow a similar practice or allow for such readings, and is far closer to the work of the contemporary German novelist, W.G. Sebald, whose fictions drop in photographs without any supporting explanation, therefore mirroring the plight of his protagonists who are engaged in memory work: both individual recovery and collective reconciliation.[23] Placement is paramount, and Kushner, unlike Sebald, confines her photographs, film, and newsreel to the closing of chapters, without commentary or explanation. But where Sebald's images go unsourced, at least in the paperback editions of his works, Kushner acknowledges her selections. These strategies can be traced to the different practice of the historical novel by the two writers: for Sebald, character and reader are engaged in the navigation of the collective trauma of World War II, and efforts to address the "conspiracy of silence" in post-war Germany.[24] Kushner, in contrast, born at the tail-end of the 1960s, a moment when, as Julian Bourg argues, revolution turned to ethics, is concerned with political rebellion and anti-capitalist protest, but approaches history through less dramatic backchannels.[25] As Myka Tucker-Abramson argues, while Lukács focalized the historical novel through a protagonist "whose participation in the making of history is allegorical of the democratization of history" this is not possible in Kushner for characters "are fantasies about capitalist regeneration under US hegemony."[26] To read *The Flamethrowers* as a historical novel, we need to read it "*against* the foreground" and "with those characters and movements that form the backdrop of the novel."[27]

A final word on the importance of the photograph and the image for Kushner: The Vintage paperback edition of the novel includes an interview with Kushner and an expository text, which she calls a curated portfolio.

Kushner proceeds through a discussion of a series of images she selected "and pinned up to spark inspiration" for the novel.[28] In an interview with Spiotta, Kushner argues that having written only two novels she has no system, but "there were elements of commonality. I'm drawn to images and seem to start with them. Or one. Something I imagine, a scene or detail, or even a photograph, something that has a charge of meaning that can't be easily reduced."[29] While there is limited ekphrasis in the novel, it is in the curated portfolio that Kushner provides a explication of these images that motivated her writing. The first is "of a woman with tape over her mouth" with "paint on her cheeks [...] the streaks of it, dripping down, were cold white shards, as if her face were faceted in icicles."[30] Interestingly, Kushner then corrects this statement about the woman having tape over her mouth: "actually Band-Aids over the photograph, and not over her lips themselves."[31]

This correction chimes with Lerner and shows a shared intentionality. In *10:04*, the author consciously does not correct earlier sections of the novel, the implication being that the manuscript is not revised in realizing taxonomical errors, and new factual discoveries.[32] In unashamedly revealing these processes of composition—compositional practices we take as sincere admissions rather than fictional constructions—the novel "becomes a novel about the writing of a novel, thereby placing it in an unusual temporality—a perpetual state of becoming."[33] In Chapter 2, I revealed how Rose uses the second trial, and her subsequent expulsion from the Communist Party, as a method to mitigate the trauma of the original in line with Freud's theory of belated action, or *Nachträglichkeit*. The revelation of compositional practices is unsurprising in the contemporary novel because many so many premier authors writing today attended writing programs and even teach such courses at college. Alongside *10:04* and *The Flamethrowers*, Jennifer Egan's *The Keep* (2006), and Teddy Wayne's *Apartment* (2020) draw upon their experiences of the creative writing program to reveal the processes of narrative composition and literature's capacity to represent lived experience, prompting Mark McGurl to consider the institutional logic of the creative writing program as a mode of production for contemporary literary fiction.

For all Kushner's interest in cinema and photography, a different strategy is at work in Chapter 13 of her book, which I will examine here. Titled the "Trembling of the Leaves," the chapter concerns the slave labor of those brought to the Amazon to harvest rubber—a process called tapping—by the Valera Company. The Tappers are required to collect and weigh the "heavy slop-promising pails" of latex, a sticky milky colored substance mined from the trees.[34] The workers have named this moment "slopossible," in reference to the moment of expectation, of hope, that the pails will come in over quota and they will not be sent back to harvest more. There are immediate parallels with John Steinbeck's discussion of cotton picking in *The Grapes of Wrath* (1939). For Kushner and Steinbeck, the weighing of produce is the discounting of human life. In Kushner's novel, those found to be committing any number of deemed discretions, including farming, collecting food from the forest floor, or consistently missing the quota, are killed, marked in the record book as having died of yellow fever. The company cannot afford to lose the profit share and Kushner reveals the strategies of enforced servitude through fear and intimidation: "The patrão's [boss's] job was to keep the Indians in line. His tools were the cheap muzzle-loaders, mock drownings with water poured over a facecloth, and various further entrenchments of the Indian's peon status."[35] These weapons are provided by the Valera company themselves, possibly at a cost, but they are "faulty equipment" and "were only good for fifty shots."[36] Like Marlowe's ceaseless demand for rivets to repair the steamboat to continue the colonial enterprise, "there was nothing to be done about it."[37] The means of ensuring exploitation are unreliable, necessitating more atavistic methods to ensure compliance.

It is instructive to turn to a 1936 essay by Georg Lukács, in which he codified the aesthetic superiority of narration over description. Description is filler, conveying detail at the expense of the temporal moment, and creating a static text where reader and narrator are mere observers. In the writing of Émile Zola, for Lukács the arch-practitioner of novelistic description, historical contradictions are "simply described [...] as *caput mortuum* [worthless remains] of a social process. Narration, by contrast, is consequence. Animated, engaged, and living, it is a stance committed to action, linking important details of the world to the fates of individual characters." Kushner's chapter begins with description, but it is not the kind of "still life" Lukács proposed. It is description, in a critical mode, of the political and economic system and of the relationality of subjects living with it. It is an objective inventory of injustices and suffering that draws relationships between peripheral and non-peripheral zones. It is the following section, however, which moves suddenly to narration, and represents a critical intervention. Kushner begins narrating the life of the tapper as if they were the reader: "Rushing, sweating, exhaustion. You wait while the patrão inspects your taps to be sure they're clean, inspects your trunk incisions to be sure they're correct."[38] The inspection of the fictional tapper becomes the inventory of the reader, momentarily pulled out of their seclusion, and instructed to wait before the patrão. This approach, made known by the New Critics, is most referred to as the affective fallacy—a reader was never to confuse the interpretation of a literary work with the feeling they had when reading it. Affective responses, they warned, led to subjective insights. In this situation, the reader was read, rather than the text itself. Stanley Fish rejected this mode of interpretation, contending a reader's response to a text activates or completes the narrative, placing the reader above the author.[39] The direct modes of address we find here in Kushner acts as a series of examinations of the reader, through the pretense of enforced action. For Lukács', narration involves action and engagement, only possible within the context of a relative freedom—that is, experience over observation—but Kushner's narration brings the reader to an enforced servitude, in which the freedom of the reading experience is halted, now subject to the demands of the patrão. By moving between these two modes, Kushner complicates Lukács' binary of narration and description.

We have discussed the ways in which Kushner's novel demands to be read through a structural practice that attends to background to grasp "the mass experience of history."[40] Early readings of the novel deplored the apathy of the main character, Reno, drawing parallels with the wilder forms of postmodern disaffection. It is difficult for the American reader to follow the complex currents of solidarity, hatred and hope involved in The Years of Lead, as Reno's impassiveness reflects. Nevertheless, as Antony Shugar argues, these experiences, particularly the kidnapping and murder of Aldo Moro, the former Prime Minister of Italy in 1978, reside at the core of the Italian psyche "in the way that the JFK assassination once did for us."[41] It is to politics, totality, and the concerns of the historical novel to which I now turn.

The Years of Lead, Totality, and the Historical Novel

Kushner's novel captures different forms of insurrectionary violence as the action oscillates between Italy and New York. Reno is eventually invited to Italy by the Valera corporation after her securing of the land speed record. It is at Sandro's opulent family villa on Lake Como that the political situation is explained to Reno. As Andrew Strombeck argues, "the threat of burning courses through this segment" and the novel crackles with easily ignitable conflicts.[42] This crisis is connected to the collapse of Fordism, fiscal crisis, and worker unrest:

> Sandro said that Roberto had instituted some of the most severe shop-floor policies of any company, and that Roberto was reviled by union leaders and workers, that nothing was going to end well. The workers, he said, came from the south, lived in miserable conditions. Their wives and children put together Moto Valera ignition sets at the kitchen table, working all night because they

> were paid by the piece, whole families contracted under piecework, which was practically slave labor. Now, poor people all over Italy—in Milan, Bologna, Rome, Naples—were setting their own prices for rent, electricity, bread.[43]

In the introduction, I argued that the gaps, inconsistencies, and internal divisions within literary texts had consistently proved to be among the most profitable and rewarding aspects of enquiry for Marxist critics. As Martin Jay remarks, "nowhere in the history of Marxism has that reliance [on totality] been as explicitly articulated and self-consciously defended as in the body of thought that is [western Marxism]."[44] United in their shared distaste for vulgar criticism, Marxists from the 1920s onwards claimed a need for totality as a goal yet to be achieved. In literary studies totality is a projected coherence, in which the text is considered complete only up until the moment one must move beyond or outside it. For Jameson, this is "the privilege of aesthetic theory, however—maybe it's the only one!—[which] lies in the fact that there, in art, beginnings and endings are demonstratable: [...] art alone seems to offer a laboratory in which these otherwise imponderables can be observed if not regulated."[45]

Kushner's novel claims the need to think within totalities, but this approach has been weakened by the apathy of the novel's main character. As such, many approaches to the text orbit the unreliable narrator. First proposed by the American literary critic Wayne C. Booth in 1961, the concept turned on a perceived proximity or distance between narrator and reader.[46] Booth argued that the "terminology for this kind of distance in narrators is almost hopelessly inadequate," relying on a perception of the narrator as reliable if they were true to the logic of the work.[47] For Booth, an unreliable narrator suffers from what Henry James defines as "insouciance": that is, they are fundamentally mistaken about themselves, and believe they possess qualities which they do not.[48] Unreliable narrators, then, at least in Booth's reading, stand apart from the text in which they exist. They may be seeking to prove something to themselves or to an imagined readership; Booth's definition thus allows for nuanced degrees on intentionality rather than simple deviance, mistruth, or misdirection.

William Riggan established a taxonomy of unreliable narrators, proposing all forms of first-person narration encourage a degree of unreliability.[49] As I have already intimated, Kushner's text does not fit neatly with such a schematic presentation, as it blends narrative modes. Reno, however, is closest to the Naif, a character type whose perception is immature, or lacking in rigor. While Tucker-Abramson does not use Riggan's classification, she pushes this ethical standpoint further: arguing that Reno's passivity, ignorance, and immaturity make her "the idiot of the novel."[50] Seizing upon Reno's immaturity, her dreamy, drifting existence, her relative lack of convictions, and her inability or refusal to create critical connections, Tucker-Abrahamson makes a distinction: while Reno does not understand the political situation in New York, the behavior of Sandro, or what is unfolding in Italy with the strikes and protests, "the novel does."[51] The unreliability of the narrator stems from a failure to possess the truth that the novel reveals: in the form of anticapitalistic protest. Such a character, however, accords with the current situation of neoliberal capital. For Tucker-Abrahamson, "the valorization of Reno is itself a symptom of the 2008 global financial crisis," which has inflicted a break-down of confidence and the formulation that capital is too difficult to know.[52]

Understandably within Kushner's novel, Reno is peripatetic, living for short periods in numerous global locales. In the following chapter I want to propose, somewhat paradoxically, that one of the strategies for coming to terms with the global complexities initiated by recent capitalist crisis is to turn to a range of texts concerned with efforts to try and stay in one place. In the following chapter, we will turn to texts about home, homelessness, and housing.

5

Dying to Buy

Evicted, Apartment, *and* Generation Rent

In her essay, "A Room of One's Own" (1929), Virginia Woolf set out the literal and figurative space required for women writers within a literary tradition dominated by men. In disclosing the necessary securities for modernist literary production, which for Woolf come in the form of access to property and a comfortable yearly income, her essay prompts readers to consider the relationships among writing, identity, and interiors. For Woolf, making sense of this connection was vital: her dream of securing the material freedoms required for women to write was tied to disclosing the "secret economies" of dwellings.[1] Woolf is initially perplexed when examining houses "on the road to Headingley," but the revelation comes, as it does for most modernists, in the flux at the heart of the city.[2] Woolf observes "four wheeled cabs [...] drawing up and depositing on the pavement corded boxes containing, presumably, the entire wardrobe of some Swiss or Italian family seeking fortune or refuge or some other desirable commodity which is to be found in the boarding-houses of Bloomsbury in the winter."[3] In the strangeness of objects assembled on the street, Woolf finds consolation. These rooms offer shelter, security, and refuge, but they are also respites from domestic drudgery. These accommodations can free women, if only momentarily, from the dual identities of wife and homemaker.[4]

These interiors are marginal, peripheral, and transient.[5] They can never be private in the same sense as a home or a domestic space. In a home, as Iris Young writes, possessions are arranged and have "personal meaning as retainers of personal narrative."[6] For Young, the interior of one's home, and the distribution of possessions within it, "supports the body habits and routines of those who dwell there."[7] Surrounded by well-chosen objects, the cherished items that make life bearable, subjectivity, argues Young, is a collection of selves, "constructed and sustained by the unique individual pathways created in the home."[8] Possessions, she writes, are "the material markers of events and relationships that make the narrative of a person or group" meaning that when "dwelling space is shared" it becomes "the space in which we dwell among the things that are *ours*."[9] It is the home, and not the bed-sits and boarding houses of Woolf's Bloomsbury, that are deemed significant of cultural and aesthetic value, because home is so often "posited as a rooted place of belonging, a transcendent signifier which cuts across cultures and identities, or a privileged location through which models of selfhood are found or forged."[10] When it comes to narratives of home, traditional, even conservative, ideas dominate. Home is premised on a bourgeoisie interiority, a place of remote, comfortable seclusion, and a space of origination, unity, and permanence. Frequently, invocations of home are predicated upon narrow models of housing.

More recent efforts have attempted to read residence beyond the ideological framework of normative domestic dwellings, while attending to the persistence of set features. Julia Prewitt Brown's investigation, beginning with the first bourgeois interior in English fiction, Crusoe's cave, argues that the "mythology of bourgeois domesticity is with us still."[11] Kate Kennedy and Hermione Lee broaden the idea of home but still see them as sites of revelation, which "tell you everything you need to know about people, whether it's the choice of wallpaper, the mess in the kitchen, the silence or shouting over meals, doors left open or closed, a fire burning in the hearth."[12] Finally, Alexander Harris has troubled the concept of home as fixed by reminding us of the "practice of regular, and synchronized moving" amongst families of the eighteenth and nineteenth centuries, and the ways in which furniture and belongings were physically altered to fit new spaces.[13] Kennedy and Lee are among the few to consider the anxieties of home ownership: the frequent and necessary repairs and daily upkeep, the meeting of mortgage payments, and the sense of being locked-in, through contracts and deposits, to a fixed place. If bourgeois sentimentality has often produced a static and naturalized imagery of home, this fixity can be a cause for apprehension and disquiet. In a March 1845 letter, the twenty-five-year-old Engels wrote to Marx of the stultifying atmosphere of his parents' home. Active in communist circles, Engels lamented the political ignorance and religious piety of his mother and father, and their "piously doleful expressions" after the arrival of each letter.[14] "I cannot eat, drink, sleep, let out a fart, without being confronted by this same accursed lamb-of-God expression," Engels fumed.[15] For Engels, engaged in the work of communist revolution, the bourgeoise home was not a conducive site for transformative politics.

This chapter is structured across three sections, exploring two texts concerned, to varying degrees of intensity, with housing, interiors, occupancy, and writing. The first section explores critical accounts of home, housing, and domesticity. The domestic interior, as a material object and discursive space, is irrevocably shaped by economic and class relations. But if this materialist tradition "profitably strips back some of the veneer of that talismanic word [...] home" it has also been less attentive to the rich symbolic nuances of dwelling, belonging and identity.[16] Several critical studies have argued the regulative and hegemonic ideology of domesticity was institutionalized in the Victorian period. As Emily Cuming writes, "the belief we are bound up with our rooms in necessarily meaningful ways, [has] never quite gone out of fashion."[17] Marx is a figure who bridges these worlds. Marx penned critical accounts of capitalist social relations, but he was also, with his wife, concerned with the distinct practicality of creating a home. As I have explored elsewhere, Marx's profession made for a taxing, itinerant existence.[18] Chased out of Germany, Paris, and Brussels, Marx and his family finally took refuge in London in 1849. For Marx, and the many other émigré families of the period, domesticity was flux, not rootedness. It encompassed exile, migrancy, surveillance, and police inspection, the volatility of rental markets, and even the trauma of eviction. Marx's chronic cough and bronchitis, coupled with the illness of his wife and daughter, required changes of climate and periods of rest, the costs of which were often defrayed by Engels. Scholarly approaches most commonly turn to the discursive context of Victorian London and Marx's immersion in the resources of the British Museum, notably the Blue Books, but it has often neglected the space of Marx's home. In combining Marx's critical explication of the paradoxes of capital with the physical, sensual, and textual experience of living and dwelling in nineteen century London, we can better arrive at Marx's reflections regarding housing and home. Novels, like houses, furnish a dwelling space. Bound to capitalism, the novel is a form of interiors and individual identity. Our categories of interpretation—content, threshold, entry point, style, perspective—are drawn from architecture, while novelist Henry James framed his fiction and writerly craft in relation to built environments.[19] The second section examines Teddy Wayne's *Apartment* (2020), a novel remarkable for the sheer extent to which it explores the relationship between writing, interiors, and housing. Set in New York City, in 1996, the novel is about the relationship of two young men (an unnamed narrator and Billy) on the MFA writing program at Columbia University. The narrator is fortuitous: he lives in an (illegal sublet) rent-controlled apartment. A friendship develops between the two (the narrator loves Billy, but this relationship never develops), and Billy is offered the use of the additional room, in exchange for non-remunerated services, such as cooking and housework. The chapter ends with Matthew

Desmond's *Evicted* (2016), an exploration of tenant rights and tumbledown houses in Milwaukee, Wisconsin, which weaves together the narratives of three families struggling to stay sheltered.

No Place like Home: Marx, Housing, Eviction

We can complicate Woolf's writings on dwellings by turning to the situation of less fortunate modernist writers, for whom exile, diaspora, and migration forced them to consider ideas of belonging.[20] Modernism was driven by unhomeliness but, as Jenny Kuhlmann argues, homelands were never fully departed, nor was belonging limited to a single place.[21] For Joyce's Stephen Daedalus, exile is a mode of life and a form of art (Joyce proclaimed he had never left Ireland) while Raymond Williams considered forced relocation a necessary condition for membership in international modernism.[22] As modernists questioned ideas of belonging, they also created homes set against conditions of change and impermanence.

Marx knew precarity particularly well. A letter to Engels in June 1862 records rent arrears, outstanding school fees, and unpaid bills to the baker, greengrocer, and tea merchant. Marx watched as his small sums from journalism were converted into the settlement of debts, recorded in the ledgers of shopkeepers and tradesmen. Often forced to face a London winter without an overcoat, Marx was sometimes unable to leave the house because his shoes were in the pawnshop. As Peter Stallybrass argues, Marx came to understand the intricacies of capital by reading in the British Library, but he learned about the domestic life of the working class through brutal first-hand experience.[23] But while Marx spent many hours in the Reading Room of the British Library, consulting the vast resources of the parliamentary Blue Books, he also worked in his rooms at home, often late into the night. Marx's thoughts on capital were made possible by the resources of the library, but they were also conceived at home.

Marx rented various unsuitable lodgings while in London. The British socialist, Henry M, Hyndman considered this a choice, writing in his reflections that the Marx family "remained in poor circumstances when power and ease and comfort were at their disposal."[24] But Marx was unsuited for any other work, and knew so himself. The house seemed shared rather than inhabited. Visitors were frequent, and not always welcome. Marx would confess to Engels his irritation and weariness with those who arrived wanting petitions or contributions. The least welcome callers were the merchants, clamoring for payment. Marx's territory was his study, on the first floor. The family moved to a terraced house on Maitland Park, North London, in 1875 having rented larger accommodations at number 1 for the last decade. Engels lived close by on Regent's Park Road. Marx's room was stuffed with books, notebooks, folios, and papers, with a small desk, chair, sofa, and space for the family's dogs. Marx had a habit of pacing when working, which could be heard downstairs. Hyndman, a frequent visitor to the family home, recalls this custom being unconfined to the study, and that Marx would stride across rooms "as if he were pacing the deck of a schooner for exercise."[25] Recollections of Marx abound. Hyndman devoted a chapter to Marx in his *The Record of an Adventurous Life* (1911). Marx's son-in-law, Paul Lafargue, provides the most detailed treatment, advising that "one must know that historic room before one can penetrate into the intimacy of Marx's spiritual life."[26] But pride of place did not translate into house-proud. The smell of tobacco ash lingered, and the discordant pile of papers was arranged to Marx's liking.

Rent, remarks David Harvey, "troubled Marx deeply."[27] For political economy, landed property has always represented a theoretical challenge, and Harvey has in mind here Marx's theoretical investigations of land, landlords, property, and ground rent, which he first mentions in *The Economic and Philosophical Manuscripts*, and later developed in the *Grundrisse* and *Capital*.[28] Marx knew that capital could not function without land ownership and rent, but he also knew that such social forms had appeared as a variety of pre-capitalist relations.[29] What Marx did not anticipate was "that new forms of capitalist rent" would evolve "within the evolutionary structures of capitalism" and these forms would go beyond "that which [Marx] found necessary and functional as well as politically tolerable."[30] We will return to debates about rents in a moment, but there is a further feature to Harvey's pronouncement which will interest us here. Marx was deeply troubled by his own precarious position, and the search for affordable lodgings, for him and his family, constituted one of the major problems. As Anna Kornblu writes, Marx was "perennially dislocated [...] unhomely at home in London for thirty-four years."[31] Both exile and émigré, Marx first stayed in a hotel popular among German refugees.[32] They were evicted from their first flat, in Chelsea, for non-payment of rent, and their belonging were taken by bailiffs.[33] The family moved to a two room flat in Dean Street, Soho, before fortuitous circumstances allowed them to take a much larger house in Kentish Town in September 1856.[34]

Marx is a figure uniquely placed to consider the critical paradoxes at the heart of capital. At times unhoused, unhomely, and once, homeless, in class society, Marx's home was also a site of production, where he worked, wrote, and received visitators. The family were complicit in this effort, and Jenny wrote of how her fingers ached copying out letters and manuscripts. But house and home are awkward neighbors, occasionally uninviting. As Cummings remarks, "housing, unlike the idea of home, is thus not primarily bound up with notions of self-identity, affect and comfortable seclusion."[35] Housing brings with it a closer consideration of economic and class relations, viewing the domestic interior as a material object and a discursive construct. Marx's writings on societies peripheral to capitalism show a fascination with dwellings.[36] He wrote extensively on lodgings, workhouses, peasant farms, the mud-walled huts of India, Irishwoman torn from their homes by pernicious landlords, abandoned houses, vacant pastures, slave dwellings, the quartering of troops, Roman villas, and domiciles of all kinds. Hegel justified property based on a connection between property and freedom. Property was essential, thought Hegel, to the development of individuality. In *Elements of the Philosophy of Right* (1820), his last major published work, Hegel outlined three relations to property (termed as taking possession, the use of the thing, and the alienation of property). These relations were all part of a successive tri-partite stage of the will's relation to the thing. For Hegel, property was an essential social institution to becoming.

Housing, Apartment, and the Contemporary Novel

There is much to be said about the political and economic processes that have shaped America's unique structures of debt and social inequality. Homeownership is clearly transformative, but generations of Black Americans have consistently been denied the right to affordable housing. Red lining, municipal ordinances, private deed restrictions, racial violence, flooding, the frequency of natural disasters, and the subprime mortgage crisis have produced shameful levels of inequality. The Housing and Economic Recovery Act of 2008 authorized $300 billion to guarantee fixed-rate mortgages for subprime owners. But in seeking to empower the poor the act did little to address regulation. The contemporary novel is responding to these developments. Annie McClanahan's study *Dead Pledges* (2017) welcomes fiction's mediation of twenty-first-century debt but only insofar as "crisis is an invaluable historical hermeneutic, compelling us to anticipate limits, to imagine alternatives, to welcome collapse, and thus to resist the 'end of history' triumphalism characteristic of capitalist ideology in boom times," crisis, she writes, "allows us to glimpse the owl of Minerva in the autumnal afternoon instead of only at dusk."[37] But for some contemporary writers, tenancy is a privilege. In Sally Rooney's

Conversations with Friends (2017), Frances lives in her uncle's Dublin apartment rent free, while Alice Kelleher, the novelist of *Beautiful World, Where Are You?* (2021), can take a house on a whim. For Rooney, rent is rarely a problem.[38]

Wayne's novel forges links among writing, interiors, and identity. The action unfolds in New York City in 1996, the same year that David Foster Wallace published *Infinite Jest*, although Billy, one of the two central characters, is oblivious to the novel, and the text itself evidences a marked antipathy to Wallace's metafictional practices, footnote technique, and reliance on academic critical discourse. I will return to *Apartment*'s disaffiliation of 1990s postmodernism and its encoding of implicit value judgments on historical forms of the novel, momentarily. The unnamed narrator of the novel is a twenty-four-year-old student on the MFA program at Columbia. The model of pedagogical practice here is the writing workshop, which takes the form of a collective, and often brutally honest, examination of a student's work. As Colombia's online catalogue explains: "All workshops are small (7 to 12 students), ensuring that all students present work at least three times per semester." Students receive substantial written responses to their work from their professors and classmates; they also have regularly scheduled one-on-one conferences with faculty. The second-year thesis workshops (6 to 10 students) are dedicated to shaping each student's work into book form.[39] Despite coming some thirty years ago, the workshop practices in the novel are remarkably similar, with each student's novel-in-progress receiving intensive and sustained exposure in a group setting.[40]

The narrator has submitted his first chapter of a four-hundred-page novel, *The Copy Chief*, which is currently being examined by the group. The response is less than ideal: the "literary references feel overdetermined" one student remarks, while another declares that the "main character's not someone I would root for."[41] For the narrator, these are less convivial criticisms than truculent barbs, exposing "an insecurity that had burrowed deeper in recent years as the gaudy excesses of the eighties had backlashed into a post–Cold War fetishization of authenticity."[42] This insecurity is his "obvious socioeconomic advantages" and is a "severe artistic drawback."[43] This defect is his middling status, "not wealthy enough to salaciously spy on the true upper crust, too cossetted to send back dispatches on the destitute."[44] The narrator's belief that he will be unable to write great fiction, or at least is severely hampered by his socio-economic status, reveals a belief in mimesis as a path to authenticity. His validation of the "broad middle swathe of America, where every adolescent experience, every chili dog eaten, every keg party in the woods, could feasibly represent some neo–Rockwellian universal."[45] There is nothing derogatory is this bringing together of representational art and prose stylistics. Rockwell's illustrations, often considered quaint, idealistic, and sentimental, are here forms of authentic art. Stranded between the extreme poles, and not sufficiently middling to access what he considers to be the materials of representational art, the narrator considers the immediacy of painting and the distinctive individual brush stroke as revealing real America.

But all this betrays a fundamental conceit, which we are asked to indulge. Namely, that the narrator cannot narrate. This stylistic can confront everything except itself. Storytelling itself becomes an art and an object, something to be learned and loving practiced. The entire novel is from the perspective of our unmanned narrator and forms the novel he could never write. And yet despite this disillusionment, our attention is never lost. There are no boring sections here (the novel is uninterrupted by chapters), no reason for the narrator to make so many leaps and bounds into tortuous philosophical discussions and abstruse rhetorical debates familiar for the reader of Thomas Mann.[46] We are to believe that the book we now have in our hands is the unrealized novel. In the workshop, writing necessarily becomes a confessional mode and inescapably bears the traces of its producer. *The Copy Chief* is narrated by "a young copy editor toiling in a freelance capacity at a glossy men's magazine in Midtown Manhattan" and supervised by "middle aged copy chief, Bart" (a homage to Melville's Bartleby).[47] These allusions demand consideration.

Firstly, and most obviously, the narrator's invocation of Melville suggests he is staking a position as a writer of literary fiction through the process of canon formation and that he hopes his novel will have similar cultural status and commercial appeal. Melville's precarious status as a writer in his own time is well known, with subsequent celebration of his work occurring after his death in 1891. The narrator of *Apartment* is relatively at peace with this model of literary success, remarking "I've always thought I'd be satisfied If I could write something that outlived me [...] Just one book, even. I wouldn't even mind if it were published posthumously, if it meant that someone would pick it up in a hundred years."[48] After the financial ruin of *Pierre* (1852), Melville was writing for a relatively small number of readers. Melville's story is not only a structuring device for *The Copy Chief* but *Apartment* as well. Like Bartleby, the narrator lacks violation, or at least prefers modes of passive resistance that have become most associated with that figure. He fails to confide his obvious attraction to Billy and does not publish his work. Dan McCall's monograph, *The Silence of Bartleby* (1989) is useful here. As befits the metafictional paradigm of *Apartment*, McCall's book appeared shortly before the fictional timeline of the novel. But it is here, at the opening, that Wayne's novel turns most perceptibly on the self-reflexive qualities of narration itself.

The workshop is a mode of pedagogical practice, in which the reader is alerted to the protocols of narrative construction. Billy is signaled out for having a "different take from everybody else" and appreciating the story.[49] The first attraction is one of a similar readerly perspective.

As I argued at the opening of the chapter, the most pressing concern of the novel is the domestic interior itself. The narrator has been illegally subletting a rent-stabilized apartment belonging to his great Aunt, and has recently learned of a loophole in New York law that would allow his aunt to cede ownership to him:

> we could transfer the lease if I had established cohabitation with my great-aunt for twelve months; a utility bill under my name would suffice. As my great-aunt planned by then to live out the rest of her days in New Jersey, she was fine with ceding ownership, and in June I doubled down on my real estate chicanery by registering the phone bill in my name. By the end of next summer, with this spurious claim of co-residency, I would be able to lay legal and permanent claim to one of the most sought-after possessions in cutthroat Manhattan: rent-stabilized housing, a powerful advantage in launching a career in the arts.[50]

The potential permeance of the apartment is reflected in the razor blades stored in the bathroom. The close of the novel returns to this object. The narrator writes, 1990–1997 on a scrap of paper, and drops it into the medicine cabinet, no doubt a desire for permeance now the apartment has been lost and an effort to heal the emotional suffering. From a purported future position, the narrator confides that "along with the discarded and immured razor blades, I would like to think it remains."[51]

The relationship between Billy and the narrator is established through a strategy of provocative contrast: while the narrator has a dwelling, Billy is practically homeless; while the narrator's father pays tuition, rent, and bills, "New York is bleeding" Billy dry. The narrator's parents are divorced but remain close, while Billy's father is "a deadbeat." The subject of their novels is equally illuminating. The narrator encodes with his text the frustrated desire of producing great art, while Billy, having been told by a previous girlfriend that he is suffering emotional consequences, is writing a book about a father and son. After a late-night drinking session at a bar where Billy works:

> He yanked a chain, and by the light of s single bulb we groped down a splintery handrail to the basement. "Watch the boxes," Billy said as we slalomed around the caches of liquor until we reached another door. He opened it and flicked on a light switch. It was an empty storage room with an air a mattress on a rug, a stack of books to its side, and some moving boxes. The space had a moldy odor of a locked room.[52]

What strikes the narrator as heart-breaking is not only "the meagerness of his possession but how neatly stored they were."[53] An invitation is extended, and Billy spends the night in the spare bedroom of the narrator's apartment. While the narrator confides that, given his precarious position of almost owning the apartment, he normally "felt a faint sense of unease, of someone encroaching upon my space" when having an overnight guest, this is not the case with Billy. Rather, the event is taken, almost unwittingly, as the next stage in a plutonic, potentially homosexual, relationship. The act of Billy staying over and sharing the interior space confreres a new intimacy. As the narrator confides, "a first sleepover, whether it was sexual or platonic, had a way of making you both more and less comfortable around the other person; you'd jumped a fence of intimacy, but now you saw each other in the blunt morning light."[54]

As mentioned above, house and home are deeply ambivalent values. But one of the primary thematics of literature about dwellings is the return home, with Homer's *Odyssey*, as the canonical text. One of the most telling incidents of the novel occurs when Billy meets a woman in a bar and stays over at her place. The following morning, he telephones the narrator admitting "I don't know how to get home."[55] While this term is ubiquitous in the novel, this utterance marks the first time it is used by Billy in conjunction with his current living arrangement. Billy spends hours navigating Staten Island and New York City public transport systems, walking from downtown Manhattan back to the apartment where the narrator waits. There are comic allusions to Odysseus's travels and Billy is welcomed home as a sailor. This term not only acts to draw parallels with figures in canonical texts who return home, but also questions the heteronormative assumptions that have, traditionally, confined women and nourished male projects.

The final section of the novel, titled "After" condenses the next forty years into a few pages, offering a vision of retrospection, closing with what seems to be the election of Trump. It is revealed that the second novel, *Camp Redwood*, is rejected, with the publisher remarking that the "brilliance and originality" of the short story did not translate into the novel. Able to afford the final year at Columbia, the narrator "had to acknowledge the truth I had been deferring all that time: I wasn't meant to be a writer, and I wouldn't leave behind a novel, post-humorously published or not."[56] The narrator is promoted, becomes a copy chief, rents a one-bedroom apartment, takes in a stray cat, and has no meaningful social life. Much of the concluding chapter is given over to Billy's accomplishments. A published author at twenty-nine, Billy continues to write successful novels and short-stories, all situated in the American mid-west, becomes an associate professor at a college in Idaho, marries, and has children. The model here is that of the frustrated *Bildungsroman*, in which a moment, or series of moments in time, is excavated as having had the potential to course correct. "Solitude," writes the narrator, "is not so bad once you come to expect it."[57] The final image is of the narrator looking into a mirror, having just re-read Billy's feedback on his stories which he has kept all these years. The "still here" recalls another pronouncement of Billy's, made when the two meet a retired playwright in a bar who has only had one play performed on Broadway, but was then unable to produce anything of value. Billy's ontological confirmation—"You're not a nowhere man. You're still here. We're all still here"—opens the potential for future commitment.

Evicted

Desmond's book proposes a narrative impulse that blends moral and ethical preachment, facts about housing, and more purely novelistic devices such as character and plot to tell the story of shelter, in the United States. I will come back to these devices or strategies in a moment, but it is important to make a quick diversion and say that this book is not interested in rent per say, which entails, as the etymology reminds us, not only regular payments in exchange for the use of land or property—an indentured relation which has proliferated in the new forms of global financial capitalism, extending not only to house payments but subscriptions serves of all kinds and therefore challenging the concept of ownership itself—but also of tearing asunder or fracture and bifurcation itself, and the fragmentation of the senses Marx remarked upon so vividly in the *Economic and Philosophical Manuscripts. Evicted*, then, tells the tale of the last stage of this desperate saga, the moment of belongings being removed, the appearance of sheriffs, court orders, and specialist eviction crews. But these are only the formal forms. Involuntary displacement—informal evictions (cheaper and easier than court appointments, like paying tenants to leave, or removing the front door of the house) landlord foreclosures and building condemnations—all "take place in the shadow of the law."[58]

Desmond does not yet dwell on this here, bracketing the discussion to later in the book, but two narrative expressions reveal the force of this reality. Rami Bahrani's *99 Homes* (2014), starring Andrew Garfield (as a recently unemployed construction worker) and Michael Shannon (as real estate operator Rick Carver) is an intimate exploration of eviction. The film's opening scene involves an "anonymous" eviction, which is for the viewer a conditioning in the procedures of this task and will be repeated throughout the film. Here the evictee has taken their life rather than be removed from the house—a minor inconvenience for Carver—and revealing the effect on communities and displaced families. It is not that Carver is unacquainted with the facts of the family, and Shannon offers a bravura performance of reciting the name and age of each family member, but simply, unashamedly, he cannot afford to care. If the film furnishes affect—the *repoussoir* of the bloody corpse and the many cherished items of the home—Desmond's account offers sociological survey:

> there is a toll that eviction takes on a person's spirit. The violence of displacement can drive people to depression and, in extreme cases, even suicide. One in two recently evicted mothers reports multiple symptoms of clinical depression, double the rate of similar mothers were not forced from their homes [...] when several patients committed suicide in the days leading up to their eviction, a group of psychiatrists published a letter in *Psychiatric Services*, identifying eviction as a "significant precursor of suicide."[59]

Carver himself cannot consider the houses homes, warning Nash: "Don't get emotional about real estate, they're just boxes, little boxes, big boxes. The more boxes you own the better."[60] It is Nash who later corrects Carver, when they celebrate their expansive housing portfolio, referring to the houses as homes. After this initiation into the procedures of eviction, the film then moves to the gutting of the Nash home. Now we have character, in the figures of Nash, his mother, and son. The act is no longer anonymous. In the first instance we do not fully glimpse the body of the suicide or see the family that has been left behind. This means, the second time, the eviction can be experienced in all its true terror.

The Depiction of Eviction

Historically, eviction has plagued Black and Hispanic neighborhoods, even as poor renting families are experiencing the worst housing crisis in decades.[61] But surely these numbers do not account for total evictions. Many are unreported, conducted without legal judgment. Ralph Ellison's *Invisible Man* (1952) articulates a radical representation of anti-eviction protest as a crowd comes to halt a forced ejection. While walking in Harlem, Ellison's narrator notes three white men moving furniture out of an elderly black couple's apartment. In witnessing the many cherished objects, torn from their habitual surroundings, the narrator makes a speech calling for non-violent action and to return these "dispossessed objects" to the home:

> "Dispossession! *Dis*-possession is the word!" I went on. "They've tried to dispossess us of our manhood and womanhood! Of our childhood and adolescence—you heard the sister's statistics on our infant-mortality rate. Don't you know you're lucky to be uncommonly born? Why, they even tried to dispossess us of *our dislike of being dispossessed!* And I'll tell you something else—if

> we don't resist, pretty soon they'll succeed! These are the days of dispossession, the season of homelessness, the time of evictions."

For Ellison, eviction constitutes a politics of violence and exclusion. Dispossession might begin with the removal of the home but quickly spreads to the socio-ontological effects of capitalist reification. This focus on treating humans as objects has prompted Cody C. St Clair to contend that Ellison deploys a collage aesthetic linking eviction to chattel slavery, while Kent proposes the novel is concerned with the protagonist's accumulative dispossession and is an "an allegory of Black struggle in American history."[62] While evictions occurred daily, Ellison's protagonist registers the sensational quality of the incident. "It was startling: the crowd watching silently, and two white men lugging the chair and trying to dodge the blows and the old woman's face steaming with angry tears [...] I couldn't believe it [...] What on earth."[63] As personal objects are placed on the curb, private property is laid bare: "we were all unwilling intruders upon some shameful event [...] we were witnesses of what we did not wish to see."[64] Despite the protagonists best efforts, his remarks incite the crowd to attack the law-enforcement officials. In Elision, the crowd are turned into an energetic collective demanding transformative action.

The passage from Elision's novel to Bahrani's film shows the fracturing of community resistance to eviction. While the number of evictions has increased dramatically, now employing specialist construction crews and mandated law-enforcement, the model of activism is one of individual conscience than group action. In the final scene, after a man barricades himself in his home and threatens his family, Nash reveals the legal document he delivered to the court is a forgery. Ultimately, in *Evicted*, we have already arrived at the past participle, the denouement, requiring a process of reverse engineering by which we return to those moments.

In *The Antinomies of Realism*, Jameson uses Barthes to argue the novel as a form is less defined by plot and character than "by the romanesque itself, by a novel-ness that extended down into the very pores of the language and the individual sentences, transforming even ostensible fact and alleged nonfiction into the inescapable connotation of the supplementary declaration, 'I am a novel.'"[65] Jameson's example is the opening sentence of a nonfictional work, Andrew Ross Sorkin's *Too Big to Fail* (2009), which is its description of a New York winter morning, "programs the reader and proposes a certain narrative and ultimately novelistic stance on what follows."[66] Such shifts are taken as a dialectic of realism's own struggle against reification, as it now takes as its adversary the realistic novel itself. Sadly, this is not the space to remark on such modulations in the realist novel, which relate to debates, first inaugurated by Tom Wolfe on the new journalism, literary journalism, or what we can term the non-fiction novel. Desmond prefaces the book with a two-line "Little Lyric" by American poet Langston Hughes: "I wish the rent // Was Heaven sent." Written in 1943, the couplet was a gesture of desperation against the discriminatory rental rates faced by Black Harlem residents in the 1930s, 40s and 50s. To mitigate the high costs the 20s saw the rise of rent parties, social gatherings which charged a fee to guests in exchange for live music and dancing, with food at an additional cost. Hughes kept a collection of rent party advertisements, tickets printed as cards which contained amusing rhymes as invitation: "not to slow and not too fast // But a real good time while it last." These can be found in his papers in Yale collections.[67] Developing Jameson then, we might say that Hughes' practice is to transpose a specific kind of sentence, the raw material of which is to be found in the rental party tickets, into a poetry of opposition and protest that is both incidental and momentary. For in Hughes, interpretation itself is thwarted. The poem is over before it begins, and the reader is left abruptly, as if they were attempting to ascend a staircase that leads nowhere. In Hughes, poetry is in circulation, like the rent. Desmond himself argues that housing has been a mechanism for institutionalized racism and the systematic dispossession of African Americans and native Americans from the land. The author's note is instructive as a form of nominative solemnity: a necessary intrusion that reminds the reader that this is a "work of nonfiction," that the events were witnessed first-hand, quotations were captured with a digital recorder, that the events of the narrative all occurred within a specific temporal frame, and that official documents have been consulted.[68] While *Apartment* offers a portrait mode, Desmond's examination is more expensive, concerned with the family, local community, and state regulations.

A guiding premise of this book regards narrative fiction as articulating an attenuation of capitalist experience in its confrontation with crisis developments. The subprime mortgage crisis of 2008 ushered in a range of fictional and filmic efforts which confronted the complexity of financial capitalism. Chapter 6 turns to one of the most important writers of contemporary U.S. fiction, Thomas Pynchon. Pynchon is a long-time practitioner of speculative postmodern historical fiction, but last novel, published in 2013, explores the dot.com boom, 9/11, and 2001 crash. While Pynchon's political sympathies have always resided with a broad constellation of left-wing efforts, his work has long been held as refusing any single political philosophy and challenging political commitment in general.

6

Fictions of Financial Crisis

Pynchon, Marx, Neoliberalism

> "The *true war* is a *celebration of markets.*"—Thomas Pynchon, *Gravity's Rainbow*[1]

As Joanna Freer argues in *The New Pynchon Studies*, the last twenty years of Pynchon scholarship have turned from post-structuralist concerns of the limits of language, the condition of meaning, and particular notions of truth to "more general theorizations" of the contemporary which include "decolonial theory, transitional theory, eco-criticism, and feminism."[2] Marx and Marxism have a less privileged place here; Sascha Pöhlmann singles out Jameson's work as a theorist of postmodernism, whose "Marxist cultural critique builds on a tradition of critiquing global capitalism that started with Marx and Engels."[3] But Jameson's contribution is less valid for his political prescriptions regarding the necessity of a Marxist theoretical practice than the ways in which his theories of cognitive mapping might be used to address Pynchon's globality, which had largely gone unremarked until the publication of *Against the Day* (2006).[4] As Tore Rye Anderson argues, we can now read Pynchon's *Gravity's Rainbow* (1973), *Mason & Dixon* (1997), and *Against the Day* as an ambitious "world-historical trilogy which tells the story of the gestation and emergence of our contemporary global reality."[5] But if Pynchon has dwelled on the negative externalities of these global realities—evidencing, as David Cowart argues, a legible distaste for capitalist practices—why is his fiction, and subsequent Pynchon scholarship, antithetical to Marx?[6]

This chapter has four main sections, with further subheadings for convenience. The first section reevaluates Marx in *Gravity's Rainbow*, proposing a more congenial theoretical relationship than has existed to date. The second argues Pynchon's first millennial novel, *Against the Day*, is central to the emergence of a new Marxist trajectory which continues into *Inherent Vice* (2009) and *Bleeding Edge*. In *Against the Day*,

Pynchon moves from the isolated, "hopeful subjunctive spaces" of *Vineland* (1990) and *Mason & Dixon* to more legible left political frameworks of working-class struggle, which the chapter will demonstrate by revealing striking formal and thematic relations with Marx's discussion of the worker in the chapter on "The Working Day" in *Capital*. Section four turns to *Bleeding Edge*, set during the bursting of the 2001 dot-com bubble. The narrative infuses the recent past with an awareness of neoliberal trends, riffing on surveillance capitalism, the regrouping of dot-com millionaires, and political resistance alloyed to class solidarity and cross-generational protest.

Pynchon & Marx

Pynchon scholarship often argues against the possibility of a meaningful theoretical partnership between Pynchon and Marx.[7] This antipathy is often located within a single textual instance—"the sly old racist" section in *Gravity's Rainbow*—which disparages the historical figure of Marx himself. Marx is mentioned twice in the novel: the first, in the form of Jewish caricature, as Leni "reminds herself that Marx was one [...] A racial affinity for the books, the theory, a rabbinical love for loud argument."[8] It is difficult to attribute sources on this issue, but Pynchon's narrator is likely aware many rabbis numbered among Marx's ancestors and mocks this genealogy through stereotype. As David McLellan argues in his foundational biography of Marx, published the same year as *Gravity's Rainbow*, and therefore not an authoritative source for Pynchon, "it would be difficult to find anyone who had a more Jewish ancestry than Karl Marx."[9] The second instance is more theoretically substantive, with the narrator attacking Marx for thinking colonial outposts are solely sources of "Cheap Labor and Overseas Markets."[10] While I will examine this latter instance in some detail, this textual moment does not constitute sufficient evidence to sustain the current incompatibility between Pynchon and Marx.[11]

Scholars have pursued post–Marxist approaches to Pynchon's novels, such as Samuel Thomas' *Pynchon and the Political* (2007), Martin Eve's *Pynchon and Philosophy* (2014), Joanna Freer's *Thomas Pynchon and the American Counterculture* (2014), and Sean Carswell's *Occupy Pynchon: Politics After Gravity's Rainbow* (2017). These are excellent additions to Pynchon scholarship, but they do not provide a sustained engagement with Marx's political philosophy, or the social, political, and intellectual contexts in which he worked and wrote. Thomas, for instance, rightly stresses the need to avoid a "programmatic Marxist" or "Libertarian

Socialist" version of Pynchon which forms "any kind of rigid party politics of the past or the present."[12] Building upon this approach, Eve contends that Pynchon's fiction exhibits "little love for Karl Marx," a point he has repeated in the *New Pynchon Studies* edited collection.[13] Freer is more sensitive to Marx's works, but argues the "message is negative as [Marx's] theory of monetary capital is deemed irrelevant to maintain freedom in the American West.[14] Finally, Carswell contends Michael Hardt and Antonio Negri's "multitude" is a "much broader" and "more appropriate" concept than Marx could ever envisage, despite making only passing reference to Marx's "proletariat" which is "the source of resistance to capital."[15] It is proposed across all these approaches that Pynchon's fiction works within legible left frameworks but eschew any party political affiliation, or indeed the elevation of the work of any single theorist or philosopher. Rather, Pynchon's fictions grapple with the problem of human freedom within the world of commodity capitalism.

"Outhouses of the European Soul": Pynchon, Imperialism, Politics

As I argued at the beginning of the chapter, Pynchon's hostility to Marx can be traced to the infamous *Gravity's Rainbow* passage. Marx argues colonial outposts can become cheap sources of labor power, allowing capitalists to fix wages below their value and forcefully migrate labor to plantation industries in different colonies. Importantly, Marx never produces an analysis of a national or colonial economy but a theory of the development of a world capitalist system. Abstraction allowed Marx to identify laws of development, as capital expanded and developed on a global scale.[16] When Marx turned to colonialism, he was concerned with economic consequences: overwork, long hours, premature death, wages below subsistence, repression, and violence.[17] He continuously affirmed anti-colonial resistance in colonized and dependent nations. Pynchon's quip about "Cheap Labor" is drawn from Marx's position on British colonialism as a historically progressive force. As Aijaz Ahmad argues, for critics seeking to argue that Marxism is exclusively concerned with modes of production and a positivistic "myth of progress," they can do little better than allude to one or two statements—ripped out of context—in Marx's writings on India.[18] In a frequently anthologized letter to the *New York Herald Tribune*, written in 1853, Marx offered both a denouncement of British colonial violence and a critique of the problems of pre-capitalist India.[19] Marx argued England "was actuated only by the vilest interests" in acquiring Hindustan [India], and "was stupid in her manner of enforcing" social and political change, but he proposed "whatever [...] the crimes of England she was the unconscious tool of history in bringing about that revolution."[20]

Marx's writings on India are often the product of financial necessity and should be read with some caution. Compelled by the misery of his life in London Marx wrote numerous articles for the *New-York Daily Tribune*—that "wretched paper," he said in a letter to Engels in 1858, creating a "great interruption" to his studies in economy.[21] In all, Marx sent thirty-three dispatches on Indian affairs to the *Tribune*, beginning in June 1853.[22] Inevitably, Marx pronounced on subjects of which he had limited factual information.[23] While horrified by the brutality of European conquest, Marx saw no use in overthrowing foreign domination simply to restore the "solid foundation of Oriental despotism."[24] For Marx, imperialism was a cruel and detestable practice but it would create new trade networks of capitalist exchange.

Like many before him, Marx did not account for the particulars of Indian history, understanding its development primarily through the intrusion of outside forces.[25] "England has to fulfil a double mission in India" Marx wrote, "one destructive, the other regenerating—the annihilation of old Asiatic Society, and the laying of the material foundations of Western society."[26] As Ahmad argues, this "double mission" should be grasped in relation to Marx's dialectics.[27] India's development is inextricable from capitalist accumulation: imperialism was but a process within the general law of capitalist accumulation on a global scale. The division of the world between the various capitalistic associations is integral to capitalist accumulation and impoverishes the working class, despite differences in national situations.

Pynchon delineates the consequences of colonialism across a variety of texts but is closest to Marx in his treatment of the United States, which had been steadily emerging over the nineteenth century as a powerful capitalist economy out of a brutal colonial dynamic and a looming Civil War. Pynchon returns to this moment in *Mason & Dixon*, a work deliberately placed at a moment when borders were being flexed. The novel follows Charles Mason and Jeremiah Dixon in their astronomical exploits to construct the Mason-Dixon Line in British North America shortly before the American Revolutionary War. The narrative is told retrospectively by the Reverend Wicks Cherrycoke—a strange clergyman, whose name recalls an ageing consumer brand label—to entertain members of his extended family on a cold December evening. Cherrycoke's tale is not official colonial history and includes on women, slaves, workers, and minorities, while the text establishes an intended anachronism through a mimesis of eighteenth-century spelling, grammar, and syntax. For Pynchon,

American predestination is the "Rubbish-Tip for subjunctive Hopes, for all that may yet be true."[28] The world of Mason and Dixon is one capitalism will destroy: it is a world where "golems stalk the land, mechanized ducks fly, men transform into magical creatures and vegetables can house whole families."[29] These magical elements form a radical place possibility; a place where fantastical solutions exist to political problems. In Pynchon, history is not the arid accumulation of facts. Facts, writes, Pynchon "are but the Play-things of lawyers [...] 'Tops and Hoops, forever a-spin'—forming not 'a Chain of single Links' [but] a great disorderly Tangle of Lines, long and short, weak and strong, vanishing into the Mnemonick Deep, with only their Destination in common."[30] To use a term from John A. McClure, *Mason & Dixon* is a late imperial romance: a space of hope, magic and enchantment "where one can excoriate imperialist adventures and yet savor their taste."[31] Pynchon's attempt to locate the "singular point in American history" where "we jumped the wrong way" becomes in *Gravity's Rainbow* an effort to find "the fork in the road America never took."[32]

Gravity's Rainbow *and the Trickster*

Gravity's Rainbow is set, primarily, in Europe in the aftermath of the Second World War, and focuses on the design, production and dispatch of V2 rockets by German military. The novel features a quest undertaken by several characters, especially the American lieutenant Tyrone Slothrop, to locate the "Schwarzgerät" (black device) installed in a rocket with the serial number "00000."[33] Revealing the emergence of new networks of military and corporate power emanating from the Second World War onwards, the novel collapses twentieth-century conflict into a singular state of emergency referred to, simply, as "the War."[34]

In this novel, Pynchon's treatment of Marx is part of a broader description of colonies that reveals the *jouissance* of imperial process:

> Where he can just wallow and rut and let himself go in a softness, a receptive darkness of limbs, of hair as woolly as the hair on his own forbidden genitals. Where the poppy, and cannabis and coca grow full and green, and not to the colors and style of death, as do ergot and agaric, the blight and fungus native to Europe. Christian Europe was always death, Karl, death and repression. Out and down in the colonies, life can be indulged, life and sensuality in all its forms, with no harm done to the Metropolis, nothing to soil those cathedrals, white marble statues, noble thoughts.... No word ever gets back. The silences down here are vast enough to absorb all behavior, no matter how dirty, how animal it gets....[35]

For Pynchon, economics incentives and affective states become complimentary, not exclusive. Homi Bhabha use Freud to distinguish two conflicting states of colonial rule: a manifest, official, conscious level, and a latent, unconscious desire.[36] The colonizer's unconscious desire for the Other is expressed in a complex pattern of attraction and repulsion, desire, and denial. Colonies become more complex spaces: sites wherein economic imperatives exploit labor and construct a libidinal playground of indulgence. Pynchon's colonialism is about Europe escaping itself, a repression resulting from the pristine "white marble" statues and ornate cathedrals of modernity.[37] But Marx too offers a striking assessment of the psychopathology of colonial rule. The relationship between capitalist metropolises and their colonies reveals the "profound hypocrisy and inherent barbarism of bourgeoisie civilization" which "lies unveiled before our eyes, turning from its home, where it assumes respectable forms, to the colonies, where it goes naked."[38] Pynchon and Marx regularly return to the notion of the colony as the true face of capitalism. Pynchon pursues the consequences of colonialism through humor, fantasy, and what Freer rightfully calls an "avowedly childish male sexism," but his critique never declines into politically ineffective parody or apathy.[39]

One of the most striking aspects of Pynchon's critique is his alignment of Marx with the trickster, inviting comparison between Pynchon's Marx and what Claudia Gutwirth has termed the "trickster problematic."[40] Prominent in oral traditions, the trickster exhibits intellect or secret knowledge, and uses it to play tricks, ruses, or otherwise disobey rules. The trickster despises social intricacies, formalities, and masks, and seeks to challenge conventions often through a crude or lewd moralism. As Roger Abrahams argues:

> The Trickster is [...] the most paradoxical of all the characters in Western narratives—at least as far as the Western mind is concerned—for he combines the attributes of many other types that we tend to distinguish clearly. At various times he is clown, fool, jokester initiate, culture hero, even ogre [...] He is the central character for what we usually consider many different types of [...] narratives.[41]

For Abrahams, the difficulties of trickster nomenclature work to increase the sphere of "hermeneutical possibilities."[42] The trickster delights in the perpetration of jokes, mischief and intellectual games, in addition to overcoming unconquerable quests and riddles, acting as a nodal point for the intersection of study across mythology, religion, anthropology and psychology.[43] William Hynes and Will Doty argue for the figure as a permanent presence across diverse cultural practices, claiming that "for centuries, perhaps millennia [...] humans have told and retold tales of tricksters, figures who are usually comical, yet serve to highlight important social values."[44] The trickster exists to provide skepticism for centrally-held beliefs, and the lack of scholarship on this figure is part of Western "bias against allowing humor to represent serious and important [...] hermeneutical (interpretative) issues."[45]

As a trickster, Pynchon's Marx delights in perpetrating frauds upon Western intellectual discourse, recalling Foucault's comment on the limitations of Marxist enquiry as an "economics of untruth."[46] "Skipping away with his teeth together and his eyebrows up," this comic gaze renders an epistemological skepticism about Marx's truth-claims. At the same time, the trickster is a figure of "cunning deception" and "chance and liberation."[47] As an "exponent of possibilities," the trickster is a powerful figure through which to address Marx's depiction of capitalist imperialist processes. In relocating psycho-sexual deviancy outside the borders of the nation-state, Pynchon renews attention to the question of embodiment in Marx's works and opens several analytical dimensions.

Most forcefully, Pynchon's trickster develops a political economy of affect, invoking "felt" qualities that give meaning and imagination to complex political and economic processes. In finding the colony a "make believe" space where it is "Cheap Labor and Overseas Markets," Pynchon's trickster reconfigures a Marxist postcolonial historiography upon an affective epistemology. For colonies, the narrator argues, are "much, much more."[48] Imperialism opens up new sites of economic domination, where "the poppy, and cannabis and coca grow full and green," but also new affective subjects, "for what's a colony without its dusky natives?"[49] The West's fascination with the colony as a space of "death and repression" where "life can be indulged" without "harm to the Metropolis" positions the colony as an enchanted space of collective longing and otherness: a necessary site for capitalist exploitation because its provides both an economic and affective release from the moral strictures of normative social democracy.[50] Like all tricksters, Pynchon's Marx is an exponent of resistance strategies, a facet made possible by the trickster's existence as a semiotic sign, "a communal signification that cannot be separated or understood in isolation."[51] The trickster is a figure of opposition and infiltration, what Simon Weaver and Raúl Alberto Mora call a "*boundary crosser*."[52] This liminality is a core feature of the trickster hermeneutic, opening a space in which Pynchon can engage with colonial development, cultural transfer, and affective economies outside the strictures of indexical relations and realist-ethical frameworks. Showing commonality rather than incompatibility, Pynchon's trickster establishes Marx as an important matrix for reading colonies, imperialism, and empire, even if he appears, at least initially, as a troublesome figure.

Class, Labor, and Capital in Against the Day

Against the Day is Pynchon's first twenty-first-century novel and marks an important shift to the history of workers, strikes, protests, and labor violence, ranging across an immense cast of characters engaged in "unequivocal class warfare."[53] Kathryn Hume argues Pynchon's turn to class reflects his "increasing desperation over the direction America is taking," a shift distinct from the subjunctive enclaves of *Mason & Dixon* and the dark humor of *Gravity's Rainbow*.[54] As Jeff Baker has noted, in this novel the struggle for America "is no longer metaphorical": dynamite is the "audible sign" of the miner's curse of "enslavement to mineral extraction" as well as "the American workingman's equalizer, his agent of deliverance."[55] Focusing on terrorism, violence, and revolution, the novel shows cynicism towards the efficacy of lawful resistance, an inclination shared, in part, by novels considered in this book, including *Dissident Gardens*, *Eat the Document*, *The City & The City*, and *New York: 2140*.

The novel covers some thirty years from the Chicago Columbian Exposition in 1893 to the closing years of World War I, incorporating features of "historiographic metafiction," such as a dependence on historical discourse, intertextuality, and literary self-consciousness, often aligned with postmodern aesthetics.[56] The plot centers on the efforts of three brothers (Reef, Frank, and Kit) to avenge the death of their father, a pro-union anarchist engineer and dynamiter named Web Traverse who is killed under orders given by the businessman Scarsdale Vibe. The search for his father's killer leads Frank to remark that he finds himself in "a dime novel of Old Mexico, featuring gringo evildoers in exile [and] sudden deaths."[57] The Western is combined with other genres including juvenile romance, hard-boiled detective fiction, and spy thrillers to make up the revisionist self-reflectional totality of the novel. Violence and political resistance are to be found in Webb's bombing campaigns. These moments are often not covered in extensive detail, much like in *Eat the Document* which I discussed in Chapter 2. Webb targets capitalists, those "who slaughter the innocent as easy as signing a check."[58] It is possible to draw connections between the concerns of Colorado mineworkers and Spiotta's invocation of violent countercultural protest as both fictions entreat readers to consider the consequences of political violence. Pynchon and Spiotta reveal sympathy for their respective protagonists, Kit and Webb, Bobby, and Mary, while acknowledging that once the cycle of violence begins it is increasingly difficult to halt. As one critic argues, neatly symbolized in the family's surname—"Traverse"—Webb's resistance to capital draws him away from friends, and family; rarely are Webb's actions located in collective action and community endeavor.[59]

Pynchon's narrative offers detailed explorations of the oppressive structures of capital. In a discussion about Kit's future, Webb offers recourse to his most prized possession: his union card. Reading from the back, he warns Kit about the hollowness of capitalist enterprise: "but if you learn nothing else, learn this by heart, what it says here—'Labour produces all wealth. Wealth belongs to the producer thereof.'"[60] "These were old, proud, and strong union people," the narrator offers, "surviving in one of the world's worst antiunion environments."[61] The discussion offers several thematic affiliations with *Capital* in which characters are spoken of, but also speak for themselves:

> The capitalist therefore takes his stand [...] suddenly, however, there arises the voice of the worker, which had previously been stifled in the sound and fury of the production process: "The commodity I have sold you differs from the ordinary crowd of commodities in that its use creates value, a greater value than it costs. That is why you bought it [...] you and I know on the market only one law, that of the exchange of commodities."[62]

Marx's personification of the worker in "The Working Day"—it is worth noting that Pynchon's choice of title is clearly a similar kind of political resistance to capitalist temporality—is a moment when Marx uses the voice of the proletariat to demand "the value of my commodity."[63] In the preface to the first edition, Marx calls attention to the use of personification, instructing readers that an awareness of this trope should govern their reading of the text:

> I do not by any means depict the capitalist and the landowner in rosy colors. But individuals are dealt with here only in so far as they are the personifications of economic categories, the bearers of particular class relations and interests. My standpoint [...] can less than any other make the individual responsible for relations whose creature he remains, socially speaking, however much he may subjectively raise himself above them.[64]

Marx's theater of voices is complex. For much of *Capital*, we are dealing with humans who are correlatives of impersonal economic processes (Marx's use of the word Träger, or bearer, seems to confirm an insistence on system rather than subject).[65] A discussion between Webb and the Finnish revolutionary Veikko furnishes a useful point from which to examine this further. Sitting atop a hill waiting to dynamite a train line, this exchange draws interesting parallels between the Tsar's regime and the forces of American capital:

> The main difference he could see was that the Russian aristocracy, after centuries of believing in nothing but its own entitlement, had grown weak,

> neurasthenic. "But American aristocracy is not even a century old, in peak of fighting condition, strong from efforts it took to acquire its wealth, more of a challenge. Good enemy."[66]

Veikko produces a fascinating convergence between the end of the Russian nobility and the consolidation of American capital which has become the enemy of the worker. When Webb asks his friend whether the capitalist occupies a position of strength too great for the average worker to surpass:

> Veikko's eyes would grow pale and illuminated from within, his voice issuing from an abundant and unkempt beard which suggested even on his calmest days an insane fanaticism. "We are their strength, without us they are impotent, we are they."[67]

The usefulness of class as an explanatory concept relies on a complex set of concrete locations within the capitalist mode of production. The most pertinent of these is the polarized location of the worker and capitalist, an analytical distinction premised on their conflicting material interests. Veikko acknowledges the Marxist tradition, noting that any compromise from class struggle produces changes in power between these two forces. The assertion that "we are they" poses challenges for class consciousness that are worth discussing here. Traditionally the "privileged nature of the worker's" situation lies, "paradoxically, in its narrow, inhuman limits":

> the worker is unable to know the outside world in a contemplative manner in one sense because he cannot know it all, because his situation does not give the leisure to intuit it in the middle-class sense; because, even before he posits elements of the outside world as *objects* of his thought, he feels *himself* to be an object, and this initial alienation within himself takes precedence over everything else.[68]

Paradoxically, it is alienation that allows the worker to overcome the limitations of neoliberal orthodoxy. The worker moves towards a new self-consciousness that permits access "to the totality or reality, to that totalising knowledge which was the stumbling block of classical [...] philosophy."[69] For the worker's previous relationship to reality and to the commodity was to see it as a static, isolated phenomenon: the finished product is understood as but a solitary moment in the process of production itself. This results in a tendency to view the world as a collection of separate unrelated things. In contrast this new relationship implies a privileged form of knowledge which resolves the epistemological dilemmas of bourgeois ethics through the union of intellectual thought and practice. The "we are they" signals a class consciousness attentive to overcoming the capital-labor relation, and the collapse of worker and capitalist, a distinction central to the capitalist mode of production.

Against the Day draws comparisons between the volatility of capital and the emergence of bomb technology. When Webb visits Merle's photographic workshop they discuss alchemy and explosives as two things which can oppose capitalism, which ironically involves some of the same materials. Webb rejects the political potential of alchemy viewing it as no longer equipped to challenge capitalist enterprise:

> "But if you look at the history, modern chemistry only starts coming in to replace alchemy around the same time capitalism really gets going. Strange, eh? What do you make of that? Webb nodded agreeably. Maybe capitalism decided it didn't need the old magic anymore." An emphasis whose contempt was not meant to escape Merle's attention. "Why bother, had their own magic, doin just fine, thanks, instead of turning lead into gold, they could take poor people's sweat and turn it into greenbacks, and save that lead for enforcement purposes."[70]

From the magic of capital, the novel uncovers a hidden "democratic" potential in bomb technology. But the intended destruction of infrastructure meets with capitalism's response, as it comes to nullify the bombs truth-value. As Webb remarks, "here was nitro, the medium of truth, being used by these criminal bastards to tell their lies with."[71] In the novel, nitroglycerine is a form of resistance, before it becomes absorbed by capitalist rationality, in a similar manner to the left political playing cards in *Eat the Document*. It is the novel's hope that the bomb offers a diegetic function, exploding the rhetoric of capitalist triumphalism and initiating a discourse of shock across the rest of the twentieth century. It is Pynchon's new political clarity that makes *Against the Day* revolutionary.

Representing Finance: Crunch-lit and Fictitious Capital

Pynchon's most recent text turns to the increasing occurrence of financial crisis in the twenty-first century.[72] The 2001 recession and 2008 crash awakened many to the precariousness of the capitalist world-system, provoking demands for tougher stances on fiscal regulation alongside premature speculations concerning the end of capitalism itself.[73] The crisis was the result of a series of poorly understood yet remarkably creative financial instruments, such as risk trenches, credit-default swaps, mortgage-backed securities, and collateralized debt obligations, which produced a "charade of fantasy valuations," which led to crisis.[74] Popular fictional texts such as *Wall Street: Money Never Sleeps* (2010), *Too Big to Fail* (2011), *Margin Call*, *The Wolf of Wall Street* (2013), and *The Big Short* (2015) followed, fostering debate about corporate greed, deregulation, and market speculation. Despite the success these works garnered, not least for their arresting presentation of a hedonistic, greedy, financial elite, the complexities of finance remained unapproachable, operating on a level incommensurable with everyday existence.[75] In these films in particular, the propensity to pass ethical judgement on financial actors was a substitute for confronting the opacity intrinsic to finance itself.

Pynchon's novels attempt to represent capital in its full complexity, showing markets in flux, prone to crisis, contradiction, and overproduction. Pynchon's framing of capitalism as a totality marks a powerful counterpoint to much of crunch-lit which uses moral and ethical responses to crisis, and which perpetuate neoliberal frames of reference. This often comes in the form of framing individual psychology, where the figure of the inhumane capitalist acts to perpetuate a timeless vision of social existence. A perfect illustration of this ahistorical impulse is given by the investment banker John Tuld (played by Jeremy Irons) in *Margin Call* (2011):

> It's all just the same thing over and over; we can't help ourselves. And you and I can't control it, or stop it, or even slow it. Or even ever-so-slightly alter it. We just react. And we make a lot money if we get it right. And we get left by the side of the side of the road if we get it wrong. And there have always been and there always will be the same percentage of winners and losers. Happy foxes and sad sacks. Fat cats and starving dogs in this world. Yeah, there may be more of us today than there's ever been. But the percentages? They stay exactly the same.[76]

Part self-justification, part naturalization, but surely one of the most influential kinds of thinking that emerges from within neoliberal ideology. Tuld's talk sweeps across the history of capital accumulation, crisis, and recession:

> Its just money; its made up. Pieces of paper with pictures on it so we don't have to kill each other just to get something to eat. It's not wrong. And it's certainly no different today than its ever been. 1637, 1797, 1819, 37, 57, 84, 1901, 07, 29, 1937, 1974, 1987—Jesus, didn't that fuck up me up good—92, 97, 2000 and whatever we want to call this.[77]

From speech to writing, the language itself is in competition with the discourse of high finance as numbers sweep across the page in the manner of ticker tapes or trading floor screens. Tuld's disquisitions fracture under the relationality of the exchange system, in which capitalist crisis is substituted for number through metonymy, and the content of experience is reduced to the intangible quality of financial discourse. Meaning fractures under the weight of non-referential number.

It is tempting to see literature as offering more compelling explanations of speculation, credit, consumption, and risk, not least because of the fundamental association between the novel and the rise of capitalism, which for Jameson is "as much a component of modernization as the importation of automobiles."[78] Unlike film, the plasticity and hybridity of the novel form enables it to incorporate multiple literary levels, genres, and modes, so that, for example, "'realist elements might be mixed with more experimental modes of narration, or older literary devices might be reactivated in juxtaposition' with new critical frames."[79] For Nicky Marsh:

> contemporary literature has been a powerful site for unraveling the assumptions that are contained within the rhetoric of money's fictitiousness. The novel's particular attention to the construction of fictitiousness has offered it a range of strategies for revealing, countering and qualifying the disabling mystification sustained by the apparent ability of money to be everywhere and nowhere, everything and nothing.[80]

While "writers select, distort, aggregate" the circumstances of economic crisis, the paradox of the literary imagination is that these "fictional works [...] tell truths about economic realities, while apparently factual works on economic realities may be infiltrated by fiction [offering] myths and fantasies, disguised dramas with heroes and villains."[81] This strategy of provocative contrast—oscillating between the villains and victims of global capital flows—defuses rather than enables an adequate representation of financial markets because it privileges a bourgeois ethics of binary relations. In short, the "good" worker and "evil" capitalist model does not go deep enough: it does not disclose the very forms of the strategies themselves as modes of ideological activity that conceal power relations and extend mechanisms of control by reproducing ideological conditions for the continuance of capitalist social arrangements. No matter how sophisticated and refined, ethics always declines into value-judgements. A reliance on moral philosophy marks crunch-lit narratives as less compelling guides to financial crisis.

As the logic of finance capital has become more complicated to think and narrate, novels on the financial crisis have tended to cede this responsibility to more experimental narrative forms. As such, crunch-lit chooses to remain within formal and narratological frameworks which privilege ethical preachment over critical engagement. Rather than narrating financial upheaval in forms conducive to its subject, a reliance on scheming, treacherous or morally indifferent investors is simply no longer able to describe the logic of the economic structure, nor is it able to provide a logical basis for narrating contemporary reality. Ultimately, this is because twenty-first-century finance capital names a distinct era beyond the dominance of industrial production and commodity exchange, where the art of money-making takes its purest form: pure in the sense that the structure of the value form and its universal equivalent, money, now stand at the forefront of the capitalist mode of production. Literary critics often remain reverential about the innate value of the realist novel, but seldom do they acknowledge the limits of realist fiction. Typically, such critics demand unapologetic "ethical heuristics trussed up in majestically lyrical prose."[82] See, for example, Liam McIlvanney and Ray Ryan's recent take on the novel:

> One can say for one thing, that the truth of novels cannot be rendered into any other form; it cannot be abstracted or codified, turned into thesis or proposition. Novelistic truth is not data, not reportage, not documentary, not philosophical tenet, not political slogan. Novelistic truth is dramatic, which means above all it has to do with character [...] In exploring character the novel's key strength is the disclosure of human interiority. To the question, what does the novel do? We might most pertinently answer: the novel does character and the novel does interiority.[83]

Character and interiority remain remarkably limited strategies with which to confront the complex abstractions of twenty-first-century financial capital. Perceived on this terrain, it is little wonder they fail. Rather the value of the novel resides, not in the kind of simple, reductive, and seemingly timeless qualities attributed to it under bourgeois liberalism, but as a distinctive method of production, a specific composition of the concrete diversity of its elements.[84] We can say, to use Terry Eagleton's reading of Pierre Macherey, the importance of the literary work consists in its ability to establish a difference, a separation from the languages, ideologies, and histories which surround it and which mark a measurable and determinable distance, which may be the object of scientific knowledge.[85] "Novelistic truth" is "not data, not reportage," but it is certainly not reducible to character and interiority. The speculative and unstable condition of twenty-first-century finance would be conveyed with greater clarity by pursuing narrative strategies which contest a reliance on the tradition of character, interiority, moralization, and realism. The requirement for a truly novel approach to the interplay of relations among finance, the market, and social and political structures can be found in the works of Pynchon, whose style and technique hold together and unify large quantities of disparate raw material, rather than seek to impose ethical heuristics on non-ethical phenomena.

Finance, Fiction, Form

Representing capital is no easy task; it strains the dimensions of all narrative models. Any serious examination of the relationship between finance and form must begin with the tumultuous period when financial speculation first began to outpace industrial production. With the new emerging cultures of financial speculation, the nineteenth-century novel was shaped by the financial contexts of the period. In his critical survey of nineteenth-century narratives, Kevin McLaughlin argues Victorian society engaged in its most intense philosophical debates about political economy during a time when the novel was at the peak of its popularity. He concludes "economic issues have never been far from British fiction" with Victorian writers producing "some of the most engaging fictions" on fiscal irresponsibility, financial temptation, and monetary crisis.[86]

Appraising their development and inhabiting their milieu, Marx explicitly aligned himself with the discursive context of Victorian London. Marx procured a Reader's Ticket to the British Library shortly after his arrival in London in 1849 and began scrutinizing issues of *The Economist* before turning to works by Shakespeare, Milton, Defoe, and Dickens.[87] Just as there could be no Dickens without London, there could be no Marx without the bustling commerce of the city. As he writes in *Capital*:

> No period of modern society is so favorable for the study of capitalist accumulation as the period of the last 20 years. It is as if Fortunatus' purse had been discovered. But of all countries England again provides the classical examples because it holds the foremost place in the world market, because capitalist production is fully developed only in England.[88]

Dickens remains a central figure in scholarship of the Victorian novel, his fictions offering critical perspectives on the centrality of finance to his characters. In *Great Expectations* (1861), a text concerned with class mobility, inheritance, and investment, the contemplation of the impersonal structures of credit and wealth produces a rather bewildered resignation: "As we contemplated the fire" remarks Pip "and as I thought what a difficult vision to realize [...] Capital sometimes was, I put my hands in my pockets."[89] As Anna Kornbluh argues, the nineteenth-century consideration of finance prompts a gesture of inward retreat, which is "emblematic of Victorian thought's struggle with fictitious capital."[90] For Kornbluh, this image of quiet introspection is "one of the seminal metaphors of modernity" as a period which saw the emergence of the modern nation's financial system—with its central bank, national debt, taxation, bonds, and paper monies—concomitantly established a turn "inward to the capital of the self [and] the construct of a psychic economy."[91] At a significant historical juncture then, when capital begins to circulate in speculative forms that are increasingly independent of their material origins, the gesture of placing hands into pockets offers a measured abdication to the cultural economy of this new financial universe. This narrative moment, which founders on the necessity to visualize capital through an inability to "pocket-it," signals an acceptance of the failure of realism to comprehend the abstractions of nineteenth-century capital and commodity.

Despite coming in the late nineteenth century, Pip's gesture of placing hands into pockets can still serve as meta-textual commentary on the current state of twenty-first-century financial comprehension. While financial operations has exerted a powerful pull on the literary imagination, the response to financial crisis in the twenty-first century has largely remained within aesthetic modes that are "comfortably quotidian" and "quaint[ly] anachronistic."[92] As Paul Crosthwaite has argued, the "very image of finance implies a frame, a set of boundaries, but what frame is capacious enough to contain something as sprawling and diffuse as finance or the market?"[93] Responding to the 2008 banking crisis, this wave of recession writings—"crunch-lit"—attempts to give shape, voice and coherence to the intricacies of global finance.[94] Despite the priority realist fiction is granted as a space equipped to evaluate the development of financial capital, "crunch-lit" typically fails to register financial processes. The possibility for unconstrained market speculation produces a corollary in the form of fiction which insists upon aesthetic and moralistic frameworks simply not up to the task:

> To imagine a narrative in which, in contrast, the protagonists are not fully realized, psychologically complex, desirous individuals but rather anonymous, inhuman systems and networks may run contrary to the traditional inclinations of the novel, but it is a task demanded by the realities of contemporary finance capital and its periodic crises.[95]

Crosthwaite cites Faulks' *A Week in December* as exemplary in this regard. The novel features an unscrupulous hedge-fund manager whose pursuit of profit leads him to take on a version of the Royal Bank of Scotland. Faulks's novel is a crunch-lit fiction which maintains a realist style whilst depicting the dynamics of the credit crisis "in profoundly counter-factual terms, attributing this structural and systematic crisis of finance capital to the actions of a small group of people, or even a single individual."[96]

The problems of using realism to reflect capital are brilliantly broached by Marx. For Marx, there is something fictitious in capital. This insight comes early in volume 1, with Marx proposing the defamiliarizing agency of capital results in the proliferation of unfamiliar agents, such as the commodity, a strange object, which both speaks and "reveals its thoughts in a language with which it alone is familiar: the language of commodities."[97] Marx comes to emphasize this estrangement beautifully, suggesting that the introduction of a monetary economy does not enhance or facilitate human interaction but gets in the way of it. Money necessitates the adoption of strange, unfamiliar language:

> To compare money with language is not less erroneous. Language does not transform ideas, so that the peculiarity of ideas is dissolved and their social character runs alongside them as separate entity, like prices alongside commodities. Ideas which have first to be translated out of their mother tongue into a foreign tongue in order to circulate, in order to become exchangeable, offer a somewhat better analogy; the analogy is then not with language, but in the foreignness of language.[98]

The strangeness of personified objects in *Capital* is one instance in which capital can only be told through unconventional narrative strategies, excessive symbolic dimensions, and strange, even uncanny, images. While Marxism accords ideas as secondary to material forces, Marx is powerfully aware of the importance of language within the structural transformations of capital. Pynchon and Marx challenge financial hegemony outside of exclusively moralistic and ethical-judgmental frameworks.[99] Pynchon's narratives are based on Menippean satire which "shapes political substructures through a stylistic multiplicity [...] fantasy and philosophy, intellection and encyclopedism, an 'anti-book' stance, a marginal cultural position, and carnivalization."[100] When considered dialectically, what can be thought of as dilemmas in Pynchon's oeuvre—his chaotic plots, two-dimensional characters, a reliance on abstruse mathematical formulae—become less matters of opinion or taste than conceptual solutions to reframing crisis in Crosthwaite's call for "unreal, impersonal and amoral" terms.[101]

David Witzling correctly reveals "the tendency among Pynchon's critics to treat characters as metonyms for ideas rather than as simulations of real people" because in Pynchon characters are artefacts of larger discursive systems that enact patterns of control, power, and ownership.[102] Pynchon's characters do not possess the innate selves assumed by the humanism of McIlvanney and Ryan. For in Pynchon:

> names do not operate as they do in, for example, Fielding in which, Thwackum or Allworthy are—or do—exactly what their names indicate [...] We usually expect to find a person in a name. In a realist book as in life, the name comes to signify a real character with unique characteristics. This goes along with the tenuous notion of the unique individual. Pynchon blows all this up. Character and identify are not stable in his fiction [...] Pynchon indicates that he can see how, in various ways, people are subject to the authority of naming: how a whole society can exercise power through naming.[103]

Pynchon must confer names on his figures, but he refuses to use character in any consistent way. Names in Pynchon can be ironic, alluding to absent qualities or traits, they can be jokes, puns, anagrams, anachronisms, they can suggest social class and identify a character as elect (saved) or preterit (damned), they can allude to people, things, phenomena or historical figures, or function as occupational or descriptive epithets.[104] For Pynchon, taxonomies can easily become strategies of containment and control.

In *The Eighteenth Brumaire*, Marx offers a list of those outside the normative structures of social ontology that is, as Patrick Hurly argues, eerily close to Pynchon's preterit dispersed across the post-war European Zone in *Gravity's Rainbow*.[105] For Marx:

> Alongside decayed *roués* with dubious means of subsistence and of dubious origin, alongside ruined and adventurous offshoots of the bourgeoisie, were vagabonds, discharged soldiers, discharged jailbirds, escaped galley slaves, swindlers, mountebanks, *lazzaroni*, pickpockets, tricksters, gamblers, *maquereaux*, brothel keepers, porters, *literati*, organ grinders, ragpickers, knife grinders, tinkers, beggars—in short, the whole indefinite, disintegrated mass, thrown hither and thither, which the French call *la bohème*.[106]

Marx considers the *lumpenproletariat* an impediment to the realization of a classless society because they do not generate socially useful production. As beggars, prostitutes, and petty criminals, they form a reactionary "class faction" composed of "outcast, degenerated and submerged elements that make up a section of the population of industrial centers."[107] For Pynchon however, this unassimilable heterogeneity is a potential form of resistance. *GR* understands this resistance as emerging out of rationally determined capitalist systems, contending that "dialectically some counterforce would have to arise."[108] Defined by the system it opposes, the Counterforce in *Gravity's Rainbow* is made up of socially excluded characters which, as Roger Mexico says, "piss on their rational arrangements."[109] In *The Crying of Lot 49* exclusion is a potential form of resistance. Oedipa Mass thinks that the old man in the derelict house might possess forms of knowledge unavailable to those in the capitalist system. As Oedipa realizes, for those citizens refusing to communicate by U.S. mail, "it was not an act of treason, nor possibly even of defiance. But it was a calculated withdrawal, from the life of the Republic, from its machinery."[110] The rejection of the socio-economic order and the refusal to generate socially prescribed value, is itself a politics, a form of resistance and revolt. Pynchon makes visible another America, the wasted America discarded under U.S. global military dominance. This exclusion is a strategic advantage to contest capital.

Pynchon, Neoliberalism, Resistance

Bleeding Edge is Pynchon's first novel set in the twenty-first century. Concomitantly, it forms the author's most direct, sustained, and explicit engagement with neoliberalism at the beginning of the new millennium. Over the last two decades Pynchon's fiction has undergone a project of repoliticization which abandons forms of postmodern metaphysical play for ideologies much closer to the Marxist tradition, if not Marxist specifically. This repoliticization is grounded in the view that, while Pynchon's novels are thick with encyclopedic historical allusions, his concern with capital and class is never obfuscated or detached. *Bleeding Edge* delineates the new networks of class resistance that have emerged to contest the hegemony of finance, corporate power, and digital technology "most notably the internet, a development that promises social control on a scale those quaint old twentieth-century tyrants with their goofy moustaches could only dream about."[111] In the novel's rejection of the techno-utopian faith in digital technologies that promise salvation, Pynchon turns to the next generation, locating hope for the future in younger characters and children. The narrative follows ex-fraud investigator Maxine Tarnow as she uncovers a conspiracy plot centered on a computer security company named hashslingrz, which is owned and operated by dotcom "boy billionaire" Gabriel Ice.[112] Ice is busy buying up failed internet start-up companies and using them as "shells for funds he wants to move around inconspicuously."[113] Maxine discovers offshore payments being made to a mysterious slush-fund in Dubai, the beneficiaries of which may have orchestrated the attacks of 9/11..

Bleeding Edge draws powerful connections between neoliberal finance, U.S. foreign policy, and terrorist violence, acknowledging the destructive consequences of fundamentalist belief and the unchecked expansion of U.S. global military power and surveillance. When Maxine reflects on the efficacy of neoliberal quantitative models that seek to explain and predict human behavior, her ex-husband Horst responds with incredulity: "how could predicting market behavior be the same as predicting terrible disaster?"[114] Maxine replies, "Maybe the two were different forms of the same thing."[115] That's "way too anticapitalistic for me," remarks Horst.[116] Horst's refusal invites consideration of the relationship between financial capitalism and terrorist atrocity. Pynchon's status as a reclusive author prohibits any authoritative attribution of texts that he may have used for research, but Laurence Wright's *The Looming Tower* (2006) may have been a key source for Pynchon's novel.[117] Published in 2006, Wright's history reveals how Al-Qaeda's escalating threats of a coordinated attack on U.S. soil had preoccupied the U.S. intelligence community long before 2001.[118] Wright situates Islamist ideology in a symbiotic relationship with the West, revealing how the failures of U.S. foreign policy, coupled with a volatile and geo-politically unstable Middle East and the growth of a virulent Islamist ideology, were central to Bin Laden's development of a terrorist network.[119] *Bleeding Edge* allocates American foreign policy a major role in the escalation of global terrorism, going so far as to situate the events within landscapes of capitalist enterprise:

> Just to say evil Islamics did it, that's so lame, and we know it. We see those official close-ups on the screen. The shifty liar's look, the twelve-stepper's gleam in the eye. One look at these faces and we know they're guilty of the worst crimes we can imagine. But who's in any hurry to imagine? To make the awful connection? [...] It would take a mind hopelessly diseased with paranoia, indeed a screamingly anti-American nutcase, even to allow to cross her mind the possibility that that terrible day would have deliberately been engineered as a pretext to impose some endless Orwellian "war" and the emergency decrees we will soon be living under. Nah, nah, perish that thought.[120]

The emphasis on paranoia is distinct from Pynchon's earlier fiction, where paranoia is dismal yet thrilling. In contrast to *The Crying of Lot 49* and *Vineland*, *Bleeding Edge* pursues existing tendencies towards conclusions. Paranoia in Pynchon's most novel is less about novelistic construction or the flight of imaginative liberty, than a serious, anxious, and reflexive encounter with the trajectory of global capitalist development. The novel is not convinced Bush was responsible for the attacks but highlights the absurdity that this possibility must be discounted.

Firstly, the novel has been positioned as a 9/11 novel, a classification that has often eschewed politics in favor of understanding trauma through marital discord.[121] Christopher Nealon has challenged this "domesticated Pynchon," arguing such readings "obscure the ways in which Pynchon has been writing, all along, about capitalism."[122] The second strand involves Emily Johansen and Alissa Karl's work on the neoliberal novel, which argues that contemporary fiction "enacts and negotiates the tendencies of neoliberal labour markets at interlocking thematic and formal levels."[123] These approached can be complimented by turning to a consideration of neoliberal power, security and surveillance. Shortly before the novel's publication, Edward Snowden leaked classified documents revealing the NSA's global surveillance program; the implication being that national security agencies, not just in the U.S., have the power to conduct mass intelligence-gathering.[124] Initial commentators quickly situated *Bleeding Edge* as a novel for the post–Snowden Era.[125] The opening pages register this subtext with the character of Reg Despard, a documentary film-maker who pirates films with a hand-held video camcorder:

> When Reg discovered the zoom feature [...] there was a lot of zooming in and out for what you'd have to call its own sake, details of human anatomy, extras in crowded scenes, hip-looking cars in the background traffic, so forth. One fateful day in Washington Square, Reg happened to sell one of his cassettes to a professor at NYU who taught film, who next day came running down the

> street after Reg to ask, out of breath, if Reg knew how far ahead of the leading edge of this post-postmodern art form he was working.[126]

Pynchon is obviously having some fun at the expense of scholarly critique, punning on the "leading edge"/ "bleeding edge" of Reg's "post postmodern art form."[127] Reg is not engaged in surveillance as such, but what is significant is how the "bootleg" tapes reveal a fractured and distorted image of individual subjects, no longer actors in the film but pictures of "human anatomy, extras in crowded scenes."[128] The "out of breath" academic that arrives to proclaim that Reg has discovered a new art form underscores Reg's distance from the efficiency of surveillance technology, which in the form of the PATRIOT Act, "heightened nationalist discourse, extended surveillance mechanisms, suspended constitutional rights, and developed forms of explicit and implicit censorship."[129]

This agenda is facilitated by government forces that, as Maxine notes in *Bleeding Edge*, "took our own precious sorrow, processed it, sold it back to us like any other product."[130] Martin Eve has suggested this moment marks the "foremost satirical representation of the academic humanities in [Pynchon's] work," claiming the "passage ridicules the academic debates over irony and sincerity that have raged in recent years."[131] Despite the comedy, the moment functions seriously as a critique of theoretical efforts which validate partial and fragmented approaches to the totality of social relations. In Reg's "post-postmodern" tapes, the attention to individual subjects "for what you'd have to call its own sake" exposes the failure to offer a situational representation "on the part of the individual subject to that totality which is the ensemble of society's structures."[132]

Reg's tapes reveal an important interplay between totality, art, and capitalism, gesturing to symbiotic forms of social control which the political theorist Stephen Gill has called "disciplinary neoliberalism."[133] This involves an array of "legal and constitutional practices" that reconstitute capital on a world scale.[134] The perceived uselessness of Reg's art reveals a need for a wider understanding of structures attentive to the interconnections between political economy, surveillance, and control.

This critique of surveillance and capital is furthered in the words of Maxine's father, specifically in his realization of an intensified Cold War bureaucratic surveillance which is personified in the narrative by FBI agent Nicholas Windhurst. "This is 2001," Ernie remarks, "the Cold War is supposed to be over, how can these people not have changed or moved on, where is such a terrible inertia coming from?[135] While we later learn that Ernie has been involved in anti–Reagan protests during the 1980s, Maxine's initiation into forms of radical left thinking comes with her father's "scary blacklist stories":

> Some kids had the Seven Dwarfs, Maxine and Brooke had the Hollywood Ten. The trolls and wicked sorcerers and so forth usually Republicans of the 1950s, toxic with hate, stuck back around 1925 in almost bodily revulsion from anything leftward of "capitalism" by which they usually mean keeping an increasing pile of money safe from the depredations of the IRS [...] Maxine often wonders if it didn't help steer her toward fraud investigation, as much as maybe it's steered Brooke toward Avi and his techie version of politics.[136]

As Maxine thinks back to Ernie's narration of these bedtime narratives, she notes, briefly, that such stories may have inculcated left political sentiments that the novel sets out to recapture. In her first meeting, Windhurst lays out recent geopolitical shifts which have been "getting the security community all nervous lately," Maxine can't help but wonder at the man's politics: "How right-wing does a person have to be to think of *The New York Times* as a left-wing newspaper?"[137] Pynchon's novel highlights practices of surveillance and control, displaying in a kind of Overton window the range of politically viable ideas Tariq Ali has recently termed the "extreme center."[138]

Windhurst is styled as a "neoliberal enforcer," and it is later revealed he has "taken positions" in the sell-off of public resources whose privatization he artfully engineered. His interest in Maxine's findings leads to a romantic interest in her. The scene is handled in characteristic Pynchon style, combining a strange mix of lurid male fantasy with female sexual freedom. After Windhurst is murdered by his bosses, Maxine later encounters a youthful avatar in the outer-reaches of DeepArcher, a "not-yet-corrupted entry level wise ass."[139] Maxine lambasts Windhurst for his ideological commitments, his belief in capitalist enterprise which paid off: "They found his careless gift of boy's cruelty and developed it," Maxine notes, "deployed and used it, by tiny increments, till one day he was a professional sadist with a GS-1800 series job and no regrets."[140] "Nothing could touch him, and he thought he could just go on, deep into his retirement years. Chump. Asshole."[141] Windhurst lost all the capital he had accumulated through nefarious business deals, but he was also tortured into pursuing these ends. Pynchon draws parallels between neoliberal doctrine and psychological discord. Capital is dependent on our compliance and goes to great levels to ensure it. In Windhurst we see the full costs of this, but also spaces of possibility and resistance, the person he could have been.

Mitchum Huehls has situated the novel within a larger left political trajectory that has concerned Pynchon since his earliest efforts, but "contrary to the Marxist dream of capitalism's finitude, in Pynchon's world, the unholy alliances of business, government and criminality always discovers more resources to exploit, more dung to convert into diamonds."[142] Huehls equates Pynchon's *penchant* for resisting narrative closure with Marx's invocation regarding the end of capital. In offering an assessment of technological momentum, Huehls reads Pynchon's texts as articulations of capitalism's ability to produce new and innovative methods of corruption and resistance: "everything changes not so much because of 9/11 but because of the Internet: even as conspiracies of capital continue to thrive, the Internet has laid them bare for all to see."[143]

It is the internet, a new means of communicative production and distribution, that is yet a space both untouched by the forces of capitalist hegemony, and one equipped with the facility to challenge global financial rule. Pynchon contrasts the relatively free and untouched space of the internet with more mainstream forms of print media:

> If you read nothing but the Newspaper of Record, you might believe that New York City, like the nation, united in sorrow and shock, has risen to the challenge of global jihadism, joining a righteous crusade Bush's people are now calling the War on Terror. If you go to other sources—the Internet, for example—you might get a different picture. Out in the vast undefined anarchism of cyberspace, among the billions of self-resonant fantasies, dark possibilities are beginning to emerge.[144]

Unlike Huehls, Pynchon considers this dialectically. The "dark possibilities" of technological innovation generate new frontiers for exploitation and profit for those brutal enough to harness them. While Huehls places emphasis on technology as a prime liberating force, he fails to underscore the many structural adjustments (spatial, temporal, and even technological) that are required to counter the tendency for profit to fall, and which ultimately require the destruction of capital to begin again.[145] In Pynchon, the virtual space of the web, like sub-Saharan Africa, is not a liberation but another "zone" to be plundered.

Liberation through the creation of new technologies is a fantasy: the promise of the internet as a universal process that could erase boundaries associated with nations, languages, and money did not occur, and likely never will. The "dark possibilities" of the internet mean it can be a space of commercialism, an apparatus for government and corporate surveillance, and an anti-democratic force. As the left-wing radical March Kellher notes, new technological innovations can still act as a wakeup call for a future of radical democratic possibilities: "that was the moment Maxi" argues March, "not when 'everything changed.'" When everything was revealed. "No grand Zen illumination, but a rush of blackness and death."[146] For March, this moment shows "us exactly what we've become, what we've been all the time [...] living on borrowed time. Getting away cheap."[147] The power to change is not imputed to technology as an independent entity. Rather, technology is a history of human actions, made up of choices and selections that determine the future.

Kellher, editor of the blog "Tabloid of the Damned," provides a powerful counterpoint to Ice's corporate greed. She appears as a "guest speaker" at Kugelblitz School, a figure Maxine's sons Ziggy and Otis consider to be a "really crazy lady," but whom Maxine recalls was "always sort of … political."[148] The narrative involves a flashback of an anti-capitalist protest, the "CO-OP—CRUEL OFFENSIVE OUTRAGEOUS PRACTICES" scandal "ten or fifteen years ago, when landlords were reverting to type and using Gestapo techniques to get […] tenants to move."[149] Maxine finds March "on a picket line of neighborhood gadflies, old lefties, tenants'-rights organizers and so forth."[150] After a hostile confrontation with the landlord, "one Dr Samuel Kriechman," March and Maxine go to a nearby bar.[151] In the ensuing discussion, March excavates what is for Maxine an unknown history of left activism and generational solidarity. As it turns out, March "used to show up at the same demonstrations" as Elaine, and Ernie. Maxine recalls it was only "years later that they felt comfortable in sharing their memories of plastic handcuffs, pepper spray, unmarked vans, the Finest doping what cops do best."[152] As Maxine appears momentarily wounded for not being asked to be involved in her parents' political activities, March responds with a comment upon the necessity of political action that avoids the strictures of left melancholy:

> Never too late to start, there's enough to do God knows, you think anything's changed? Dream on. The fucking fascists who call the shots haven't stopped needing races to hate each other, it's how they keep wages down and rents high, and all the power over on the East Side, and everything ugly and brain dead just the way they like it.[153]

Maxine's questioning of March's political efforts—as least as she relates them to the two boys—comes under further scrutiny when Pynchon aligns the creation of these new, potentially democratic forms in technology, with the political efforts of his favorite decade: the 1960s. As March demonstrates, class continues in the virtual: "their idealism … their youth, Maxi I've never seen anything like it since the 1960s. These kids are out to change the world. Information must be free—they really mean it." On the other side are the agents of capital, the "greedy fucking dotcommers make real-estate developers look like Bambi and Thumper."[154]

The virtual world of "DeepArcher" exists, at least for the moment, beyond Ice's search for profitable investment. Young idealists must decide whether to sell the source code for a profit or pass it on to the benefit of all: the "same old classic dot-com dilemma," Pynchon writes, "be rich forever or make a tarball out of it and post it around for free, and keep their cred and maybe self-esteem."[155] As in all his fiction, Pynchon is troubled by the movement of capital away from an exploitation-free universal prosperity. We can conclude this discussion by turning to the end of the novel, which features Maxine's flashback to a moment "not so long ago in DeepArcher, down in their virtual hometown of Zigotisopolis."[156] This fictional city, which puns on the fertile (zygote) has been created by Ziggy and Otis. "Zigotisopolis" is a fictional Manhattan located in the Deep web, a place where dotcom venture capitalists and real-estate developers are replaced with utopia, community zones, and families.[157] The novel ends with transferring radical hopes to the next generation, as Maxine watches her sons walk to school in "precarious light."[158] Pynchon end what may be his last novel by placing hope in the hands of the next generation.

It is to young people we now turn.

7

Growing Up, Growing Old, in *Red at the Bone* and *Another Brooklyn*

A writer of young adult fiction, Jacqueline Woodson's *Red at the Bone (2019)*, *Another Brooklyn* (2016), and *Brown Girl Dreaming* (2014) remain rich and demanding explorations of Black women growing up in New York City. *Another Brooklyn*, her first adult novel in twenty years, follows August, a young girl who moves with her father and brother from Tennessee to the Bushwick in Brooklyn (Woodson lived there and the novel is dedicated to Bushwick). In *Brooklyn Fictions* (2015), James Peacock examines the "coming-of-age in the community" novel; this narrative form provides the reader with the protagonist's awareness of the historicity of their surroundings by developing characters "individual sovereignty."[1] If community has been troubled in recent years, authenticity, argues Peacock, becomes essential, and Woodson's novel, like others, turns to the past to comprehend the present while recognizing that community is known but never static. August grows up to become an anthropologist immersed in death rites and rituals. She has "seen death in Indonesia and Korea" and "death in Mauritania and Mongolia." She had "watched the people of Madagascar exhume the muslin-wrapped bones of their ancestors, spray them with perfume, and ask those who had already passed to the next place for their stories, prayers, and blessings."[2] This serious study of non-western conceptions of death rejects narrative in normative terms; the novel itself does not proceed through a linear structure but unfolds through a series of seemingly unconnected vignettes. August's knowledge of human development better equips her to understand her own life narrative, seeing her childhood, adolescence, and adulthood as intimately connected non-chronological prisms rather than disparate, procedural stages.

One morning August meets an old friend on the subway and this encounter prompts recollections of her childhood, and childhood friends,

Angela, Gigi, and Sylvia. Much of the girls' time is split among handling respective family strife, imaging the future, and avoiding dangers on Brooklyn streets. It is inevitable that Woodson's novel be read against a landmark fiction in the American coming-of age tradition, Toni Morrison's *The Bluest Eye* (1970). Morrison's novel is about a young Black girl, Pecola, living in 1940s Ohio and features an extensive catalogue of racism, incest, poverty, and child molestation. Ashamed of being black, Pecola develops a desire for blue eyes which she equates with the legal and cultural freedoms of whiteness. Both novels are formally experimental, concern childhood friendships, and explore complex forms of oppression connected to race, sex, and gender. Both concern specific forms of sexual predation as August and Pecola face perpetual threats as young girls and woman. Adam Dawson has argued that while Morrison depicts the dangers the white gaze poses to young Black girls, Woodson chronicles the perils of the "adultifying gaze, which reads Black girls as always already adults and therefore sexually available."[3] Drawing upon a number of troubling statistics which see Black children misperceived as legal adults, Dawson traces these concerns to the model of "the prematurely knowing Black girl" in nineteenth-century writing, as extreme hardship and danger dog Black youth in the present moment. The retrospective frame of *Another Brooklyn* and *The Bluest Eye* allow August and Claudia (Morrison's narrator) to establish a distance to work through their respective childhood trauma.

The freedoms, liberations, and experiences of 1970s Bushwick meet with many racial, sexual, and class oppressions, weathered by girlhood friendships and new networks of support generated by the family's recent conversion to Islam. At age eight, August and her father are approached while waking on the street by a member of the Nation of Islam, a black nationalist and religious organization. Called "a black queen," the man refers to August's body as a "temple" that "should be covered."[4] August feels exposed, sexualized, by the man's comments and this moment begins her rejection of the organization, while both her brother and father firmly place their trust in the group's patriarchal identity. Like others in her community, August's childhood is ruptured as she is subjected to racialized modes of sexual innocence and transgression. Threat lurks behind seemingly safe spaces, including church, school, and local stores. August, Angela, Gigi, and Sylvia must warn each other of people and places where unwanted sexual attention takes place.

August's mother died back in Tennessee and haunts the text as a recurring absence and space of imaginative potential, as reflected in the novel's title. August loses her mother, gains admission to an Ivy League college, studies anthropology, falls pregnant, and endures the death of her father. As a professional anthropologist by the time of the novel's narration, this training, she confides, mitigates the loss of loved ones but not the general experience of becoming: "Death didn't frighten me. Not now. Not anymore. But Brooklyn felt like a stone in my throat."[5] The novel is a work of memory and, as Peacock argues, events "simply happen [in the narrative but] it is their mental revisiting that gives them affective power."[6] The novel has a clear concern with kinship, inventory, cultural systems, and the symbolic excavation of the past. Its form is fractured, relating each memory in strikingly short scenes or episodes which often seem unconnected. Only through a shifting of these incidents can one construct a meaning of these events. The close of chapters has occasional recourse to anthropological comparison, with August's narration positioning the habits, routines, and rituals of her family against the customs and practices of ancient societies and other cultures, particularly in their treatment of the dead. For August, these cross-cultural typologies offer imaginative modes of working through the loss of her mother and childhood oppression.

Another Brooklyn was followed by *Red at the Bone*, another adult novel that weaves together the recollections from three generations of a black Brooklyn family, focusing on individual and collective traumas originating in the Tulsa Massacre. Occurring in Oklahoma in 1921 and considered one of the single worst incidents of racial violence in the United States, the violence began after a black shoeshiner, Dick Rowland, was falsely accused of attempting to rape a 17-year-old white girl. Mobs of white residents were deputized, given guns by city officials, and attacked black residents and neighborhoods. By the close of the following day, thousands of homes and businesses were destroyed, and around three hundred people were dead.[7] The novel, another work of memory, narrated by several characters, is concerned with two black families coming together when Iris and Aubrey, two teenagers, become pregnant. Iris is from a wealthy middle class black family and "even as a child, [had] never doubted that she'd one day go to college."[8] Iris keeps the baby, Melody, while Aubrey moves into the family home in Brooklyn and takes a job. Iris quickly becomes dissatisfied with her new life. She wants to go to college, leave Aubrey, and forge a career, "some fancy job where she dressed cute and drank good wine at a restaurant after work."[9] *Red at the Bone* is less a novel about a missing mother than the constraints of sex, class, motherhood, and a concomitant desire for female freedom. Woodson reverses stereotypes—mothers in Woodson often have no wish to mother—and has Melody raised by her father.

Woodson's other important work, *Brown Girl Dreaming*, a novel for young people written in verse, is like many of her fiction drawn from the author's childhood, growing up as a Black woman in the 1960s and 70s in Ohio, South Carolina, and New York. The narrative invokes the radicalism of the U.S. civil rights movement, often naming key figures by their first names only, showing an intimacy with protest and the worldliness of political discourse. In Chapter Two, I argued that Colson Whitehead's *The Nickel Boys* (2019) crafted the arena of the unlived life as Elwood Curtis, a promising African American student, is wrongly convicted and imprisoned in a brutal juvenile reformatory, Nickel academy, and later killed while trying to escape. While Whitehead's fiction arrests Elwood's development, Woodson's poems connect the Civil Rights movement to an ongoing autobiographical project. Using the writings of Martin Luther King, Jr, and the actions of Rosa Parks, Woodson uses Civil Rights as a formal feature through which to construct more imaginative modes of personal identity. In the second part of the book, in a section titled "South Carolina at War," Woodson writes of the ubiquitousness of violence and civil rights protest in the city:

> We can't go to downtown Greenville without
> seeing the teenagers walking into stores, sitting
> where brown people still aren't allowed to sit
> and getting carried out, their bodies limp, their faces calm.[10]

But family elders caution against the sole use of violence which must be complimented with other forms of political protests and radical action. As Woodson's grandfather says, "You can't just put your fist up. You have to insist / on something / gently. Walk toward a thing / slowly."[11] Rather than think that personality exists before pen is put to page, Woodson frames her autobiographical works through affirmative moments of protest. As Woodson moves South to live with her grandmother she is exposed to segregation. In this narrative, and indeed elsewhere in her work, Woodson pursues a strategy of provocative contrast, exposing drastic differences between regions, between country and city life, and between freedom and restriction. Much of the novel dwells on the difficulties of considering the South, with its complex racial and colonial legacies, home. Woodson later returns to Brooklyn, is reunited with her mother, and begins to craft a career as a fiction writer.

While Woodson's three works are formally experimental, in the construction of an often fragmented and episodic narrative structure, there are stylistics at work. I want to argue here that Woodson's writing gives weight to the isolated perception, and is closer to the poet's vision of single, exceptional image or moment rather than the generic comprehension or world building of the novelist, although undoubtedly these perceptions create a world. For the reader must continually fit together fragments, thrown out unexplained in the course of the text. It is almost as if the troubles and racial oppressions of the past cannot be rendered into seamless prose, but require a new temporality, and an extended consideration of the individual sentence, which demands to be read in isolation. Woodson achieves this partly through her innovative use of the page itself, a spatial form perhaps closest in tone and time to Claudia Rankine's *Citizen* (2014), in which the many micro-oppressions, which render visible Black experience, are given heightened consideration by the layout of the page (in which text is surrounded by white space). Woodson's novels, at least the ones considered here, are less about formal cohesion or unity, than moment; more about the weight of single, overriding images—two girls walking, arm in arm, down the street; the years of domestic violence represented in the glimpse of a father's damaged hands; the awakening of sexual desire by the view of other girls from the apartment's window—over narrative composition. These "poem-novels," in their preference for isolated perceptions, show hardship, uncertainty, transition, danger, and beauty as components in Black childhood experience, an experience Woodson is working to fit together.

Despite the similarities sketched at the outset between Morrison and Woodson, some critics have argued that the latter's narratives are an important break in the tradition of African American writing. For Dawson, this concern with representing human growth through non-linear forms shows that teleological narrative is a generic imposition rather than an accurate reflection. He proposes that "Woodson employs a model of coming of age that queer theorist Kathryn Bond Stockton terms 'growing sideways,'" such a model "suggests the width of a person's experience or ideas, their motives, or their motions, may pertain at any age."[12] Instead of the teleological linearity of standard coming-of-age accounts, which chart a course toward stature, marriage, reproduction, and the relinquishing of childish ways, growing sideways understands human development through "odd lingerings, wayward paths, and fertile delays."[13] These retrospective encounters forge links between the past and the contemporary self that Dawson calls autobiography in reverse. Using the work of Paul de Man, who notes the structure of a life is not inherent in it, but rather imposed upon it by the constraints of form, Dawson argues the rejection of linear narrative is based upon the "adultification of Black girls [...] not seen as children in the first place due to the adultifying gaze."[14] If the coming of age novel relies on the complex progression from adolescence to adulthood, then this is denied to the characters of Woodson's works, and to girls in particular, and by extension, as we saw in *The Nickel Boys*, to black youth in general.

Unlike the other authors considered in this study, it is this deliberate, willed, and self-conscious apprenticeship in children's and young adult's literature, and working across forms including memoir, illustrated books, television scripts, and novels, that has allowed Woodson a marked ability to imaginatively detail loneliness, prejudice, predation, segregation, racial division, interracial relationships, and class distinction, so commonly excluded from much of children's fiction. For here, in Woodson's three novels, form is itself transient, moving between the dual polls of the developed adult text (however we may define this) and the pull of simpler narrative forms, which André Jolles has shown to be a structuring principle of narrative and everywhere present, a distinction unsatisfactory as much as it is necessary.[15] The young adult novel attempts to capture this state of transition, of becoming. But in Woodson's use of a fragmentary form, the narrative is like a jigsaw that refuses to render a finished picture.

In a book that has dwelt extensively on left politics and literary criticism, it is worth noting that Fredric Jameson never provided any sustained consideration of children's literature or young adult fiction, only occasionally invoking the Alice books as conceptual metaphors in reference to the absurdities of contemporary capital.[16] Another passing reference to young readers is made in *The Antinomies of Realism* in relation to Tolstoy's education of the peasant pupils and the "unerring precision with which the children isolated a single 'trait'-physiological or linguistic, a habit or a sudden interjection-ta characterize their imaginary figures."[17] As Jameson observes, Tolstoy recorded his thoughts on education and noted children had taught him more than he could ever hope to teach them.[18] These educational experiments were often short lived, but children, noted Tolstoy, could become particularly perceptive readers, and this brings us to Jameson's famous pronouncement about naïve readers (the latter of which, he reminds us, we all are from time to time). For Jameson: "The presupposition here is that undergraduates—as more naïve or unreflexive readers (which the rest of us are also much of the time)—never confront a text in all its material freshness; rather, they bring to it a whole set of previously acquired and culturally sanctioned interpretive schemes, of which they are unaware, and through which they read the texts that are proposed to them […] The student's first confrontation with a classic, therefore—with *Heart of Darkness*, with Jane Austen, with Vonnegut or with Hemingway—will never really involve unmediated contact with the object itself, but only an illusion of contact, whose terminus turns out to be a whole range of interpretive options."[19] The naïve reader brings to a text a whole host of received thoughts and opinions, which they rarely consider in themselves. The task of the critic argues Jameson, it to understand this process, and confront these institutional interpretations. Mindful of these prescriptions, I now turn to one such moment in *Another Brooklyn*, in which August undergoes a kind of political awakening by linking her situation with conflict in West Africa. Specifically, it is worth considering whether this naivety, which Jameson diagnoses as a critical error, can prompt new progressive forms of empathy and progressive political consciousness.

Brooklyn and Biafra

Another Brooklyn examines postcolonial subjectivities in turning to the legacy of the Nigerian-Biafra War. Often ignored or forgotten in cultural discourse, Biafra was a nascent state in West Africa, formed from the nationalist aspirations of the Igbo people. Established in 1967, it was subsumed back into Nigeria after three years of brutal, savage war.

Nigerian Independence came in 1960, but regional tensions, exacerbated by colonial policy, persisted. Political campaigning and elections were marked by crime, violence, and fraud. Britain had left Nigeria in 1963, but war, ethno-religious conflicts, and military coups continued. The worst episodes of these events were captured in the work of the African novelist Chinua Achebe, who considered the Nigerian Civil War, which lasted until January 1970, to be among the defining experiences of his life. In his reflections on these events, *There was a Country*, written some forty years after the conflict, he argued the kinship of politics and art:

> Writing has always been a serious business for me. I felt it was a moral obligation. A major concern of the time was the absence of the African voice. Being part of that dialogue meant not only sitting at the table but effectively telling the African story from an African perspective—in full earshot of the world.[20]

Achebe was an Igbo, from the East of Nigeria, and presents the people and culture in his work as often progressive, democratic, and communal. When the British arrived in Nigeria in the nineteenth century, Igbo culture was dismissed and judged as possessing no valid political, or religious institutions. The British imposed colonial rule through District Commissioners, who themselves appointed Igbos as chiefs and clerks. No democratic method was employed. The result was lasting social ferment, resentment of colonials, and hatred of any collaborators who assisted the administration. This system survived until Independence in 1960.

As other critics have identified, the fundamental theme of Achebe's *Things Fall Apart* (1958) and *Arrow of God* (1964) is the "demonstration and dignity and validity of Igbo culture," with his work covering the history of Nigeria, from colonization to coup.[21] For Achebe, African literature should reflect national values and concerns, restoring a humanity that had been crudely distorted by colonialists. It should be, as the poet and stateman, Leopold Senghor argued, "functional, collective, and committed."[22] In *Another Brooklyn*, the conflict happens remotely, involving no member of the family, but it is experienced intimately. August confronts these images at a moment when she was "too young to understand what it meant to be a child."[23] It nevertheless acts as a traumatic and transformative moment in which August observes the marginalized voices of the Igbo people and the starvation of the children, caused by blockading forces. As August observes:

> In 1968, the children of Biafra were starving. My brother was not yet born and I was too young to understand what it meant to be child, to be Biafran, to starve. Biafra was a country that lived only inside my mother's admonitions—*Eat your peas, there are children starving in Biafra*—and in the empty-eyed, brown, big-bellied children moving across my parents' television screen.[24]

The events of the conflict occur rapidly in part due to their presence on the television but "long after Biafra melted back into Nigeria, the country from which it had fought so hard to secede, the faces and swollen bellies of those children haunted me."[25] The event underscores the failure of imaginative solutions to political crisis, with August asking, "How do we dream ourselves out of this?"[26] More importantly, August considers the exploitations and oppressions of the Biafra conflict to establish structural similarities or homologies with the characters in Brooklyn. Initially this might seem an absurd pronouncement, but August quickly qualifies this comparison. "No, we were not poor like this. Our bellies were filled and taut. Our legs were thin but muscled. Our hair was oiled, clean. But still."[27] This conjunction is symbolically rich. It implies a connection even as it recognizes a contradiction. August's material comforts deny any direct equivalence—she has enough to eat, her hair is clean—but furnish forms of empathy and connection. Woodson end her vignette with this clause, placing it at the top of a sperate page. The refusal to pursue this thought any further gives it a reverberating symbolic resonance. A different form of nourishment and understanding is required for Woodson's characters.

August is further confronted with a copy of *Life* magazine which has "two genderless children on the cover and the words STARVING CHILDREN OF THE BIAFRA War blared across the ragged white garment of the taller child."[28] Shortly afterwards, two children are brough to August's family door and left with her while the mother leaves for an undisclosed purpose. "The children were tiny and silent, staring up at my brother and me with huge eyes […] Whatever we put in front of them, they ate."[29] Many hours pass, and the mother returns "sleepy-eyed, scratching at her arms and legs, her wig at a strange angle."[30] The children are retuned, and August can hear them quietly crying through the apartment's floorboards. While Woodson dramatizes a scene of domestic discord, poverty, neglect, and child welfare (a result of tremendous structural challenges in poor inner-city neighborhoods), showing the starving children, and poverty and hardship that occur in both regions. The depiction of the mother's struggles to raise her children—as she abandons them to August to find comfort in cocaine—work to bridge the geographical "remoteness" between the Brooklyn and Biafra.

Raw Emotions in Red at the Bone

Red at the Bone opens in media res in 2001 with Melody's coming-of-age ceremony. In my reading of *Another Brooklyn,* I discussed the importance of poetic perception and the isolated image—the novel is "pure poetry" claims one reviewer, filled with "incantatory repetitions, soaring cadences, burnished images"—contending that Woodson's work and her choice of form was closer to these concerns than the prose and world building of the novelist.[31] In *Red at the Bone* music dominates. An orchestra is playing, and the family's brownstone is filled with music which spills out through opened windows across the block while smaller sounds filter in (unexpectedly the choice of music for the ceremony causes dispute and there is no vocalist). "Black fingers pulling violin bows and strumming cellos, dark lips around horns, and a small brown girl with pink nails on a flute."[32] Called siren-like "curious white people" stop in front of the building to listen.[33] We have the sense here that the text is composed rather than written, as the novel unfolds in the manner of a musical accompaniment. Melody's name invokes musical tones and establishes a sense of harmony in what is otherwise a complex, disordered, and somewhat fractious life.

The novel concerns five characters, spanning three generations. At the beginning of the novel, Melody must undertake her ceremony wearing a dress originally made for her mother, Iris, in a celebration that never happened. For Iris was already pregnant and shame replaced joy. The performative aspect of this day prompts reflection. "Maybe" remarks Melody, "this was the moment when I knew I was part of a long line of erased stories. A child of denial. Of magical thinking."[34] As Melody is obviously aware, Iris's teen pregnancy is treated as family tragedy. Failing to represent the families' hopes, Melody is positioned—often against her will—as the culmination of deferred dreams. As other critics have noted, Woodson evokes a black formalism, a post-reconstruction aesthetic culture which highlights black dignity though dress, style, and tradition, and which includes ritual practices, embedded norms, codes of conduct, and dignified modes of being. This complex legacy of vexed and violent intrusion is further reflected in the characters of Sabe and Sammy, Melody's grandparents, who narrowly escaped the 1921 Tulsa massacre. Sabe's family lost everything here as the prosperous business district, Greenwood—known as Black Wall Street—was destroyed at the hands of a violent white mob, erasing years of Black success. A promising antidote to racial oppression, the destruction of Greenwood and the massacre of Black residents is regarded as one of the worst racial attacks in the modern history of the U.S. The financial toll of the day was some 1.8 trillion dollars in property loss claims. As in the other fictions here, there is the enduring loss of what could have been, as black generational wealth which was destined to secure the fortunes of future children was destroyed, and political progress arrested, and forgotten. Given the destruction of property and forced bankruptcy, Sabe no longer has any trust in financial institutions and secures her money "everywhere. In secret sewn-in coat pockets, inside those suede shoes you don't wear anymore."[35] The story of the massacre circulates throughout the family and is told at numerous points with Sabe hearing it "a hundred times by the time I was school age [...] and I made sure Iris knew [...] and Melody knows too."[36] The story becomes part of the children growing up in the house "becoming a part of their blood. Their memory."[37] These momentous events are passed on in narrative form to future generations with the instruction that they save and store objects of value and to hold on to what is yours because "my people's lives and dreams [became] ash."[38]

The proximity between poetry and sound is well established, and the novel is replete with repetitions and aurally pleasing passages. The text itself furnishes its own kind of critical apparatus, in which we consider the narrative in relation to musical devices such as pitch, tone, length, and volume. Chapters do not interrupt the "score" and gathering crescendo, and the novel is replete with musical moments of levity, and transition. Discussions between mother and daughter unfold at the start of the novel, upstairs, while the orchestra is "warming up," a kind of instrumental introduction or overture in which the reader is acquainted with the kinds of approach and the text's own logic. "Maybe," remarks Melody, "all over the world there were daughters who knew their mothers as young girls and old women, inside and out, deep."[39] But, she confides, "I was not one of them [...] my memory of her [...] is only halfway here."[40] Melody is a child that was hidden from her grandparents, but this veiling was a strategy for survival: "*That's how you get here. They were hella good Catholics back then, but you would have been dust.*" The pregnancy bump is cloaked by "your granddad's button-down shirts, telling them it was the style."[41] Melody, then, was "a child of denial. Of magical thinking."[42] It is this pregnancy, which is considered, by Iris, and others, to be a terminus: "Two words spoken early enough, *I'm pregnant*, would have meant the end of my beginning. The end of so many beginnings."[43] The dancing that occurs at the end of the opening chapter belies the coordination and "sync" of the participants. Melody realizes that her situation is narratological. "I am not Melody who is sixteen," she remarks, "not my parents' once illegitimate daughter—I am a narrative, someone's almost forgotten story. Remembered."[44]

8

Capital, Liquidity, and Revolution in *New York: 2140*

> "It is worse, much worse, than you think. The slowness of climate change is a fairy tale, perhaps as pernicious as the one that says it isn't happening at all and comes to us bundled with several others in an anthology of comforting delusions: [...] that we live today somehow outside or beyond or at the very least defended against nature, not inescapably within and literally overwhelmed by it."—David Wallace-Wells, *The Uninhabitable Earth* (2019)[1]

This final chapter of this book turns to the work of Kim Stanley Robinson, one of the most important political novelists of our time and, along with the British author China Miéville, a writer well versed in Fredric Jameson, climate change, and left politics.[2] In Robinson's *New York:2140*, two major climate disasters—named pulses—have seen sea levels engulf coastal areas, displacing wildlife, and killing millions. The water accumulations mean Manhattan is a drowned city, with boat taxis, skybridges, intertidal zones, and submerged skyscrapers. Financial capitalism persists, of course, and has sought out new and profitable investment opportunities, betting on coastlines, global tides, and the frequency of typhoons. Amid this crisis, the novel brings together several characters who trigger a financial crash to nationalize banks, divert climate catastrophe, and embark on unknown post-capitalist futures. Before turning to Robinson's novel, the chapter dwells on the formal problems of conventional climate fiction, arguing it is only through a grasping of the conceptual limits, paradoxes, and aporias within such conventional representational forms that new and more complex problems can be staged and considered. As I have argued throughout this book, drawing my position from both Jameson and Marx, the dialectic exists to overcome such representational dilemmas, and to coordinate seemingly incompatible modes of thought through the staging of the union of opposites, and the switching of sides, so that what was once affirmative can become negative and so on again in a series of ever widening critical climaxes.

As a premier political novelist, Robinson is also a science-fiction writer, and has done much to move the genre, and the climate novel, towards a greater respectability by invoking a recognizable present or near future in which climate catastrophe poses immediate political and economic dilemmas, which are then countered by a concord of science and progressive politics. As critics have been quick to note, this realist impulse is underwritten by a set of "highly conventional and canonical novelistic techniques" that are "grounded in identification and empathy," committed to notions of coherent subjectivity, individual agency, and imaginative projection.[3] If real action is to be taken, politicians and tech giants need to care. Such empathetic procedures are much more consistent with the domestic taxonomies of realism than the imaginative estrangement of scientific fiction per se. Such varied conceptualizations of the climate change novel, then, often have recourse to a set of storytelling conventions that "are not always, after all, transparently or straightforwardly beneficial to the kinds of reflections and behaviors demanded by the Anthropocene."[4] The richest fictional examinations of climate change are ones that effectively probe the boundaries and representational limits of the form.

Robinson's fiction certainly draws on these familiar techniques, and holds together contradictory and compromised possibilities, but his work also articulates greater formal innovations than has often been released.[5] Robinson began his career in the 1980s, and by the close of the millennium had already produced two major trilogies. The first, *Three Californias*—formed of *The Wild Shore* (1984), *The Gold Coast* (1988), and *Pacific Edge* (1990)—are distinctly regional narratives, playing out possible futures (post-apocalyptic dystopian, and utopian) on the West Coast of the United States among young, hopeful, and optimistic characters. The second set of works, *Red Mars* (1993), *Green Mars* (1994), and *Blue Mars* (1996), are hard science-fictions that chronicle a future history of planetary colonization through terraforming. Told through numerous character viewpoints across a temporal span of two centuries, *Red* begins with the "First Hundred" colonists (technically 101, including the stowaway Desmond "The Coyote" Hawkins) travelling to Mars, and the creation of a Martian civilization through a variety of political, scientific, and infrastructural projects, many of which cause fractious debate about the ecological future of the planet. *Green* and *Blue* chart the gradual process of moving away from violent revolution towards consensus building and the creation of utopia, although it is made clear that this not a fixed or final state but a constantly renewed process. To overcome this extended temporal frame, Robinson introduces "longevity treatments," which extend the lifespan of individuals into a collective multiplicity corresponding with the physical and political development of the planet itself.[6] We should note here that collective subjects are a staple of Robinson's trilogies. He regularly refuses narrative investment in any one character in preference to brief and periodic moments of focalization. As Adeline Johns-Putra writes, "the nature of Robinson's collaborative and coalitional utopian vision does not require exclusive reader identification."[7] In his eschewal of individual enterprise and character psychology, Robinson's novels complicate many of the convictions of the realist novel, and its sub-species, the *Bildungsroman*. In the twenty-first century, Robinson has been equally prolific, having written eleven novels and another trilogy, among them *The Years of Rice and Salt* (2002), *Science in the Capital* series—featuring *Forty Signs of Rain* (2004), *Fifty Degrees Below* (2005), *Sixty Days and Counting* (2007)—and later condescend to become *Green Earth* (2015), *Shaman* (2013), *Aurora* (2015), *Red Moon* (2018), and *Ministry for the Future* (2020). Each narrative has come with the receipt of honors, among them the Hugo, Nebula, Locus, and John W. Campbell Memorial Award, with the last novel selected as recommended reading by President Barack Obama.[8] Robinson's fiction is most established for its anti-capitalist commitments to a range of pressing issues, including ecology, stewardship, education, democracy, and welfare. He completed his doctorate in literature on the works of Philip K. Dick with Fredric Jameson at the University of California–San Diego in the 1970s, resulting in a Marxist pedagogical approach to political issues and literary criticism. Jameson and Robinson remain close friends. Jameson has dedicated two later works, *The Antimonies of Realism* (2013) and *Allegory and Ideology* (2019), to Robinson, while Robinson has acknowledged Jameson in *New York: 2140*. Jameson's collection of essays on science-fiction, *Archaeologies of the Future*, features a single essay on the *Mars Trilogy*, while Robinson's first volume of the same work deploys the Greimas Square, a favorite device of Jameson's.[9] Robinson's understanding of utopia nevertheless departs from Jameson in provocative ways, but Jameson's tutelage was central to Robinson's political and professional development.

Most of Robinson's prominent characters are scientists of one kind or another, and are closely engaged in scientific, pursuits, goals, and activities. Many are engaged in the practices of, or have expertise in, STEM subjects (Science, Technology, Engineering, and Mathematics) and are employed in this capacity by scientific and technical institutions such as the National Science Foundation, or in the case of the *Mars* books, have been selected by selected for service by international committee. Those unable to hold scientific posts, often for reasons of maturity, are however no less engaged in the pursuit of science and the application of scientific reasoning, often pursuing science for its utopian potential. Such figures undoubtedly include the two homelessness boys, Stefan, and Roberto, in *New York: 2140*, who despite their youth remain scientists of a certain kind. To plunder the submerged streets of Manhattan for sunken treasure, the boys must build and operate a diving bell, a task that involves more than a passing familiarity with oceanography, geology, materials science, and chemistry. Science for the boys has a secondary use however, in that they must rely upon their ingenuity to survive in the drowned city, for Robinson having created a new economic situation in which "capital having considerably more liquidity than water, slid."[10] These debates are particularly pressing when we turn to the dilemmas of conventional climate fiction.

Ecology, Climate Fiction, Form

It is a sobering thought that the next few decades will decide whether humanity can continue to survive on Earth. While the current climate crisis is unprecedented in its magnitude, pace and severity, its problems are also uniquely formal, as indicated by David Wallace-Wells, in the epigraph that begins this chapter. Firstly, there is the nature of the representational relations which govern the discourse of climate change, and which have, so far, largely failed to convey the seriousness of the situation, not through a failure of the apocalyptic imagination, which seems everywhere present, but because environmental disasters are so often still glimpsed as mere episodes or isolated incidents in which it is easy to pinpoint a single causal line which may have been different. There is a still limited sense of climate catastrophe possessing its own deeper rhythm or logic that is beyond human-made confines, a problem which is as much characterological as it is about scientific facts, value, and prestige.

For climate change itself is so frequently bracketed as an event that can still be deferred, and that the vast resources of capital can be put to solving the problem through funding schemes, early detection technology, and carbon neutral programs. Political change is the lifeblood of Marxism and everyone evident in Marx's writings, which posit the dialectical connection between humans and the natural world; capitalist production, Marx writes in *Capital* "disturbs metabolic reaction between man and the earth" and develops "only by sapping the original sources of all wealth—the soil and the worker."[11] In *The Manifesto*, Marx makes such change binary, arguing epochal struggle will end "in the revolutionary reconstruction of society or in the mutual destruction of the contending parties."[12] *Capital's* study of a single mode of production proposes the cooperation and organization of the workers towards mutual association, with Marx asking us to imagine, while it is still possible, "an association of free men, working with the means of production held in common, and expending their different forms of labour-power in full self-awareness as one single social labour force."[13] But these resources have never been mobilized in the manner of the craze or compulsion for relentless expansion which Marx carefully demarcates. There is no sense of the diachronic, in which a fateful destiny can be understood and still averted, rather than simply proffer small and local changes to human social relations in the twenty-first century.

Alongside the exhortations of prominent scientists, cultural and literary critics, and the increasingly obvious manifestations of climate change, it is hoped that the proliferation of novels, short-stories, dramas, and children's literature, will promote a wider and deeper climate consciousness which will then translate into transformative politics.[14] Climate fiction is often "assumed to have a positive ecopolitical influence through the exercise of the imagination, 'enabling readers to imagine potential climate futures and persuading them of the gravity and urgency of climate change.'"[15] A case in point is the disaster film which paradoxically enthuses the very destruction it would seek to avert, only to relegate the process of rebuilding outside the logic of the text. In the climate action thriller, there is little sense here of any reflexive or conscious procedure by which the texts give some heightened attention to their own material.

Wallace-Wells also dwells on the problem of temporality, or rather the tension between everyday experience and the perceived slow time of planetary change. This perception of slowness is an ideological fiction, we are told, and needs to be inverted and pressed into service to construct a whole host of new registering apparatuses that aim not for a politics of shock or estrangement but the building of a consensus. Anna Kornbluh's book on political formalism, which I have returned to across this book, makes the case for rethinking the dominant logic of literary and cultural studies "which has maintained the truly underlying orientation of taking things apart" instead of form-building and "constructivist projects."[16] Amitav Ghosh has called our present moment *The Great Derangement* (2016), proposing that narratives about climate crisis are often regulated to the genre of science-fiction as a strategy for dispensing with the seriousness of their content. If realism is foremost the indexical reiteration of the existent world, science-fiction's concern with the future brackets a comforting space of freedom and choice where these issues can be endlessly deferred; in reality, this possibility forecloses the space of possible change: an awareness that we can act at any time guarantees we will never actually do it. For Ghosh, "if certain literary forms are unable to negotiate these waters, then they will have failed—and their failures will have to be counted as an aspect of the broader imaginative and cultural failure that lies at the heart of the climate crisis."[17] In this reading, genres are less useful heuristics than strategies for containment, in which the force of the problem is relocated and where nature, and ecological devastation in particular, are given "an illusionary apartness from ourselves."[18] We are, Ghosh writes, "suddenly confronted with a new task: that of finding other ways to imagine the unthinkable beings and events of this era."[19]

Those of us in literary studies are forced to confront whether the novel itself can indeed register irreversible planetary devastation, and whether the current tools and methods used in reading texts are adequate to the task. Laurence Buell has shown how the politics of canonization have largely ignored considerations of nature, environmental destruction, and geographical regions where poor and marginalized groups live.[20] It is easier, it is often said, to imagine the end of the world than the end of capitalism. Mark Fisher argued realism is the preferred literary mode of capitalism; realism in the contemporary became capitalist realism: "the widespread sense that not only is capitalism the only viable political and economic system, but also that it is now impossible even to imagine a coherent alternative to it."[21] Fisher does not consider realism to be inherently conservative, as "little more than a sophisticated technology for capitalism to secure its continued existence and expansion," but a recognition regarding the seeming permeance of capital.[22] Indeed, the novel for Jameson is not successful in dealing with generations: "All of diachronic time is compressed into this single apocalyptic instant, which the narrative relates as [...] memory"; there are strategies for "suggesting *durée* or the passage of time (in their systems of verbal tenses but also by way of the length of their books)" but characters do not serve "efficiently as registering apparatuses for the slow changes in historical time."[23] Generations are represented through "sheer length, sheer reading time," a structural device uniquely at odds with narrating the urgency of climate change.[24] Jameson follows his comment, noted above, about the limitations of the novel form by arguing that Robinson is instructive in this regard. Robinson's texts are obliged to grapple with these representational challenges and invent solutions for them.

Most commonly, this is considered through revolution—variously described as an event, process, or desire—and forms a constituent feature of Robinson's work. Of course, revolutions are formed by specific historical events, and remain unique in their individual character. They can range from more moderate constitutional changes to sudden and dramatic transformations. It is the latter sense of the term that dominates contemporary thought, with revolution a synonym for "violent uprisings," including "rebellions, civil wars and sometimes coups" which can be "unsuccessful (abortive and failed)" can "last decades" or be "relatively non-violent."[25] Robinson's narratives go further than simply staging acts of political resistance, however. Read collectively, Robinson's novels and short-stories present revolution through a full range of richly developed test cases, reconstructing moments of scientific and technological change, political insurrection and revolt, and more subtle shifts in meanings and values (*Werteswandel*).[26] Numerous examples of this abound. In *Galileo's Dream* (2009), the crafting of the telescope plays a fundamental role in initiating the scientific revolutions of the seventeenth century, revealing new phenomena in the galaxy, questioning traditional geocentric astronomy, and shifting authority in the observation of nature from humans to instruments. In *2312* (2012), scientific advances have led to human settlement on other planets, eventually leading to the establishment of a radical green politics which sets out to restore an ecologically compromised Earth through the re-introduction of thousands of animal species. Robinson's fiction thus forms a constellation that represents revolution in multiple spatial, temporal, and historical dimensions, and it is now I turn to the novel in greater detail.

New York: 2140

I stated at the outset of this book that many of the fictions considered in these pages locate their action in some version of New York City and this is no less the case for much of contemporary fiction dealing with climate catastrophe. Robinson's novel joins Nathaniel Rich's *Odds Against Tomorrow* (2013) and Lev Rosen's *Depth* (2015) to reimagine urban space and reveal a "post–Anthropolis" or a "vaster, unfamiliar, less human-centered eco-polis" than previously known.[27]

The distinctive formal properties of Robinson's novel demand particular attention, and here I must disagree with Anna Kornbluh's otherwise excellent essay on Robinson. Proposing the novel is impelled by Fischer's comments on capitalist realism, Kornbluh argues it "represents horrific capitalist longevity in long-ago passé literary realism."[28] But despite this outmoded narrative mode, the novel is not without jouissance:

> the book severs capitalist realist mode from capitalist realist mood, since it trades depression for ebullience *apres le deluge*. *Business Insider* calls it "surprisingly fun!" Activating Austenian irony and Dickensian omniscience and Melvillean hyperbole in a 634-page situation comedy of immortal capitalism

> after legion death, *New York 2140* disrupts capitalist realist affect while accepting its world-trappings; it mediates capitalist realism as world-structuration rather than world-regard. The novel [...] ventilates the suffocating totalizations of capitalist realist depression with new winds of political will, denaturalizing the very medium of ecocide, atmosphere itself.[29]

The sheer fun or jauntiness of the text is for Kornbluh its saving grace, its "metafictional insouciance, unforgivable puns, and value theory badinage"—the "humor's crack of depression crush," she writes—act as a powerful counterpoint to the kinds of climate depression sketched out by Wallace-Wells at the outset.[30] This fun extends beyond this particular novel, and there is much import in Robinson's celebrations, gatherings, festivals, and parties; in a phrase, collective and communal events of all kinds, which are so often the sources of his novelistic material and furnish some of the most important moments. It is also the mobilization of the senses, the enthusiasm of enquiry, and the celebration of hard-won gains. The form-building impulse in Robinson's novel is a rebuilding of the world based on its utopian potential. As in other novels, Robinson characters come to form a collective subject to challenge capitalist frameworks, but what is unique in this text is how the formal properties constitutes a kind of layering, or brick-by-brick assemblage. Kornbluh has centered this impulse on the character of Vlade, the Met Life's building supervisor, whose daily task is the security of the building itself.

This troubling of realist practice is most evident, I think, in the use of the isolated perception, or epigraphs which seem to begin or conclude each chapter. For how are we to read these quotations? As merely digressions or comedic interludes? Perhaps Robinson is giving us the necessary theatrical-critical equipment for plunging ahead? these Benjamin-like collections, or mosaics, problematize contemporary realism. One of the important themes of this text is a kind of frustrated excavation or archology, the recovery of sunken treasure that so animates the boys' sections of the novel. The novel is an allegory of excavation itself, a kind of dredging operation in which Robinson as novelist casts out a net and to collect perceptions which might float by.

Let us take the stand-alone pronouncement, made early in the novel: "To be brief about it—proposed Henry James."[31] A disconcerting announcement, part provocation, for there is scarcely a moment of brevity in James. James is the chronicler of new and intense subjective experiences and ever narrowing interior geographies, the master of point of view, theoretician of the novel in *The Art of Fiction*, and writer of criticism. There is nothing in James to suggest brevity, his whole work, his very life, a testament to density, difficulty, obstacles, fascinatingly complex and wildly excessive, all of which became a sign of distinction and prestige. These seemingly isolated perceptions are a cleansing of the palate. There is nothing destabilizing or metafictional here, no consciousness reference to postmodern play, no hermeneutics of suspicion or crisis of interpretation, but a humorless interlude against the most painstaking and unyielding of novelists. But this very anecdote cannot help but reconstruct the whole mass of James' work. This chapter opened with a rather realist and gloomy official seriousness about climate change, and we may well feel that it is left to Robinson to furnish some powerful vision of hope, some politically positive and energizing vision of the future in keeping with his belief in utopia and commitment to progressive transformation. Indeed, in there is no left melancholy in Robinson, no real sense of sadness, or missed opportunities, or mourning of political and cultural losses. I examined this critical-thematic strain in chapter 1, proposing selected fiction writers had treated recent left political defeats as a creative wellspring for seizing radical change in the present. But Robinson chooses to celebrate not the failure of grand political gestures but rather gradual and reformist efforts—a kind of "socialist incrementalism"—in which small advances are made and recognized. In Robinson, the past is not a resource but an obstacle to be overcome, as new and more progressive modes of interaction and existence ever beckon.

Robinson's work, then, is a fully positive resource. His love of celebrations, spectacles, in a word, *carnival*, permeates his fiction, and it seldom a literary work of his ends without communal festivities of one or another kind. Jameson's comment that "the privilege of aesthetic theory [...] lies in the fact that endings are demonstrable" is of course confined to formal properties of the text, the physical ending of pages which confronts even the most gargantuan texts. In truth, in texts, all endings are beginnings. The most obvious is the seemingly inexhaustible creativity of Joyce, whose *Finnegan's Wake* (1939) refuses such distinctions and "brings us by a commodius vicus of recirculation back to Howth Castle and Environs."[32] The question is of disembarking, rather than ending. But in endings, Joyce is closer to Hegel's dialectic of intensification, where Robinson is more of Marx's expansion and progressive enlargement. Robinson is less interested in returns, rather privileging change, development, and transformation. It is in this sense that to speak of endings in Robinson is a difficult task: endings hinge on the transference of a transformatory politics to the reader, not necessarily through action or spectacle, but in the long-durée of commitment.

In the conclusion to Johns-Putra's *Climate Change and the Contemporary Novel* (2019), the author returns to Frank Kermode's *The Sense of an Ending* (1967). Both books seek to impart a critical awareness of endings, "for even critical readerly journeys must end: they may not be resolved, but they necessarily reach the final page."[33] For Kermode, we render existence and time significant by seeking endings, and in turn privilege narratives concerned with finality, resolution, and closure. Kermode's book however is also about the often-arbitrary strategies we invent for perceiving such endings. In a now classic example: when we listen to the ticking of a clock, Kermode writes—a technology seldom seen, if almost impossible to hear[34]—we "provide the fictional difference between the two sounds."[35] We see shape and rhythm, organize duration, and impose narrative structure (tick-tock; beginning, end; genesis, oblivion) on non-narrative phenomena so that fictions "confer organization and form on the temporal structure."[36] Jameson remarks that the pleasure of the aesthetic is the recognition that is has an end, while Kermode is concerned with the psychological impulse that fuels the search for finality.

My reading of Robinson has suggested a series of formal innovations which challenge the often deceptively conventional fictions of climate change. For it is clear we need urgent and ambitious action at every level, from governments submitting to increased national commitments to, to greater public and private investment and tax collection, divesting from fossil fuels and increased green energy investments, to the action of individual citizens and compulsory civic education to establish climate literacy. In *The German Ideology*, Marx and Engels presented a post-pastoral vision of the future in which humans are free from the tyranny of work and able to pursue conscious and creative activity in any branch they wish. One could rear cattle in the morning, fish in the afternoon, and criticize after dinner. But Marx's vision is in danger. As Gregory Claey remarks, if we fail to act on the climate crisis, "there will be nothing to fish or hunt, but plenty to criticize."[37] While we have passed the final warning, it may not be too late to avoid some of the worst effects.

Epilogue

A guiding premise of this book is that the left critical tradition offers an essential resource for coming to think about the contemporary novel. As I have already argued, any sustained account of contemporary literary studies, and the field's Marxist modes of theoretical influence, must reckon with the monumental work of Fredric Jameson, whose career long "project of dialectical criticism" ranges across the last sixty years.[1] The fictions considered here offer provocative engagements with Jameson's critical positions. The essential movement of all dialectical criticism is reconciliation, but, as I have suggested here, Marxist criticism is supremely enriched when positioned in dialogue with the new literary and cultural constellations of textual relationships, in a manner that builds upon its own uses as so many provisional formulations in an unfolding dialectical relationship. It is through the grasping of limitations, of accepting failures rather than holding out for impassioned successes, that we can advance critical thought in the contemporary.

This book has argued for a fresh engagement with Marx's writings, alongside a close examination of selected British and American fictions that pursue, develop, and extend Marxist critical concerns in numerous and novel ways. It is in this sense, then, that this book has been as much about the work of Jameson and Marx as about the manifestations of anti-capitalist commitment in contemporary narratives. Marx is both necessary and insufficient to the profound and urgent problems we face today, and yet the most incisive modes of Marxist literary criticism are those that remain attentive to the remarkably rich theoretical investigations first developed and pursued by Marx himself. This book has set out a scholarly commitment to refresh a body of critical and theoretical knowledge that remains central to challenging capital in the twenty-first century. Three central propositions. Firstly, Marxist critical concerns are explored with striking precision in a range of contemporary Anglo-American fictions. In reading a range of texts written at a social, political, historical, and geographical remove from the centers of state-socialism, selected British and

American fiction establishes a critical consciousness that aims towards the recuperation and regeneration of the Marxist intellectual tradition. All the texts considered here collectively examine the situation of oppressed subjects through a rigorous critique of seemingly natural, yet exploitative, capitalist relations; an awareness of how economic concepts and the mode of production determine personal relationships, feelings, and social values; and the creation of individual and collective acts of political resistance alongside the desire for self-empowerment and realization. Secondly, this study has shown how the present moment, commonly considered as arriving after postmodernism, affords scholars and critics an extraordinary opportunity for a fresh re-engagement with Marx's writings, and the Marxist intellectual tradition more broadly. More than any other body of work, Marx captures the impact and influence of global capitalist structures upon individual subjects and, crucially, reveals how the individual is located and constituted within the broader matrix of capitalist social reality. Marx offers an acute observation of the development of capitalism, while the level and rigor of his analysis suggests, on a wider disciplinary level, the continued validity of Marxist critique in the present moment. Thirdly, this book has argued Marxism remains the most productive and epistemologically rich framework for literary interpretation. Marxist dialectical criticism can take many forms, but its fundamental task is twofold; first, to expose and supersede the principal ideological instruments and sources of mystification that are the cause and target of Marxist critique; secondly, to reconsider the terms of the analytical apparatus by revealing the unstable nature of the terms and categories employed in critique. Through articulating the limitations and strengths of any given philosophical position, dialectics ventures a new solution—a new mode of perceiving the problem—through a reflexivity that is genuinely comparative.

Apart from China Miéville, I have not argued for any of these writers as being committed Marxist intellectuals; certainly, none of the fictions under consideration here can be considered orthodox expressions of revolutionary struggle. Rather, this book has explored the multiple and varied manifestations of Marxist intellectual commitment, contending that these, at times very different narrative representations, collectively demonstrate the extraordinary range and diversity of Marxism in the contemporary. At the end of the final chapter, however, I gestured towards the process by which fictional narratives produced shortly before the end of the twentieth century inescapably accrue new meanings in the years and decades to come. This relationship is, of course, reciprocal: for if recent economic, ecological, and political crisis change how we read and examine the past, then so too might fictional works assume a new critical potency in the face of global neoliberalism. Marxism constitutes one of the most pressing and relevant tasks within literary scholarship today. Marxism establishes a concrete political intervention which grounds cultural productions within the economic development of capital. Its epistemological vocation lies in its ceaseless and unmatched ability to describe capitalism's historical originality, structural contradictions, and create an alternative social, political, and economic vision. There are few intellectual movements that have known as many internal schisms and debates, and Marxism ranges from the highly theoretical to the practical, demotic, and vulgar. There is certainly an ethical dimension here, but Marx takes as his subject the dialectical form of capitalism, which is simultaneously destructive and progressive, celebrated, and decried, new, and old. Marx must therefore remain a central component of critique, one able to think capital historically without resorting to ideological simplifications and ethical polarities. We must continuously strive to maintain a critically rich conversation with, against, and beyond the writing of Marx. The contemporary moment affords an exciting opportunity to develop a more pluralist Marxism than that of the twentieth century, a process which returns us to rediscovering Marx, and the striking philosophical originality of his works. As Peter Osborne argues, the present "heralds the possibility of a new life for Marx's texts [...] a life of interpretation freed from the political authority of orthodoxy."[2] For Osborne, the most powerful response to this situation is, quite simply, reading:

> Reading is an established way of challenging orthodoxies. Codification requires interpretations that will never be intellectually adequate to the subtleties and contradictions of the texts on which it grounds its authority. The idea of reading, reading as interpretation, reading *against orthodoxy*, has played a central role in Enlightenments movements for the reform of education, [...] In this respect reading has enjoyed a special place in theoretical disciplines in the humanities since the libertarian movements of the 1960s. Marx's texts have been no exception; indeed, they have been exemplary.[3]

Reading: well and carefully, closely, critically. As literary critics, we can reserve some small space for celebration here. But it is to ways of thinking about the future, in the sense of making it, which are important now.

Appendix

The following section may prove useful for the student and surveys some of the work that has been done in areas this book touches on.

As the excesses of global capitalism have become more increasingly acute, it is perhaps unsurprising that one of the most striking changes in recent decades has been the return of communism as a political force and intellectual presence, a project most forcefully registered in the new range of writings by Alain Badiou, Jodi Dean, Antoni Negri, Michael Hardt, Jacques Rancière, Jean-Luc Nancy, Bruno Bosteels, and Alberto Toscano, many of which were first given long ago at the "Idea of Communism" conferences, hosted in London, New York, and Seoul.[1] As the principal organizers argued, the gathering was not meant to "deal with practico-political questions of how to analyze the latest economic, political, and military troubles" but to instigate a movement of "more radical questioning" which will "deal with communism as a philosophical concept" as the only "idea worthy of a philosopher."[2] Further contributions have come in the form of Raphael Samuel's re-examination of the history of British Communism, while Shannon Brincat has edited a three volume study exploring the resurgence of communist theory and practice across the globe.[3] As Alan Johnson has argued, common ground for these approaches is that the crisis of capitalist societies—ecological degradation, financial turmoil, the loss of trust in the political class, exploding inequality—are systemic, interlinked, not amenable to legislative reform, and requiring revolutionary solutions.[4]

Class, Communism, and the Collected Works

It is proper, and necessary to give some further acknowledgment of the diverse range of interdisciplinary scholarship on Marxism in the twenty-first century, but in the limited space available it is impossible to do this criticism the full justice it deserves. My outline is therefore necessarily brief, but it will have become clearer in the previous chapters how my readings have developed extant scholarly work. For the purposes of clarity, I have situated developments in Marxist scholarship around a triumvirate structure: class, communism, and the collected works, before adding a fourth in the form of my own field of literary and cultural studies, and the contemporary novel. Firstly, it is increasingly clear that class is reemerging in the twenty-first century as a legitimate method of engaging the practices of global neoliberal austerity, with scholars demonstrating a new interest in class identity, class exploitation, and class conflict. For at least three decades, particularly in Britain, but also in the United States, class was delegitimized through a "Thatcher-Reagan" rhetoric of class denial. Moral character and personal capacity replaced economic processes as explanations for individual agency, leading some scholars to assert that "class as a concept is ceasing to do any useful work," or even more stridently, proclaiming the "death of class."[5]

Concerns with the displacement and disarticulation of class were powerfully raised by both Terry Eagleton and Alex Callinicos, who argued that the adoption of postmodernism in the academies and in popular culture has enacted abstruse forms of critical enquiry which increasingly revealed their distance from ideologies of class struggle and radical politics.[6] Once timely, postmodern theories of capitalism have become increasingly indistinguishable from the neoliberal faith in market efficacy and self-regulation. As Doug Henwood argues, taking sight at Jean Baudrillard and his reading of Marx in *The Transparency of Evil* (1990), "financial markets may seem fanciful, appearing detached not only from production, even from social relations, but they are actually institutions that consolidate ownership and control among the very rich of the world."[7] David Harvey has similarly positioned free-market economics as a political project carried out by a corporate capitalist class that felt increasing pressure from labor at the end of the 1960s.[8] Baurillard's giddy, indiscriminate revelry in the omniscient status of finance offers any number of metaphors that overlap with neoliberal discourses of the market.[9] Indeed, this was a period in which, as the American novelist Benjamin Kunkel writes, "it often seemed easier to spot the contradictions of Marxism than the more famous contradictions of capitalism."[10]

More recently, scholars and critics have constructed class critiques that respond to the revitalization of agency and belief in political alternatives. Marxist sociologist Erik Olin Wright has reconnected class to work, gender, and lived experience, using class as an analytical tool, explanatory concept, and vital axis of political mobilization to understand systems of economic inequality.[11] Domenico Losurdo has reinterpreted class struggle, social conflict, and liberation movements in the works of Marx, Engels, and Lenin, moving beyond classical oppositions to a general theory of social conflict.[12] Class has, once again, become a foundational concept to understand society and chart a course for future political development, with many Marxists seeking to complement the study of contemporary economic contexts (immigration, the plight of refugees, youth employment, poverty, and UK-EU relations) with explorations of race, nationality, gender oppression, sexual exploitation, and citizenship, all of which are increasingly considered intrinsic to, rather than external of, the logic of capital.[13]

As the financial crash and neoliberal austerity accelerated a crisis in political hegemony, we have witnessed the emergence of a left-wing radicalism (and a far-right nationalism), which Chantal Mouffe has called a "populist moment."[14] In Britain, Jeremy Corbyn was elected as Leader of the Labour Party in 2015, building a platform based on youth support, the rejection of austerity, and working-class socialism, before a seismic defeat in the 2019 General Election. In the U.S., the democratic socialist Bernie Sanders mounted progressive campaigns that sought to secure universal healthcare, address economic inequality, and move to clean energy, but these movements have failed, twice, to secure him the Democratic nomination for President. The discontents of capitalism, austerity, inequality, ecological crisis, and political corruption remain strikingly acute, but they have not transmitted into electoral success.[15] Increasingly, left political parties are seeking to build fairer, more democratic, and more sustainable societies by seeking substantial structural shifts in capitalism rather than individual, minor reforms.

Completing class and communism, examinations of Marx's manuscripts have posed new challenges for traditional Marxism. The Standard English edition of the Collected Works of Marx and Engels, the *Marx-Engels Collected Works* (MECW), published its final volume in 2004.[16] The international collected works project, the *Marx–Engels Gesamtausgabe* (MEGA), is an ongoing project, but almost complete. Access to unpublished documents reveals fundamental changes in Marx's thought over time, suggesting that many of the conceptual discords between Marxism and other critical approaches arise more from miscommunication than opposition.[17] It is increasingly clear that many political parties largely obscured Marx's original position on revolution, forging a connection between Marx and the "Marxist" language of violent overthrow. As Gareth Stedman Jones has argued, political leaders conducted their strategies upon what they conceived to be a correct reading of a small number of Marxist texts, all of which were taken from the years before *Capital* and Marx's involvement with the International. From the 1860s onwards, Marx considers revolution to be a process rather than an event: "successful revolution meant the political ratification of changes which had already occurred or were already occurring in civil society. The greater the extent of such changes," he argues, "the greater the possibility of imagining a revolution that did not need to be violent."[18] Marx, of course, famously claimed that he was no Marxist, a formulation that returns us to his work rather than the history of Marxism itself.[19] As I have argued elsewhere, this moment can be welcomed insofar for it renews our commitment to a reading of the original and still forthcoming texts, so that we can judge his insights for ourselves.[20]

Marxist Literary Criticism

In 2009, *Mediations* featured a collection of essays by Nicholas Brown, Nell Larsen, Imre Szeman, and Sarah Brouillette, that sought to "define the project and concrete praxis of Marxist literary criticism today" and to extrapolate the "methodological and disciplinary conclusions" of this enquiry to "arrive at general indications regarding major disciplinary concepts."[21] Self-consciously situated within a moment of disciplinary crisis, featuring fractious debates about the role of critique, theory, and the efficacy of deep reading practices, these theoretical interventions sought to gesture to the "range of potentiality contained in literary study" and ask what these "challenges might mean for Marxist literary criticism."[22] Szeman's essay complicated this question, arguing that Marxist literary criticism possessed no singular set of considerations, aims, or objectives that adequately define it. But to understand this argument, we must first briefly turn to Marx's initial formulations on aesthetics.[23] Marx, and Engels, maintained the importance of art, literature, and culture in their discussions of history, philosophy, and economics, but Marx's remarks on aesthetics are often tentative, occasionally in conflict, and dependent on some of the most complex concepts in Marxist theory, such as ideology.[24] As John Berger argues, the relationship between culture and economics is ultimately a "question which Marx posed but could not answer: if art in the last analysis is a superstructure of an economic base, why does its power to move us endure long after the base has been transformed?"[25] Marx "began to answer" this question, but then "broke off the manuscript and was far too occupied ever to return."[26] While more interested in political revolution than aesthetic criticism, Marx never demanded literature provide tactical support to his efforts. As Edward Wilson argues, "Marx and Engels, unlike some of their followers, never attempted to furnish socio-economic formulas by which the validity of works of art might be judged."[27] Marx responded to literary works on their respective artistic merits and considered literature to be a realm of relative freedom. As such, for Szeman:

> There is no such thing as *a* Marxist literary criticism: no established approaches, no clear methodology, no agreed-upon ideas about how to approach a text or what count as appropriate texts to read, or, indeed, no clearly established sense of why one might expend energy on literary analysis to begin with. It is difficult even to establish a core set of interests and commitments that mark it off from other forms of literary criticism. Marxist literary criticism need not even refer back to Marx.[28]

Nevertheless, there are discernible patterns—"modes of intervention"—that "Marxist literary criticism has taken."[29] Beginning in the 1920s with the early work of Adorno, Benjamin, Bloch, and Lukács, Marxist literary criticism began by working with, rather than against, received approaches to texts, becoming "one of a handful [of approaches] which can be substituted for one another depending on context or even an individual critic's analytic sensibilities."[30] Marxist literary criticism then developed a greater attention to the function of institutions, professional organizations, and university departments, endeavoring to map out historical shifts by focusing attention on form rather than content. Szeman's third stage, associated with the work of Eagleton and Jameson, is concerned with the tensions between "the repudiation of culture as an ideological category" and "a belief in its potential redemptive" possibilities.[31]

On Marxist literary criticism now, Szeman recognizes various positions. He ends his essay by contending that the study "of literature within universities may not be the main site for such transformations to be better understood or actualized."[32] This "isn't the same as saying such studies don't have any value" but a recognition that the position from which critics address literature seems "unexpectedly immune to reformism."[33] We might contend that such a position is dialectical: we struggle to think beyond the ideology of the text, but can glimpse, briefly, a potential future for Marxist literary criticism in the contemporary.[34] This, then, is the basis for the argument that contemporary fictional narratives are among the new centers of Marxist political commitment. While the academy still has an obligation to foster alternative forms of politic critique and keep open the space of possibility for other kinds of social existence, literary culture itself has increasingly risen to the challenge to demarcate a Marxist political radicalism. My contribution to this debate has been to explore a wide array of literary texts that use Marxist frames of interpretation to offer imaginative formal experiments in fictional narrative, aimed at fostering human capabilities and freedoms.

Chapter Notes

Introduction

1. See Philip Mirowski, *Never Let a Serious Crisis Go to Waste: How Neoliberalism Survived the Financial Meltdown* (London: Verso, 2014).

2. See Adam Tooze, *Crashed: How a Decade of Financial Crises Changed the World* (London: Penguin, 2018). Financial crisis has become a regular feature of the United States and global landscape since deregulation began in earnest in the late 1970s: from the stock market crisis in 1987, the Savings & Loan bailout in 1990, the emerging markets crisis of 1997, and the bursting of the dot-com bubble in 2001. See Robert Pollin, "The Wall Street Collapse and Return of Reality-Based Economics," *Monthly Review* 62.5 (2010), ppl–17, p. 2.

3. See Mark Blyth, *Austerity: The History of a Dangerous Idea* (New York & Oxford: Oxford University Press, 2013).

4. See William Davies, "The New Neoliberalism," *New Left Review*, 101, September-October 2016 [online] https://newleftreview.org/II/101/william-davies-the-new-neoliberalism [accessed 20/02/2018]. For a study of Brexit fiction see Kristian Shaw, *Brexlit: British Literature and the European Project* (London: Bloomsbury Academic 2021).

5. See Loïc Wacquant, *Punishing the Poor: The Neoliberal Government of Social Insecurity* (Durham, NC: Duke University Press, 2009), Johann Hari, *Chasing the Scream: The First and Last Days of the War on Drugs* (London: Bloomsbury, 2016), Matthew Desmon, *Evicted: Poverty and Profit in the American City* (London: Penguin, 2017), and Chloe Temperley, *Generation Rent* (Surrey: Canbury Press, 2020). For an excellent filmic representation of the U.S. housing crisis see *99 Homes*, directed Ramin Bahrani (2014).

6. See Zara Dinnen, *The Digital Banal: New Media and American Literature and Culture* (New York: Columbia University Press, 2018) and Nina Schiick, *Deepfakes and the Infocalypse: What You Urgently Need to Know* (London: Monoray, 2020).

7. See Elle Hunt, "Paris Climate Agreement: Trump pulls out of Global Accord," *The Guardian* [online] https://www.theguardian.com/environment/live/2017/jun/01/donald-trump-paris-climate-agreement-live-news [accessed 20/02/2018].

8. Nancy Fraser, "Behind Marx's Hidden Abode: For an Expanded Conception of Capitalism," *New Left Review*, 86 (March–April 2014), pp. 55–72, p. 55.

9. *Ibid.*, p. 55.

10. See, for instance, Guy Standing, *Basic Income: And How We Can Make It Happen* (London: Pelican Books, 2017).

11. Bruno Latour, "Why Has Critique Run out of Steam? From Matters of Fact to Matters of Concern," *Critical Inquiry* 30 (Winter 2004), pp. 225–248, p. 227.

12. Stephen Best and Sharon Marcus, "Surface Reading: An Introduction," in "The Way We Read Now," ed. Sharon Marcus and Stephen Best, *Representations*, 108 (2009), pp. 1–21, p. 5/2.

13. See Jason M. Baskin, "Soft Eyes: Marxism, Surface, and Depth," *Mediations*, 28.2 spring (2015), pp. 5–18.

14. Fredric Jameson, *Allegory and Ideology* (London: Verso, 2019), p. 1.

15. Jameson includes within Marxism the "great themes of Hegel's philosophy—the relationship of part to whole, the

opposition between concrete and abstract, the concept of totality, the dialectic of appearance and essence, the interaction of subject and object" which also seem inescapable to me. See Jameson (1971), p. xiv.

16. Anna Kornbluh, "Conclusion: Theory Presents," *Criticism*, 61.4 (2019), pp. 587–594, p. 588.

17. *Ibid.*, p. 588.

18. Patrick Deneen has explored the contradictions of liberalism, arguing it claims equal rights while fostering profound levels of material inequality, its political legitimacy is built on consent and yet it discourages civic commitments in favour of the pursuit of individual autonomy, and has actively undermined citizenship, see Patrick J. Deneen, *Why Liberalism Failed?* (New Haven: Yale University Press, 2019).

19. See Karl Marx, *Capital: A Critique of Political Economy*, volume 1, trans. by Ben Fowkes (London: Penguin, 1990).

20. Karl Marx, *The Grundrisse: Foundations of the Critique of Political Economy (Rough Draft)* (London: Penguin, 1993), p. 83.

21. For an excellent account of this novel see Franco Moretti, *The Bourgeois: Between History and Literature* (Verso: London, 2013), pp. 25–58.

22. Crusoe of course brings with him the political and ideological relations of his time. After rescuing Friday from captivity, he immediately confers upon him the name and his status as a slave, see Daniel Dafoe, *Robinson Crusoe* (Oxford: Oxford World Classics, 2008).

23. *Ibid.*, p. 100.

24. A recent and fascinating book proposes that the various strains of twentieth century literary theory can all be traced to the thought of Hegel. See M.A.R. Habib, *Hegel and the Foundations of Literary Theory* (Cambridge: Cambridge University Press, 2018).

25. Two books by Marcello Musto deserve mention here. *The Marx Revival*, edited by Marcello Musto (Cambridge: Cambridge University Press, 2020) and Marcello Musto, *The Last Years of Karl Marx: An intellectual Biography* (Stanford: Stanford University Press, 2020). A forthcoming work will discuss Marx's newly published notebooks on ethnology.

26. Warren Breckman, *Adventures of the Symbolic: Post-Marxism and Radical Democracy* (New York: Columbia University Press, 2013), p. 2.

27. *Ibid.*, p. 2.

28. *Ibid.*, p. 2. For a serious effort see Christopher Hitchens, "The Revenge of Karl Marx: What the author of *Das Kapital* reveals about the current economic crisis," *The Atlantic* [online] https://www.theatlantic.com/magazine/archive/2009/04/the-revenge-of-karl-marx/307317/ [accessed 02/06/2017].

29. See China Miéville, *October: The Story of the Russian Revolution* (London: Verso, 2018).

30. See Fredric Jameson, *Representing Capital: A Reading of Volume 1* (London: Verso, 2014), David Harvey, *A Companion to Marx's Capital* (London: Verso, 2010), Alex Callinicos, *Deciphering Capital* (London: Bookmarks Publications, 2014), and Slavoj Žižek, Frank Ruda, and Agon Hamza, *Reading Marx* (London: Polity Press, 2018).

31. See Jonathan Sperber, *Karl Marx: A Nineteenth-Century Life* (New York & London: Liveright Publishing, 2013), Gareth Stedman Jones, *Karl Marx: Greatness and Illusion* (London: Penguin Books, 2017), and Sven-Eric Liedman, *A World to Win: The Life and Thought of Karl Marx* (London: Verso Books, 2018).

32. See Rachel Holmes, *Eleanor Marx: A Life* (London: Bloomsbury Publishing, 2014), Mary Gabriel, *Love and Capital: Karl and Jenny Marx and the Birth of a Revolution* (London: Little Brown, 2012), and Yvonne Kapp, *Eleanor Marx* (London: Verso, 2018).

33. Terry Eagleton, *Why Marx Was Right*, second edition (London: Yale University Press, 2018) and Gregory Claeys, *Marx and Marxism* (London: Pelican, 2018), p. 7.

34. David Harvey, *A Companion to Marx's Capital: The Complete Edition* (London: Verso, 2018).

35. "Marx@200,"https://marx200.org/en

36. See Rupert Woodfin and Oscar Zarate's *Marxism: A Graphic Guide* (London: Icon Books, 2018), Martin Rowson's *The Communist Manifesto: A Graphic Novel* (London: SelfMadeHero2018), David N. Smith and Phil Evans, *Marx's Capital: An Illustrated Introduction* (London:

Haymarket Books, 2014), Kat Evans *Red Rosa: A Graphic Biography of Rosa Luxemburg* (London: Verso, 2015).

37. Kevin B. Anderson, *Marx at the Margins: On Nationalism, Ethnicity, and Non-Western Societies* (Chicago: University of Chicago Press, 2010), p. 1.

38. Fredric Jameson, *A Singular Modernity: Essays on the Ontology of the Present* (London: Verso, 2013), p. 182.

39. See, for instance, Anna Kornbluh, "On Marx's Victorian Novel," *Mediations*, 25.1 (2010), pp. 15–38, and Fredric Jameson, *Representing Capital: A Reading of Volume 1* (London: Verso, 2011).

40. Sharae Deckard, Nicholas Lawrence, Neil Lazarus, Graeme McDonald, Upamanyu Pablo Mukherjee, Benita Parry, and Stephen Shapiro, *Combined and Uneven Development: Towards a New Theory of World Literature*, WRec, Warwick Research Collective (Liverpool: Liverpool University Press, 2015), p. 75. One should of course add here the work of wife and daughter as both amanuensis and interlocutors. For an account of Marx's relationship here see Mary Gabriel, *Love and Capital: Karl and Jenny Marx and the Birth of a Revolution* (London: Little, Brown, 2012).

41. *Ibid.*, p. 74.

42. Elizabeth Stuart Phelps, *The Silent Partner* (University of Michigan: University Library, 2005), p. vi.

43. Anna Kornbluh demonstrates how "prevailing conceptions of realism cohere around the conviction that it is first and foremost the indexical reiteration of the extant world." See Kornbluh (2019), p. 171.

44. William Lynn Watson, "'The facts which go to form this fiction': Elizabeth Stuart Phelps's 'The Silent Partner' and the Massachusetts Bureau of Labor Statistics Reports," College Literature 29.4 (2002), pp. 6–25, p. 7.

45. Anna Kornbluh, *The Order of Forms: Realism, Formalism, and Social Space* (Chicago: University of Chicago Press, 2019), p. 7.

46. *Ibid.*, p. 54

47. WReC, p. 75.

48. Marx, 1990), 279–280.

49. Fredric Jameson, "Antimonies of the Realism-Modernism Debate," *Modern Language Quarterly* 73.3 (2012), pp. 475–85, p. 479. That is, as several influential accounts of the novel form have shown, liberal capitalism. See Ian Watt, *The Rise of the Novel: Studies in Defoe, Richardson, and Fielding* (Berkeley: University of California Press, 1957), Lionel Triilling, *The Liberal Imagination: Essays on Literature and Society* (New York: New York Review Books, 2008), and Benedict Anderson, *Imagined Communities: Reflections on the Origin and Spread of Nationalism* (London: Verso, 2016).

50. Nicholas Brown, "One, Two, Many Ends of Literature," *Mediations*, 24.2 (2009), pp. 90–101, p92.

51. *Ibid.*, p. 92.

52. See, for instance, Emily Johansen and Alissa Karl, *Neoliberalism, and the Novel* (Routledge: New York, 2019).

53. WRec, p. 49. See also Immanuel Wallerstein, *The Modern World System*, volumes 1–4 (Berkeley, California, University of California Press, 1974–1989).

54. Shonkwiler (2017), p. 124.

55. Wai-chee Dimmock, *American Literature in the World: An Anthology from Anne Bradstreet to Octavia Butler* (New York: Columbia University Press, 2016).

56. Liam Kennedy and Stephen Shapiro, *Neoliberalism & Contemporary American Literature* (New Hampshire: Dartmouth College Press, 2019), p3./ Mitchum Huehls, *After Critique: Twenty-First-Century Fiction in a Neoliberal Age* (Oxford: Oxford University Press, 2016).

57. Jeffrey T. Nealon, *Post-Postmodernism: or, The Cultural Logic of Just-in-Time Capitalism* (Stanford, California: University of California Press, 2012), p. 150.

58. Alison Shonkwiler and Leigh Claire La Berge, *Reading Capitalist Realism* (Iowa: University of Iowa Press, 2014), p. 3.

59. Joseph North, *Literary Criticism: A Concise Political History* (Cambridge, Massachusetts: Harvard University Press, 2017), p. 197.

60. Fredric Jameson, *A Singular Modernity* (London: Verso, 2012), p. 29.

61. Liam Kennedy and Stephen Shapiro (2019), p. 13.

62. Mitchum Huehls and Rachel Greenwald Smith, edited, *Neoliberalism and Contemporary Literary Culture* (Baltimore: John Hopkins University Press, 2017), pp. 1–18, p. 10.

63. Theodore Martin, *Contemporary*

Drift: Genre, Historicism, and the Problem of the Present (Columbia: Columbia University Press, 2017), p. 6.

64. See Nicholas Dames, "The Theory Generation," n+1, issue 14, *Awkward Age* (Summer 2012), https://nplusonemag.com/issue-14/reviews/the-theory-generation/

65. Jacques Derrida: *Specters of Marx: The State of Debt, the Work of Mourning and the New International* (London: Routledge, 2006), p. 18.

66. Jameson in Mark Laffey and Kathryn Dean, "A Flexible Marxism for Flexible Times" in *Historical Materialism and Globalisation: Essays on Continuity and Change*, edited by Mark Rupert and Hazel Smith (London: Routledge, 2016), pp. 90–110, p. 92.

67. For an examination of the work of Kim Stanley Robinson in relation to Marxist critical concerns see my forthcoming, *Kim Stanley Robinson: Revolutions in, against, and beyond Capital* (Liverpool University Press).

68. The distinction between form and content is far from simple, however. As Fredric Jameson argues: "Everyone understands that to emphasize either one of these terms—form or content—in the absence of the other one will lead to results that are distorted and unhelpful (however much they may be suggestive for future work [...] As a bad word, formalism is often restricted to designating an emphasis on pure form as such, in the absence of any content [...] The exclusionary emphasis on content, meanwhile, is inevitably and insensibly transformed into a prescription for this or that specific type of content, a prescription for which form is transparent and unproblematic, but whose failures (and occasional successes) might well tend to reawaken some productive sense of the ways in which form is a precondition for content just as content is a precondition of form." See Fredric Jameson, *The Modernist Papers* (London: Verso, 2016), p. xiii. One can never fully isolate the two; formal categories are inextricable from their textual enactment. It is therefore a question of degree and emphasis, but it seems to me those recent developments in Marxist literary criticism nevertheless point to a revival of content after many years study of form.

69. Rita Felski, *The Limits of Critique* (Chicago: The University of Chicago Press, 2015), p. 6

70. *Ibid.*, p. 24.

71. Nico Baumbach, Damon R. Young, and Geneviere Yue, "For a Political Critique of Culture," *Social Text*, 34.2 (2016), p. 7.

72. *Ibid.*, p. 7.

73. Elizabeth Weed, "The Way We Read Now," *History of the Present*, 2:1 (2012), p. 95.

74. Jason Potts. "Editor's Note." *Mediations* 28.2 (Spring 2015), pp. 1–3, p. 2.

75. Pynchon's encyclopedic cast of bizarre character names challenge the representational limits of the novel form. As Patrick Hurley has shown, characters names can be comic, ironic, descriptive, subversive, or ordinary. See Patrick Hurley, *Pynchon's Character Names: A Dictionary* (Jefferson: McFarland & Company, 2008). We may question whether character is a suitable term in relation to Pynchon's fiction.

76. Ben Lerner, *10:04* (London: Granta, 2014), p.

77. See for instance, Katy Shaw, *Crunch Lit* (London: Bloomsbury, 2015), Shonkwiler (2019), and Leigh Claire La Berge, *Scandals and Abstraction: Financial Fiction of the Long 1980s* (Oxford: Oxford University Press, 2015).

78. Fredric Jameson, "A New Reading of *Capital*," *Mediations*, 25.1 (Fall 2010), pp. 5–14, p. 5.

79. *Ibid.*, p. 6.

80. Fredric Jameson, *Allegory and Ideology* (London: Verso, 2019), p. 361. I want to consider textual logics in a forthcoming work, provisionally titled *Literature and Logic*, for Cambridge University Press.

81. *Ibid.*, p. 126.

82. Joshua Clover raises this possibility in relation to the work of Jameson and turns to poetry as a literary form registering narrative's ongoing displacement. See Joshua Clover, "Autumn of the System: Poetry and Financial Capital," *Journal of Narrative Theory*, 41.1 (2011), p. 34–52.

83. Ben Lerner in Karl Smith, "Tome on the Range: Time is a Flat Circle, Ben Lerner Interviewed," 8th February 2015 [https://thequietus.com/articles/

17190-ben-lerner-interview-1004-leaving-atocha-station-poetry-time-knausgaard].

84. Rachel Kushner in *World Literature, Neoliberalism, and the Culture of Discontent*, edited by Sharae Deckard and Stephen Shapiro (London: Palgrave, 2019), p. 211/ Treasa De Loughry, *The Global Novel and Capitalism in Crisis: Contemporary Literary Narratives* (London: Palgrave, 2020), p. 186.

85. Jameson (1971), p. xii

86. Paul Crosthwaite, *The Market Logics of Contemporary Finance* (Cambridge: Cambridge University Press, 2019), p. 106.

87. Sally Rooney, *Normal People* (London: Faber & Faber, 2019).

88. Rooney, 2019.

89. For histories of the American Left see Paul Buhle, *Marxism in the United States: A History of the American Left* (London: Verso, 2013), Michael Denning: *The Cultural Front: The Laboring of American Culture in the Twentieth Century* (London: Verso, 2011), Richard Flacks, *Making History: The American Left and the American Mind* (New York: Columbia University Press, 1988), John Patrick Diggins, *The Rise and Fall of the American Left* (New York: Harcourt Brace Jovanovich, 1992), Jack Ross, *The Socialist Party of America: A Complete History* (Lincoln: University of Nebraska Press, 2015), and Rhodri Jeffrey-Jones, *The American Left: Its Impact on Politics and Society since 1900* (Edinburgh: Edinburgh University Press, 2013). See also the "Mapping American Social Movements" project, organized by James N. Gregory, University of Washington, https://depts.washington.edu/moves/

90. Breckman (2013), p. 192.

91. See *China Miéville: Critical Essays*, edited by Caroline Edwards and Tony Venezia (London: Glyphi, 2015).

92. Edwards and Venezia, "UnIntroduction: China Miéville's Weird Universe" in *Ibid.*, p. 1/2.

93. Carl Freedman, *Art and Idea in the Novels of China Miéville* (Canterbury: Gylphi, 2015), p. xi.

94. Ruby Mendenhall, "The Political Economy of Black Housing: From the Housing Crisis of the Great Migrations to the Subprime Mortgage Crisis," *Black Political Economy*, 40.1 (Spring 2010), pp. 20–37, p. 20.

95. Shonkwiler (2017), p. 32.

96. Brian McHale argues "so ubiquitous is Pynchon in the discourse of postmodernism that we might go so far as to say, not that postmodern theory depends on Pynchon's fiction for exemplification, but that, without Pynchon's fiction, there might never have been such a pressing need to develop a theory of literary postmodernism in the first place." Brian McHale, "Pynchon's Postmodernism" in *The Cambridge Companion to Thomas Pynchon*, edited by Inger H. Dalsgaard, Luc Herman, and Brian McHale (Cambridge: Cambridge, University Press, 2011), pp. 97–111, p. 97.

97. Inger H. Dalsgaard, Luc Herman, and Brian McHale in Martin Eve, *Pynchon & Philosophy* (Basingstoke: Palgrave Macmillan 2014), p. 1.

98. *The New Pynchon Studies* (Twenty-First-Century Critical Revisions), edited by Joanna Freer (Cambridge: Cambridge University Press, 2019).

99. The most recent criticism of which argues Pynchon displays "an aversion to Marxist dialectical materialism as a perverse (il)logical crutch used to garner authority to leadership," see Joanna Freer, *Thomas Pynchon and the American Counterculture* (New York: Cambridge University Press, 2014), p. 11.

100. For a more detailed account of Robinson's oeuvre see my *Kim Stanley Robinson: Apprenticeships in Narrative*, forthcoming with Liverpool University Press.

101. Kim Stanley Robinson, *New York: 2140* (London: Orbit, 2017), p. 206

102. *New York: 2140*, p. 206.

Chapter 1

1. See Kornbluh (2019), Felski (2015), Carol Levine, *Forms: Whole, Rhythm, Hierarchy, Network* (Princeton: Princeton University Press, 2015), and Marjorie Levinson, "What is New Formalism?" *PMLA*, 122.2 (2007), pp. 558–569.

2. See Tom Eyers, *Speculative Formalism: Literature, Theory, and The Critical Present* (Evanston, Illinois: Northwestern University Press, 2017), p. 1.

3. Levine (2015), p. xiii.

4. *Ibid.*, p. 47.

5. Kornbluh (2019), p. 8.
6. Kornbluh (2019), p.
7. Tom Eyers, *Speculative Formalism: Literature, Theory, and The Critical Present* (Evanston, Illinois: Northwestern University Press, 2017), p. 1.
8. Tom Eyers, "The Revenge of Form: Review of C. Levine's 'Forms: Whole, Rhythm, Hierarchy, Network'" Boundary2 (May 2018), https://www.boundary2.org/2018/05/tom-eyers-the-revenge-of-form-review-of-c-levines-forms-whole-rhythm-hierarchy-network/. For a useful contemporary overview of revenge see Kyle Wiggins, "Introduction" in *American Revenge Narratives: A Collection of Critical Essays*, edited by Kyle Wiggins (London: Palgrave: 2018), pp. 1–20.
9. Terry Eagleton has written that Jameson "composes rather than writes his texts, and his prose [...] carries an intense l*ibid*.inal charge, a burnished elegance and unruffled poise, which allows him to sustain a rhetorical lucidity through the most tortuous, intractable." Terry Eagleton, "Fredric Jameson: The Politics of Style," 12.3 (1982), pp. 14–22. See also Daniel Hartley, *The Politics of Style: Towards a Marxist Poetics* (London: Brill, 2016).
10. Jameson (2007), p. xi.
11. Fredric Jameson, *Valences of the Dialectic* (London: Verso, 2009), p. 102.
12. Jameson (1971), p. x.
13. *Ibid*., p. 45.
14. *Ibid*., p. 306.
15. Marx (1990), p. 44.
16. Jameson (1971), p. xiii.
17. Sartre takes this to extremes in *The Critique of Dialectical Reason*. An early reviewer remarks that the boredom of Sartre's text was so great, it had plagued their dreamlife. One sympathizes.
18. Jameson (1991), p. 289.
19. See Andrew Rowcroft, *Karl Marx* (London: Routledge, 2021).
20. See Fredric Jameson, "Criticism in History" in *The Ideologies of Theory* (London: Verso, 2008), pp. 125–143.
21. Evan Watkins, "Generally Historicizing" in *On Jameson: From Postmodernism to Globalization*, edited by Carren Irr and Ian Buchanan (Albany: SUNY Press, 2006), pp. 15–25, p. 15.
22. In contrast to these other efforts, Marxism is profoundly historical, able to comment on the conditions of its existence and its own conceptual instruments. In the twentieth century, Marxism was imbued with the force of a totalisation, with Antonio Gramsci considering Marxism an "absolute historicism" while Sartre called it the untranscendable horizon of his time, which one could ignore but not surpass. In the *Critique of Dialectical Reason* (1961), the French philosopher and existentialist Jean-Paul Sartre sought to reinterpret the philosophical categories first staked out in *Being and Nothingness* (1943) by connecting them firmly to the materialist tradition, during period of Stalinist orthodoxy.
23. Jameson (1971), p. 365.
24. Jameson (2009), p. 3.
25. *Ibid*., p. 3.
26. Jameson (1971), p. x.
27. See Georg Wilhelm Fredrich Hegel, *The Science of Logic*, trans. and edited by George di Giovanni (Cambridge: Cambridge University Press, 2015).
28. See G.W.F Hegel, *Phenomenology of Spirit*, trans. by A.V. Miller, forward by J.N. Findlay (Oxford: Oxford University Press, 1977).
29. Bhaskar (2008), p. 3.
30. Robert Albritton, "Introduction: The Place of Dialectics in Marxian Political Economy" in *New Dialectics and Political Economy*, edited by Robert Albritton and John Simoulidis (Hampshire & New York: Palgrave Macmillan, 2003), p. xi–xix, p. xi.
31. Ernest Mandel, "Introduction" in Karl Marx, *Capital* (London: Penguin, 1990), pp. 11–93, p. 19. In a letter of 1858 to Engels, Marx reveals his desire, "if ever the time comes when such work is again possible, [...] to write 2 or 3 printers sheets making accessible to the common reader the rational aspect of the method which Hegel not only discovered but also mystified." See Karl Marx & Fredrick Engels, *Collected Works*, volume 40, Letters, 1856–1859 (London: Lawrence & Wishart, 2010), p. 249. See also Vladimir Ilyich Lenin, "Plan of Hegel's Dialectics (Logic)" in Robert C. Tucker, *The Lenin Anthology* (London & New York: W.W. Norton & Company, 1975), pp. 115–120.
32. Marx (1990), p. 102.
33. Jameson (1971), p. 309.
34. *Ibid*., p. 333.

35. Marx (1990), p. 102.

36. David MacGregor, *The Communist Ideal in Hegel and Marx* (London & New York: Routledge, 2015), p. 11.

37. Frederic Jameson, *The Hegel Variations: On the Phenomenology of Spirit* (London: Verso, 2010), p. 22.

38. Marx (1990), p. 102.

39. Jameson (1971), pp. 307–308.

40. Jameson (2007), p. xii.

41. Jameson (1971), p. xiii.

42. Marx in Bhaskar (2008), p. 313.

43. See Christopher Arthur, *The New Dialectic and Marx's Capital* (Cambridge, Massachusetts: MIT Press, 2000), Jim Kincaid, "The New Dialectic" in *The Critical Companion to Contemporary Marxism*, edited by Jacques Bidet and Stathis Kouvelakis (Boston: Brill, 2008), pp. 385–412, and Fred Moseley, Marx's Method in Capital: A Re-Examination (London: Prometheus, 1993).

44. Hegel completed two versions of *The Science of Logic*. The first was serialized from 1812 to 1816. A second, shorter version was published in 1831. As Kincaid argues, "it is common ground in the new-dialectic reading of *Capital* that Marx enlists the help of Hegel's *Logic* to organize his argument as a series of moves involving some kind of *necessity*." Kincaid (2008), p. 393.

45. Kincaid (2008), p. 385. Kincaid is referring to Moseley's rejection of Engel's interpretation. To Moseley: for Engels, Marx's logical categories in *Capital* correspond with an idealized periodization of the actual process of history. The clearest and most influential aspect of this interpretation is its assumption that the subject of Part 1 of Volume 1 is not capitalism but rather a pre-capitalist "simple commodity production in which producers own their own means of production and there is no wage labour." See Moseley (1993), p. 1.

46. Christopher J. Arthur, "Contradiction and Abstraction: A reply to Finelli," *Historical Materialism* 17 (2009), pp. 170–182, p. 170.

47. Arthur (2004), p. 243.

48. Arthur (2004), p. 244.

49. *Ibid.*, p. 243

50. In *The Phenomenology of Spirit* (1807) Hegel argues that "When we want to see an oak with all its vigor of trunk, its spreading branches, and mass of foliage, we are not satisfied to be shown an acorn instead [...]the actual realisation of this abstract whole is only found when those previous shapes and forms, which are now reduced to ideal moments of the whole, are developed anew again, but developed and shaped within this new medium, and with the meaning they have thereby acquired. See Hegel, *The Phenomenology of Spirit*, edited and trans. by Terry Pinkard (Cambridge: Cambridge University Press, 2018), p. 9. For a discussion of the dialectical transformation of the acorn into an oak see Alexandre Kojève, *Introduction to the Reading of Hegel: Lectures on the "Phenomenology of Spirit,"* edited by Allan Bloom, trans. by James H. Nichols, jr. (Ithaca: Cornell University Press; 1980), p. 199.

51. Bhaskar (2008), p. 1.

52. *Ibid.*, p. 1.

53. Marx, "Letter to Engels, January 14th 1858" in *Marx Engels Collected Works* (2010), p. 186.

54. *Ibid.*, p. 186.

55. Stuart Hall, "Reading of Marx's 1857 Introduction to the Grundrisse."

56. Stephen Best and Sharon Marcus, "Surface Reading: An Introduction," *Representations*, 108.1 (2009), pp. 1–21, p. 1. For an overview of these numerous critical approaches, including Franco Moretti's "distant reading," Michael Ward's "uncritical reading" and those of Best and Marcus see Sarah Kay, "Surface Reading and The Symptom That is only Skin Deep," *Paragraph* 35.3 (2012), pp. 451–459.

57. Jeffrey J. Williams, "The New Modesty in Literary Criticism," *The Chronicle of Higher Education* (2015), https://www.chronicle.com/article/The-New-Modesty-in-Literary/150993 [accessed 17/01/2019].

58. *Ibid.*

59. Best and Marcus (2009), p. 9.

60. Emily Apter and Elaine Freedgood, "Afterword" in *Representations* 108.1 (2009), pp. 139–146, p. 139.

61. *Ibid.*, p. 2.

62. See Edgar Allan Poe, *The Purloined Poe: Lacan, Derrida & Psychoanalytic Reading*, edited by John P. Muller & William J. Richardson (Baltimore: John Hopkins Press, 1988), pp. ix.

63. *Ibid.*, p. ix
64. Best and Marcus (2009), p. 18.
65. *Ibid.*, p. 18.
66. Jason M. Baskin, "Soft Eyes: Marxism, Surface, and Depth," Dossier: Surface Reading in *Mediations*, 28.2 (Spring 2015), pp. 5–18, p. 10.
67. *Ibid.*, p. 10.
68. *Ibid.*, p. 10.
69. Poe, Edgar Allan *Tales of Mystery and Imagination* (Herefordshire: Wordsworth Classics, 1993), p. 225.
70. *Ibid.*, p. 224.
71. Caroline Lesjak, "Reading Dialectically" in *Contemporary Marxist Theory* (2014), p. 407–439, p. 414.
72. *Ibid.*, p. 409.
73. *Ibid.*, p. 414.
74. *Ibid.*, p. 432.
75. Baskin (2015), p. 11.
76. Breckman (2013), p. 191.
77. Derrida (2006), p. 95.
78. Slavoj Žižek, "Melancholy and the Act" in *Critical Enquiry*, 26.4 (2000), pp. 657–681, p. 659–660, my italics.
79. *Ibid.*, p. 659.
80. *Ibid.*, p. 660.
81. Freud refers to certain psychical processes as "theoretical fictions" in that "so far as we know, no psychical apparatus exists which possesses a primary process only." See Sigmund Freud, *The Interpretation of Dreams*; trans. by James Strachey (New York: Avon Books, 1965), pp. 642–643.
82. Traverso (2016), p. xiv.
83. *Ibid.*, p. 7.

Chapter 2

1. Michel Foucault in Gilles Deleuze, *Foucault*, trans. and edited by Sean Hand (London: Continuum, 1999), p. vii.
2. Rosa Luxemburg, "Order Prevails in Berlin" in *Socialism or Barbarism: The Selected Writings of Rosa Luxemburg*, edited by Helen C. Scott and Paul Le Blanc (London: Pluto, 2010), p. 267.
3. Walter Benjamin, "Left-Wing Melancholy (On Erich Kästner's New Book of Poems)," in *Screen* 15.2 (1974), pp. 28–32.
4. See Enzo Traverso, *Left-Wing Melancholia: Marxism, History and Memory* (New York: Columbia University Press, 2016).
5. Fredric Jameson, *The Benjamin Files* (London: Verso, 2020), p. 69. *Marxism and Form* was one of the first major American studies of Benjamin, with Jameson imbuing the former with a strong melancholic dimension that sought cathartic expression: "So the melancholy that speaks from the pages of Benjamin's essays—private depressions, professional discouragement, the dejection of the outsider, distress in the face of a political and historical nightmare—searches the past for an adequate object [to] can find momentary, if only aesthetic, relief." Jameson (1971), p. 60.
6. Benjamin (1974), p. 30.
7. Walter Benjamin in Jameson (2020), p. 69.
8. Jameson (2020), p. 68.
9. Fredric Jameson, "Foreword: A Monument to Radical Instants" in Weiss (2005), pp. vii–xix, p. xvii. Jameson, I think, also puns on the nature of progression ("Forward") through an examination of the past.
10. Breckman (2013), p. 3. The movement was one of civil disobedience: activists did not accept the legitimacy of existing political and economic structures, but they were not advocating changes, or making a specific set of demands.
11. *Ibid.*, p. 3.
12. Maria Cristina Melgar in *On Freud's "Mourning and Melancholia,"* edited by Leticia Glocer Fiorini, Thierry Bokanowski, and Sergio Lewkowicz (London: Karnac Books, 2009), pp. 110–122, p. 110.
13. *DG*, p. 37.
14. Jodi Dean has discussed the attempt, by late capitalism, to reduce communisms to the singular "dictatorial synonym" of Stalinism. See Dean (2012), p. 29. For an account detailing the distinctions between Marx and Stalinism see Alex Callinicos, *The Revenge of History: Marxism and the East European Revolutions* (Oxford: Polity Press, 1991).
15. Walter Benjamin, *Illuminations*, edited by Hannah Arendt, trans. by Harry Zohn (London: Fontana, 1992), pp. 245–255, p. 249.
16. See Walter Benjamin, *The Writer of Modern Life: Essays on Charles Baudelaire*, edited by Michael William Jennings (Cambridge, Massachusetts: Harvard University Press, 2006) and Walter

Benjamin, *Charles Baudelaire: A Lyric Poet in the Era of High Capitalism*, trans. by Harry Zohn (London: Verso, 1997).

17. Walter Benjamin, "Left-Wing Melancholy (On Erich Kästner's New Book of Poems)," in *Screen* 15.2 (1974), pp. 28–32, p. 30./ Walter Benjamin, "The Author as Producer" in *The Work of Art in the Age of its Technological Reproducibility*, edited by Michael W. Jennings, Brigid Doherty, and Thomas Y. Levin (Cambridge, Massachusetts: Harvard University Press, 2008), p. 88.

18. Benjamin (1974), p. 29.

19. See Fredric Jameson, *Post-modernism Or, The Cultural Logic of Late Capitalism* (London & New York: Verso, 2009), Linda Hutcheon, *The Politics of Postmodernism* (London & New York: Routledge, 2002), and Patricia Waugh, *Metafiction: The Theory and Practice of Self-Conscious Fiction* (London: Methuen, 1984).

20. Kelly, Adam "'Who Is Responsible?' Revisiting the Radical Years in Dana Spiotta's *Eat the Document* in 'Forever Young'": *The Changing Images of America*, edited by Philip Coleman and Stephen Matterson (Universitatsverlag: Winter, 2012), pp. 219–230, p. 220.

21. *Ibid.*, p. 220.

22. Nicoline Trimmer, *Do You Feel It Too? The Post-postmodern Syndrome in American Fiction at the Turn of Millennium* (Amsterdam: Rodopi, 2010), p. 51–52.

23. *Ibid.*, p. 52.

24. *Ibid.*, p. 13.

25. Lionel Trilling, *Sincerity and Authenticity* (Cambridge, Massachusetts: Harvard University, 1972), p. 93.

26. Jameson (2016), p. xix.

27. Fredric Jameson, *The Ideologies of Theory* (London: Verso, 2008), p. 89.

28. See Paul Blackledge, *Marxism and Ethics: Freedom, Desire, and Revolution* (New York, Albany: Suny Press, 2012).

29. Marx in Kenan Malik, *The Quest for a Moral Compass: A Global History of Ethics* (London: Atlantic Books, 2014), p. 230.

30. Marx in *Ibid.*, p. 230.

31. *Ibid.*, p. 230.

32. See Elizabeth Markovits, *The Politics of Sincerity: Plato, Frank Speech, and Democratic Judgment* (Pennsylvania: Penn State University Press, 2008).

33. Harry G. Frankfurt, *On Bullshit* (Princeton; New Jersey: Princeton University Press, 2005), p. 66.

34. *Ibid.*, p. 66.

35. *Ibid.*, p. 66.

36. Jonathan Lethem in Paul Laity, "Interview: I've always thought of myself as a dark writer, but this is utterly different," *The Guardian* [online] https://www.theguardian.com/books/2017/feb/10/jonathan-lethem-interview-the-blot [accessed 05/06/17].

37. James N. Gregory, "Remapping the American Left: A History of Radical Discontinuity," *Labor: Studies in Working-Class History of the Americas*, 17.2 (2020), pp. 11–45, p. 12.

38. I must here insist on the distinction between novels focusing on the American Left and working-class literature, which has a much wider focus.

39. Marx noted a distinction between bourgeoise and proletarian revolutions when he wrote that the former ran "swiftly from success to success" while the latter "constantly interrupted themselves in their own course, returned to the apparently accomplished, in order to begin anew." Karl Marx, "The Eighteenth Brumaire of Louis Bonaparte," volume 11 in *Collected Works*, 50 Volumes (London: Lawrence & Wishart, 1979), p. 107.

40. Nick Witham explores these challenges in detail, demonstrating that despite Reagan's popular appeal and unheralded success, his presidency was marked by domestic protest, civil unrest, anti–interventionist sentiment, and a wave of revolutions sweeping the Central Americas. See Nick Witham, *The Cultural Left and the Reagan Era: U.S. Protest and Central American Revolution* (London: I.B. Tauris, 2015).

41. *DG*, p. 366. Italics in original.

42. *Ibid.*, p. 4. Italics in original.

43. As Marx writes, "Hegel remarks somewhere that all great world-historic facts and personages appear, so to speak, twice. He forgot to add: the first time as tragedy, the second time as farce." Karl Marx, "The Eighteenth Brumaire of Louis Bonaparte" in *Surveys from Exile* (2010), p. 143. As Susan Buck-Morss argues, "For Marx, history legitimates political revolution. The suturing of history's narrative discourse transforms the violent

rupture of the present into a continuity of meaning." See Susan Buck-Morss, *Dreamworld and Catastrophe: The Passing of Mass Utopia in the West* (Massachusetts: MIT press, 2002), p. 45.

44. *DG*, p. 6.
45. *Ibid.*, p. 7/3.
46. *Ibid.*, p. 7. Italics in original.
47. *Ibid.*, p. 9.
48. *Ibid.*, p. 9–11.
49. *Ibid.*, p. 4/p. 15.
50. *Ibid.*, p. 15.
51. J. Laplanche and J.B. Pontalis have defined *Nachträglichkeit* as a term "frequently used by Freud in connection with his view of psychical temporality and causality: experiences, impressions and memory-traces may be revised later to fit in with fresh experiences or with the attainment of a new stage of development. They may in that event be endowed not only with a new meaning but also with psychical effectiveness." See J. Laplanche and J.B. Pontalis, *The Language of Psychoanalysis*, trans. by Donald Nicholson-Smith (London: Karnac Books, 1988), p. 111.
52. Sigmund Freud, "From the History of an Infantile Neurosis [The 'Wolfman']" in *The Penguin Freud Reader*, edited by Adam Philips (London: Penguin Classics, 2006), pp. 196–309, p. 221.
53. *Ibid.*, p. 226.
54. Peter Nicholls, "The Belated Postmodern: History, Phantoms, and Toni Morrison" in *Psychoanalytic Criticism: A Reader*, edited by Sue Vice (Cambridge: Polity Press, 1996), pp. 50–67, p. 53.
55. See Stef Craps and Stijn Vanheule, "*Nachträglichkeit*: A Freudian Perspective on Delayed Traumatic Reactions" in *Theory & Psychology*, 24.5 (2014), pp. 668–687, p. 668–9.
56. *DG*, p. 268.
57. In a letter to Wilhelm Fliess, Freud writes of *Nachträglichkeit*: "I am working on the assumption that our psychical mechanism has come to being by a process of stratification: the material present in the form of memory-traces being subjected from time to time to a *re-arrangement* in accordance with fresh circumstances." See Sigmund Freud, "Letter to Wilhelm Fliess, December 6th 1896" in J. Laplanche and J.B. Pontalis (1988), p. 112.
58. *Ibid.*, p. 7.
59. *Ibid.*, p. 16.
60. Peter Nicholls, "The Belated Postmodern: History, Phantoms, and Toni Morrison" in *Psychoanalytic Criticism: A Reader*, ed. by Sue Vice (Cambridge: Polity Press, 1996), pp. 50–67, p. 53.
61. For a discussion of the spectrum of metafictional practice see Patricia Waugh, *Metafiction: The Theory and Practice of Self-Conscious Fiction* (London: Routledge, 1984).
62. Sigmund Freud, "Mourning and Melancholia" in Sigmund Freud, *The Standard Edition of the Complete Psychological Works*, Volume XIV, 1914–1916, edited and trans. by James Strachey (London: Hogarth Press, 1957), pp. 243–258.
63. *Ibid.*, pp. 243–244.
64. *Ibid.*, p. 244.
65. *Ibid.*, p. 245.
66. *Ibid.*, p. 246
67. *Ibid.*, p. 245.
68. *Ibid.*, p. 247.
69. Eng and Kazanjian (2003), p. 3.
70. The relation between psychoanalysis and politics is one of considerable debate. Sean Homer states that although psychoanalysis can engage a "continuing critical dialogue with political and social theory" its inability to develop a positive sense of ideology means the [im] possibility of a psychoanalytic political theory." Likewise, Elizabeth Bellamy has argued that despite an acute analytical potential, psychoanalysis does not offer further opportunities for political action. Both these accounts are discussed in Chris Macmillan, *Žižek and Communist Strategy: On the Disavowed Foundations of Global Capitalism* (Edinburgh: Edinburgh University Press, 2012), p. 12.
71. Vamik Volkan, "Not Letting Go: From Individual Perennial Mourners to Societies with Entitlement Ideologies" in *On Freud's "Mourning and Melancholia"* (2009), pp. 90–109, p. 98.
72. *Ibid.*, p. 98.
73. *Ibid.*, p. 98.
74. *Ibid.*, p. 98–99.
75. *Ibid.*, p. 100.
76. *Ibid.*, p. 100.
77. *Ibid.*, p. 100.
78. *DG*, p. 41.
79. *Ibid.*, p. 41.
80. *Ibid.*, p. 41.

81. *DG*, p. 43.
82. *Ibid.*, p. 43.
83. James Berger, *After the End: Representations of Post-Apocalypse* (Minneapolis: University of Minnesota Press), p. 106.
84. Maurice Blanchot, *The Writing of Disaster*; trans. by Ann Smock (Lincoln: University of Nebraska Press, 1995), p. 47. Italics in original.
85. Elie Wiesel, *From the Kingdom of Memory: Reminiscences* (New York: Summit Books, 1990), p. 166.
86. Jonathan Lethem in Sarah Anne Johnson, "Interview with Jonathan Lethem" in *Conversations with Jonathan Lethem*, edited by Jamie Clark (Jackson: University of Mississippi Press, 2011), pp. 78–99, p. 90.
87. Theodor W. Adorno, "The Meaning of Working through the Past" in *Critical Models: Interventions and Catchwords*, trans. by Harry W. Pickford (New York: Columbia University Press, 1998), p. 89–104, p. 89.
88. Freud (1917), p. 244.
89. Fredric Jameson, "Marx's Purloined Letter" in *New Left Review* (January–February 1995), http://newleftreview.org/I/209/fredric-jameson-marx-s-purloined-letter.
90. *DG*, p. 44.
91. Susan Buck-Morss (2002), p. 48.
92. The statue of Lenin in East Berlin (*Leninplatz*) was officially removed in 1992.
93. Slavoj Žižek, *In Defense of Lost Causes* (London: Verso, 2009), p. 64.
94. *Ibid.*, p. 64.
95. *DG*, p. 41.
96. Roger Hillman, "Goodbye Lenin: History in the Subjunctive," *Rethinking History* 10.2 (2006), p. 221–238, p. 224.
97. *DG*, p. 44.
98. V.I. Lenin, "Our Revolution" in *The Lenin* Anthology, edited by Robert C. Tucker (New York & London: W.W. Norton & Company, 1975), p. 705. Lenin begged Stalin for strychnine after his first stroke rendered his political future uncertain. Stalin took the matter to the Politburo, but the request was denied. For Charity Scribner, this moment gestures to the Party's instrumentalisation of the individual in the service of History. See Charity Scriber, "Left Melancholy" in *Loss* (2003), pp. 300–323, p. 312.
99. Bunker, played by Carroll O'Connor, was originally a character in the television series *All in the Family* (1971–79) and later its spin-off *Archie Bunker's Place* (1979–83). A working-class World War Two veteran popular for his racism, bigotry, sexism, and stubbornness, Bunker routinely levelled acerbic barbs against "Commies," hippies, homosexuals, Jews, Catholics, and Polish-Americans or "Polacks."
100. *DG*, p. 262.
101. *Ibid.*, p. 261.
102. *Ibid.*, p. 262. Italics in original
103. *Ibid.*, p. 264.
104. *Ibid.*, p. 265.
105. *Ibid.*, p. 272.
106. *Ibid.*, p. 272.
107. *Ibid.*, p. 272.
108. Dana Spiotta, *Lightning Field* (New York: Scribner, 2002), p. 85.
109. Dana Spiotta, *Stone Arabia* (Edinburgh: Canongate, 2011), p. 2/p. 220.
110. See Dana Spiotta in John Emrys Eller, "A Conversation with Dana Spiotta," *12th Street: The Journal of Writing and Democracy* (2012), available at http://www.12thstreetonline.com/2012/11/27/a-talk-with-dana-spiotta/ [accessed 21/02/17]. For an account of the Weather Underground see Bryan Burrough, *Days of Rage: America's Radical Underground, the FBI, and The Forgotten Age of Revolutionary Violence* (New York: Penguin, 2015).
111. Kelly (2011), 4F is a classification given to a U.S. military registrant indicating that they are not fit for service in the Armed Forces due to medical reasons. Henry intentionally fails the hearing test and is therefore disqualified from service in the Vietnam War.
112. *ETD*, p. 61.
113. See Aliki Varvogli, "Radical Motherhood: Narcissism and Empathy in Russell Banks's *The Darling* and Dana Spiotta's *Eat the Document*," *Journal of American Studies*, 44 (2010), pp. 657–673.
114. Mark Musa, "An Introduction to Dante and His Works" in Dante Alighieri, *The Divine Comedy, Volume 1: Inferno*, trans. and introduced by Mark Musa (London: Penguin, 1984), pp. 15–56, p. 37.
115. Dorothy Sayers in Dante, *The Divine Comedy: Hell* (London: Penguin Classics, 1977), p. ix.

116. Dana Spiotta, *Eat the Document* (London: Scribner, 2006), p. 73.

117. *Ibid.*, p. 245.

118. Walter Benjamin, "Unpacking my Library" in Benjamin (1992), p. 62.

119. *Ibid.*, p. 22.

120. *Ibid.*, p. 22.

121. Lauren Berlant, "Cruel Optimism: on Marx, Loss, and the Senses," *New Formations* 63 (Winter 2007), pp. 33–51, p. 33.

122. *Ibid.*, p. 33.

123. *ETD*, p. 266.

124. Berlant (2007), p. 33.

125. *Ibid.*, p. 33.

126. *ETD*, p. 266.

127. *Ibid.*, p. 266.

128. *Ibid.*, p. 289.

129. *Ibid.*, p. 298

130. *Ibid.*, p. 298.

131. *Ibid.*, p. 290.

132. For a more detailed account of Benjamin's intellectual odyssey see Richard Wolin, *Walter Benjamin: An Aesthetic of Redemption* (New York: Columbia University Press, 1982) and Richard Dellamora, "Introduction" in *Postmodern Apocalypse: Theory and Cultural Practice at the End*, edited by Richard Dellamora (Philadelphia: University of Pennsylvania Press, 1995), p. 1–14, p. 1.

133. Ilit Ferber, "Melancholy Philosophy: Freud and Benjamin" in *EREA* (*Discourses of Melancholy)* 4.1 (2006), pp. 66–74.

134. Kästner was a highly regarded poet, journalist, and novelist during the Weimar period.

135. Walter Benjamin, "Left-Wing Melancholy (On Erich Kästner's New Book of Poems)," in *Screen* 15.2 (1974), pp. 28–32, p. 30./ Walter Benjamin, "The Author as Producer" in *The Work of Art in the Age of its Technological Reproducibility*, edited by Michael W. Jennings, Brigid Doherty, and Thomas Y. Levin (Cambridge: Harvard University Press, 2008), p. 88.

136. Benjamin (1974), p. 29.

137. *Ibid.*, p. 30.

138. *Ibid.*, p. 30.

139. *Ibid.*, p. 257.

140. As Benjamin notes of Kastner's poetry in a later essay, "The Author as Producer," such writing "has made the struggle against misery a consumer good." Walter Benjamin in Jodi Dean, "Communist Desire" in *The Ends of History: Questioning the Stakes of Historical Reason*, edited by Amy Swiffen and Joshua Nichols (London: Routledge, 2014), pp. 5–22, p. 6.

141. *ETD*, p. 258.

142. *Ibid.*, p. 259.

143. *Ibid.*, p. 259.

144. *Ibid.*, p. 260. In *Dissident Gardens*, as Cicero begins to pay regular visits to Rose in the nursing home, she recalls fragments from her life. She too offers a begrudging acceptance of capitalism as a form of constriction on revolutionary movements: "Capitalism wouldn't get out of the way. We couldn't breathe, we couldn't begin to exist. It filled all available space." Cicero' s assuagement can only rest on an acknowledgment of the ontological condition, rather than any achieved gains: "You did okay, though Rose. You existed for a while. It's in the record books." See *DG*, p. 348.

145. *ETD*, p. 259/p. 261.

146. Walter Benjamin, "The Author as Producer" in Walter Benjamin, *Understanding Brecht*, trans. by Anna Bostock (London: Verso, 1998), p. 87–103, p. 91.

147. Dean, *The Ends of History* (2014), p. 11.

148. *Ibid.*, p. 11.

149. *Ibid.*, p. 237.

150. ETD, p. 237. / Dean in *The Ends of History* (2014), p. 11.

151. *ETD*, p. 261.

152. Anna Hartnell, "From Civil Rights to #BLM" in *The Routledge Companion to Twenty-First Century Literary Fiction*, edited by Daniel O'Gormon and Robert Eaglestone (London: Routledge, 2018), pp. 298–310, p. 300.

153. Fredrick C. Harris in Hartnell, p. 299.

154. Hartnell, p. 299.

155. Christopher Lloyd, "Colson Whitehead" in *The Routledge Companion to Twenty-First Century Literary Fiction*, edited by Daniel O'Gormon and Robert Eaglestone (London: Routledge, 2018), pp. 434–445, p. 434.

156. Ron Charles, "In Colson Whitehead's *The Nickel Boys* an Idealistic Black Teen Learns a Harsh Reality," *The Washington Post*, July 9, https://www.washingtonpost.com/entertainment/

books/in-colson-whiteheads-the-nickel-boys-an-idealistic-black-teen-learns-a-harsh-reality/2019/07/09/bab00918-a19b-11e9-b732-41a79c2551bf_story.html

157. Sean McCann, "'The Mound of His Back': The Profession of Literature and the Fear of the Mob," *American Literary History*, 35.1 (2023), pp. 350–363, p. 350 and Paula Martín-Salván, "'A Jail within a Jail': Concealment and Unveiling as Narrative Structure in Colson Whitehead's *The Nickel Boys*," *Critique: Studies in Contemporary Literature*, 63.2 (2022), pp. 204–219.

158. Aminatta Forna, "The Nickel Boys by Colson Whitehead Review—Essential Follow-up to the Underground Railroad." *The Guardian*, 26 Jul. 2019. Web.

159. Colson Whitehead, *The Nickel Boys* (London: Fleet, 2020).

160. *The Nickel Boys*, p. 87.

161. Paula Martín-Salván argues the novel's structure of unveiling prompts "a series of readjustments in the reader's ethical judgment of what has been read." Paula Martín-Salván (2022), p. 205.

162. See Stefan M. Bradley, *Upending the Ivory Tower: Civil Rights, Black Power, and the Ivy League* (New York: NYU Press. 2018) and Jon N. Hale, *A New Kind of Youth: Historically Black High Schools and Southern Student Activism, 1920–1975* (Chapel Hill: The University of North Carolina Press. 2022).

Chapter 3

1. Alain Badiou in Judith Butler, Ernesto Laclau, and Slavoj Žižek, *Contingency, Hegemony and Universality: Contemporary Dialogues on the Left* (London: Verso, 2011), p. 90.

2. See Costas Douzinas, Costas and Slavoj Žižek *The Idea of Communism* (London & New York: Verso, 2010).

3. As I stated in the introduction, the dialectic can be considered a gothic structure, a phantasmagorical staging of cultural contradictions that exists in peripheral vision, will dissolve if examined too closely, vanishes when it has served its purpose, only to appear again in a new form.

4. China Miéville, *The City & The City* (London: Pan Books, 2009), p. 161

5. *Ibid*., p. 12.

6. David McNally *Monsters of the Market: Zombies, Vampires, and Global Capitalism* (London: Haymarket Books, 2011), p. 113.

7. *Ibid*., p. 113.

8. China Miéville, "Marxism and Halloween—Socialism 2013" [podcast] 30th October 2013 https://www.youtube.com/watch?v=paCqiY1jwqc [accessed 11/04/2017].

9. For an excellent exploration of early attempts to theorise Gothic Marxism see Margaret Cohen, *Profane Illumination: Walter Benjamin and the Paris of Surrealist Revolution* (Berkley: California Press, 1993).

10. Fredric Jameson, *Marxism and Form: 20th Century Dialectical Theories of Literature* (Princeton: Princeton University Press, 1971), p. 333.

11. *Ibid*., p. 311.

12. Jameson in Mark Laffey and Kathryn Dean, "A Flexible Marxism for Flexible Times" in *Historical Materialism and Globalisation: Essays on Continuity and Change*, edited by Mark Rupert and Hazel Smith (London: Routledge, 2016), pp. 90–110, p. 92.

13. Lucie Armitt, *Twentieth-Century Gothic* (Cardiff: University of Wales Press, 2011), p. 1.

14. Cohen (1993), p. 11.

15. *Ibid*., p. 1.

16. *Ibid*., p. 2.

17. See Mark Neocleous, "The Political Economy of the Dead: Marx's Vampires," *History of Political Thought* 24.4 (Winter 2003), pp. 668–684.

18. Francis Wheen, *Karl Marx: A Life* (London: W.W. Norton & Company, 2010), p. 304.

19. Anna Kornbluh, *Realizing Capital: Financial and Psychic Economies in Victorian Britain* (New York: Fordham University Press, 2014), p. 17.

20. Marx: let us "leave this noisy sphere, where everything takes place on the surface and in full view of everyone, and follow them into the hidden abode of production, where on whose threshold there hangs the notice 'No admittance except on business.'" Karl Marx, *Capital: A Critique of Political Economy*, volume 1, trans. by Ben Fowkes (London: Penguin, 1990), p. 279–280.

21. Anna Kornbluh, "On Marx's Victorian Novel," *Mediations* 25.1 (2010), pp. 15–37, p. 21. Italics in original.

22. Marx, Karl and Friedrich Engels, *The Communist Manifesto* (Oxford: Oxford University Press, 1992), p. 2.

23. *Ibid.*, p. 8. /p. 16.

24. Marx (1990), p. 342.

25. *Ibid.*, p. 367.

26. Scott Brewster, "Gothic and the Question of Theory, 1900–Present" in *The Gothic World* (London: Routledge, 2013), p. 308–320, p. 316.

27. See Brian Psiropoulos, "Victorian Gothic Materialism: Realizing the Gothic in Nineteenth-Century Fiction," PhD Dissertation, University of Oregon, 2013.

28. Jameson (1991), p. 289. See also Alex Link, "The Mysteries of *Postmodernism*, or, Fredric Jameson's Gothic Plots," *Gothic Studies* 11.1 (2009), p. 70–85.

29. See Jacques Derrida, *Specters of Marx: The State of Debt, the Work of Mourning, and the New International* (London: Routledge, 2006).

30. A comprehensive list of gothic features, themes, and ideas is given by Eve Kosofsky Sedgwick, *The Coherence of Gothic Conventions* (London: Methuen, 1986), p. 2. See also Allan Lloyd Smith, *American Gothic Fiction* (London: Continuum, 2004), p. 133.

31. Cohen (1993), p. 2.

32. Lawrence Grossberg and Cary Nelson, "Introduction: The Territory of Marxism" in *Marxism and the Interpretation of Culture*, edited by Cary Nelson and Lawrence Grossberg (Basingstoke: Macmillan Education, 1988), pp. 1–16, p. 3.

33. Raymond Williams, "Base and Superstructure in Marxist Cultural Theory," *New Left Review* 1.82 (1973), p. 6.

34. Miéville left the party in January 2013 in response to the leadership's handling of rape allegations against an SWP member.

35. China Miéville in John Newsinger, "Fantasy and Revolution: An Interview with China Miéville," *International Socialism* 88 (2000), pp. 153–63, p. 155.

36. China Miéville, "Marxism and Fantasy: Editorial Introduction," *Historical Materialism* 10.4 (2002), pp. 39–49, p. 43–44. See also Darko Suvin, *Metamorphoses of Science Fiction: On the Poetics and History of a Literary Genre* (New Haven: Yale University Press, 1979).

37. By 2005, Miéville refuted the term "New Weird" as a marketing ploy, although it has continued to be used by other writers, critics, and readers. See VanderMeer (2008), p. xiii. In a recent interview Miéville has stated, "I don't think you can distinguish science fiction, fantasy, and horror with any rigour, as the writers around the magazine Weird Tales early in the last century (Lovecraft in particular) illustrated most sharply. So, I use the term 'weird fiction' for all fantastic literature—fantasy, SF, horror and all the stuff that won't fit neatly into slots." See China Miéville, "China Miéville's Top 10 Weird Fiction Books" *The Guardian* [online] Thursday 16th May 2002 [accessed 25/04/17].

38. See Carl Sederholm and Jeffrey Weinstock, *The Age of Lovecraft* (Minneapolis: University of Minesota Press, 2016), Mark Fisher, *The Weird and the Eerie* (London: Repeater Books, 2016) and Eugene Thacker, *In the Dust of this Planet: Horror of Philosophy,* volume 1 (London: Zero Books, 2011).

39. For the gothic's engagement with contemporary capitalism see *Neoliberal Gothic: International Gothic in the Neoliberal Age*, edited by Linnie Blake and Agnieszka Monnet (Manchester: Manchester University Press, 2017).

40. Miéville (2013).

41. McNally (2011), p. 253.

42. *Ibid.*, p. 2.

43. Miéville (2009), p. 86.

44. *Ibid.*, p. 160.

45. *Ibid.*, p. 160

46. *Ibid.*, p. 160.

47. *Ibid.*, p. 160.

48. *Ibid.*, p. 160.

49. See Fredrick Taylor, *The Berlin Wall, 13th August 1961–9th November 1989* (London: Bloomsbury, 2006), pp. 196–199.

50. Mark Bould and Sheryl Vint, *The Routledge Concise History of Science Fiction* (London: Routledge, 2011), p. 202.

51. Miéville (2009), p. 51/See Alain Badiou and Slavoj Žižek "Have Michael Hardt and Antonio Negri Rewritten the *Communist Manifesto* for the Twenty-First Century?" *Rethinking Marxism* 13.3 (2001), pp. 190–198.

52. Miéville (2009), p. 31.

53. China Miéville in Geoff Manaugh, "Unsolving the City: An Interview with China Miéville" [online] http://www.bldgblog.com/2011/03/unsolving-the-city-an-interview-with-china-mieville/ [accessed 10/04/2017].

54. Miéville (2009), p. 57.

55. Carl Freedman, *Art and Idea in the Novels of China Miéville* (Canterbury: Gylphi Limited, 2015), p. 89.

56. Miéville (2009), p. 280.

57. *Ibid.*, p. 278.

58. *Ibid.*, p. 328.

59. *Ibid.*, p. 279.

60. Jameson has written on Walter Benjamin's "spatial sentences" as forms of breach in the manner I discuss here. See Fredric Jameson, *The Benjamin Files* (London: Verso, 2020), pp. 17–42.

61. *Ibid.*, p. 51.

62. *Ibid.*, p. 373.

63. Freedman (2015), p. 103.

64. *Ibid.*, p. 307.

65. See Douzinas and Žižek (2010).

66. See Douzinas and Žižek (2010), Žižek (2013), and Žižek and Taek-Gwang Lee (2016).

67. See Verso: Radical Press [online] http://www.versobooks.com/series_collections/11-pocket-communism [accessed 19/04/17].

68. Alain Badiou, "The Idea of Communism" in Douzinas and Žižek (2010), pp. 1–14, pp. 2–3. / Nicholas Thoburn, "Do Not Be Afraid, Join Us, Come Back? On the 'Idea of Communism' in Our Time," *Cultural Critique* 84.1 (2013), pp. 1–34, p. 3.

69. *Ibid.*, p. 2

70. Karl Marx and Friedrich Engels, *The German Ideology*, edited by Christopher John Arthur (London: Lawrence & Wishart, 1970), p. 57.

71. Karl Marx and Friedrich Engels, *The Communist Manifesto* (New York: Oxford University Press, 1992), p. 38.

72. Thoburn (2013), p. 4.

73. *Ibid.*, p. 31.

74. *Ibid.*, p. 5.

75. Jameson (1971), p. 367.

76. *Ibid.*, p. 37.

77. *Ibid.*, p. 14.

78. Paul March-Russell, "Signatures of the Invisible: Reading between *The City & The City* and Christopher Priest's *The Glamour*" in *China Miéville: Critical Essays*, edited by Caroline Edwards and Tony Venzia (Canterbury: Gylphi Press, 2015), pp. 139–158, p. 146.

79. Miéville (2009), p. 14.

80. Derrida (2006), p. 21.

81. Miéville (2009), p. 373.

82. Adam Turl, "A Thousand Lost Worlds: Notes on Gothic Marxism," *Red Wedge: Rekindling the Revolutionary Imagination* [online] http://www.redwedgemagazine.com/evicted-art-blog/a-thousand-lost-worlds-notes-on-gothic-marxism.

83. Miéville (2009), p. 20.

84. Leon Trotsky in Sharae Deckard, Nicholas Lawrence, Neil Lazarus, Graeme Macdonald, Upamanyu Pablo Mukherjee, Benita Perry, and Stephen Shapiro, *Combined and Uneven Development: Towards a New Theory of World Literature* (Liverpool: Liverpool University Press, 2015), p. 10.

85. Miéville (2009), p. 94.

86. *Ibid.*, p. 79.

87. *Ibid.*, p. 78.

88. Michel Foucault, *Discipline and Punish: The Birth of the Prison*, trans. by Alan Sheridan (New York: Vintage, 1995), p. 227.

89. Miéville (2009), p. 310.

90. *Ibid.*, p. 310.

91. *Ibid.*, p. 194.

92. *Ibid.*, p. 45.

93. *Ibid.*, p. 95–96.

94. Douzinas and Žižek (2010), p. vii.

95. David Punter, "Introduction: of apparitions" in *Spectral Readings: Towards a Gothic Geography*, edited by Glennis Byron and David Punter (Basingstoke: Macmillan, 1999), pp. 1–8, p. 2.

Chapter 4

1. Rachel Kushner, *The Flamethrowers* (London: Vintage, 2014).

2. *Ibid.*, p. 1.

3. *Ibid.*, p. 2

4. *Ibid.*, p. 2.

5. *Ibid.*, p. 9.

6. Jean-Paul Sartre, *Words* (London: Penguin, 2000), p. 123.

7. *Ibid.*, p. 121.

8. *Ibid.*, p. 141.

9. Jean-Paul Sartre, *Nausea* (London: Penguin, 2000).
10. *Ibid.*, p.
11. See David Seed, *Cinematic Fictions: The Impact of the Cinema on the American Novel Up to World War II* (Liverpool: Liverpool University Press, 2009).
12. Roland Barthes, *S/Z: An Essay*; translated by Richard Miller (London: Hill and Wang, 1991), p.
13. Jameson (1992), p. 3.
14. *Ibid.*, p. 17.
15. Fredric Jameson, *Signatures of the Visible* (London: Routledge, 2007), p. 82.
16. For a discussion of the road narrative see Ann Brigham, *American Road Narratives: Reimagining Mobility in Literature and Film* (Charlottesville: University of Virginia Press, 2015).
17. *Ibid.*, p. 1.
18. Jameson (2007), p. 107.
19. Jameson compares this strategy to photography itself, which "has no vanishing point and whose perspective shifts ceaselessly across its immense expanses." Jameson (2020), p. 178.
20. Benjamin, p.
21. Hamilton Carroll, "'On the Very Edge of Fiction': Risk, Representation, and the Subject of Contemporary Fiction in Ben Lerner's *10:04*" in *Neoliberalism & Contemporary American Literature*, edited by Liam Kennedy and Steven Shapiro (Hanover, New Hampshire: Dartmouth College Press, 2019), pp. 92–113, p. 109.
22. *Ibid.*, p. 96.
23. For a discussion of memory, trauma, and complicity in literary fiction see Ivan Stacey, *The Complicit Text: Failures of Witnessing in Postwar Fiction* (Rowman and Littlefield: Lexington Books, 2021).
24. W.G. Sebald in Uwe Schütte, *W.G. Sebald* (Liverpool: Liverpool University Press, 2018), p. 5.
25. See Julian Bourg, *From Revolution to Ethics: May 1968 and Contemporary French Thought*, second edition (London: McGill-Queen's University Press, 2007). Bourg's study is specifically located in French political and intellectual culture, but his arguments of course have wider implications for contemporary global experience.
26. Myka Tucker-Abramson, "*The Flamethrowers* and the Making of Modern Art" in Kennedy and Shapiro (2019), pp. 73–91, p. 89.
27. *Ibid.*, p. 89.
28. Kushner (2014), p. 392.
29. Rachel Kushner in Dana Spiotta, "A Psychotic Pattern of No-Pattern: A Conversation Between Rachel Kushner and Dana Spiotta" (March 2016), https://tinhouse.com/a-psychotic-pattern-of-no-pattern-a-conversation-between-rachel-kushner-and-dana-spiotta/.
30. *Ibid.*, p. 392.
31. *Ibid.*, p. 392
32. See Hamilton Carroll in Kennedy and Shapiro (2019), pp. 102–103.
33. *Ibid.*, p. 102.
34. *Ibid.*, p. 214.
35. *Ibid.*, p. 214.
36. *Ibid.*, p. 213.
37. *Ibid.*, p. 213.
38. Kushner (2014), p. 214.
39. Stanley Fish, *Surprised by Sin: The Reader in Paradise Lost*, 2nd ed. (Cambridge, MA: Harvard University Press, 1998).
40. Tucker-Abramson in Kennedy and Shapiro (2019), p. 89.
41. Antony Shugar, "Wanna Be Like Everyone: Italy in the Years of Lead," *The Paris Review*, https://www.theparisreview.org/blog/2014/10/14/wanna-be-like-everyone/
42. Andrew Strombeck, "The Post-Fordist Motorcycle: Rachel Kushner's The Flamethrowers and the 1970s Crisis in Fordist Capitalism," *Contemporary Literature*, Volume 56, Number 3, Fall 2015, pp. 450–475, p. 465.
43. Kushner (2014), p. 250.
44. Martin Jay (1984), p. 23.
45. *Ibid.*, p. 126.
46. Wayne C. Booth, *The Rhetoric of Fiction* (Chicago: University of Chicago Press, 1961), p. 158–159.
47. *Ibid.*, p. 158.
48. *Ibid.*, p. 159.
49. See William Riggan, *Picaros, Madmen, Naifs and Clowns: The Unreliable First-Person Narrator* (Norman, Oklahoma: University of Oklahoma Press, 1981).
50. Tucker-Abramson in Kennedy and Shaprio (2019), p. 86.
51. *Ibid.*, p. 87.
52. *Ibid.*, p.

Chapter 5

1. Virginia Woolf, *A Room of One's Own and Three Guineas* (Oxford: Oxford University Press, 2015), p. 14. Hermione Lee calls the essay Woolf's "own disguised economic biography." See Hermione Lee, *Virginia Woolf* (London: Chatto and Windus, 1996), p. 557. Woolf's room is also problematic. As scholars of working-class culture have shown, we need consider the precarious aesthetic placement of narrative forms composed in different locales and widen the parameters of cultural production beyond that which is composed in the quiet of a "room of one's own." See *American Working-Class Literature: An Anthology*, edited by Nicholas Coles and Janet Zandy (New York: Oxford University Press, 2006).

2. Woolf writes: "What was the truth about these houses, for example, dim and festive now with their red windows in the dusk, but raw and red and squalid, with their sweets and their bootlaces, at nine o'clock in the morning? [what] was the truth, which was the illusion about them? I spare you the twists and turns of my cogitations, for no conclusion was found on the road to Headingly." Woolf (2015), p. 12.

3. *Ibid.*, p. 20.

4. Emma Short has demonstrated how the hotel room functions for many writers and female protagonists in fiction as "a room of one's own," a private space away from the demands of the domestic sphere. See Emma Short, *Passing Through: Mobility and the Hotel in Modernity Literature* (London: Palgrave, 2019).

5. Woolf acknowledges this when she writes that "We were all being shot backwards and forwards on this plain foundation to make some pattern." See Woolf (XXXX). Emma Short has demonstrated how, in contrast, the hotel room functions for many writers and female protagonists in fiction as "a room of one's own," a private space away from the demands of the domestic sphere. See Emma Short, *Passing Through: Mobility and the Hotel in Modernity Literature* (London: Palgrave, 2019).

6. Iris Marion Young, *On Female Body Experience: "Throwing Like a Girl" and Other Essays* (Oxford: Oxford University Press, 2005), p. 139.

7. *Ibid.*, p.

8. Short (2019), p. 58.

9. Young (2002), p. 157. Woolf was quite cutting when it came to the domestic spaces of less financially secure writers, writing to Vanessa Bell that Elizabeth Bowen's house was "merely a great stone box [...] full of decayed eighteenth-century furniture," in which Bowen "insisted on keeping up a ramshackle kind of state, dressing for dinner and so on." See Virginia Woolf, *The Letters of Virginia Woolf*, ed. by Nigel Nicolson, 6 volumes (London: Hogarth Press, 1979), V, pp. 299–300.

10. Emily Cuming, *Housing, Class, and Gender in Modern British Writing 1880–2012* (Cambridge: Cambridge University Press, 2016), pp. 1–2.

11. Julia Prewitt Brown, *The Bourgeois Interior: How the Middle Class Imagines Itself in Literature and Film* (Charlottesville and London: University of Virginia Press, 2008), p. 6.

12. Hermione Lee, "Preface" in *Lives of Houses*, edited by Kate Kennedy and Hermione Lee (Princeton: Princeton University Press, 2020), pp. xiii–xvii.

13. Alexander Harris, "Moving House" in *Lives of Houses*, edited by Kate Kennedy and Hermione Lee (Princeton and Oxford: Princeton University Press, 2020), pp. 3–17, p. 5.

14. Engels in Karl Marx and Friedrich Engels, *Collected Works*, volume 38, Letters: 1844–51 (London: Lawrence and Wishart, 2010), p. 29.

15. *Ibid.*, p. 29.

16. Marxist feminist scholars have provided rich accounts of gender, marriage, housework, domesticity, the bourgeois family, patriarchy, and capitalism. The relationship between Marxism and feminism has, however, often been fractious. In a 1979 essay, Heidi Hartman famously deployed the metaphor of divorce to call for a more progressive and equal union between the two critical methods. For further works examining Marx, Marxist, and feminist perspectives on these issues see Heather Brown, Marx on Gender and the Family (London: Haymarket, 2013), Michèle Barrett, *Women's Oppression Today: The Marxist/Feminist Encounter* (London: Verso, 2014), and Silvia Federici, *Caliban and the*

Witch: Women, the Body and Primitive Accumulation, New York: Autonomedia, 2004).

17. Cuming (2016), p. 6.

18. See Andrew Rowcroft, *Karl Marx* (London: Routledge, 2021).

19. Chiara Briganti and Kathy Mezei, "Reading the House: A Literary Perspective," *Signs* 27.3 (2002), p. 839. On James" image of the "house of fiction" see Henry James, *Literary Criticism: French Writers Other European Writer Henry James: Literary Criticism: French Writers, Other European Writers, the Prefaces to the New York Edition* (New York: Library of America, 1984), p. 1130.

Kornbluh read architecture in relation to her theory of modelling, writing it "does not represent, depict or refer—it rather takes places, makes space, composes shape." (Kornbluh, 2019), p. 42.

20. Woolf was particularly cutting of her fellow writers. After visiting Elizabeth Bowen, Woolf remarked in a 1934 letter to Vanessa Bell that the house was "merely a great stone box [...] full of decayed eighteenth-century furniture," in which Bowen "insisted on keeping up a ramshackle kind of state, dressing for dinner and so on." Such comments reflect Woold prejudices as a member of the English upper class. See Virginia Woolf, *The Letters of Virginia Woolf*, ed. by Nigel Nicolson, 6 vols (London: Hogarth Press, 1979), Volume V, pp. 299–300.

21. See Jenny Kuhlmann, "Analytical Concepts in Migration Studies" in *The Routledge Handbook of Transregional Studies*, edited by Matthias Middell (London: Routledge, 2018), pp. 392–399.

22. See James Joyce, *A Portrait of An Artist as a Young Man* (London: Penguin, 2000), John McCourt, "Joyce and Ireland: Home Thoughts from Abroad," *Radharc*, volume 4 (2003), pp. 59–80, and Raymond Williams.

23. Peter Stallybrass, "Marx's Coat" in *Border Fetishisms: Material Objects in Unstable Spaces*, edited by Patricia Spencer (New York: Routledge, 1998), pp. 183–207.

24. Henry M. Hyndman, *The Record of an Adventurous Life*.

25. Henry M. Hyndman, *The Record of an Adventurous Life*.

26. Paul Lafargue, *Reminiscences of Marx and Engels*, edited Institute of Marxism-Leninism p. 73.

27. David Harvey, *A Companion to Marx's Capital*, 2010.

28. For an overview of recent discoveries see Susumu Takenaga, "Marx on Rent: New Insights from the new MEGA," *The European Journal of the History of Economic Thought*, 25.5 (2018), pp. 926–960.

29. David Harvey, *Marx, Capital, and the Madness of Economic Reason* (London: Profile Books, 2017), p. 37. Harvey mentions land owned by the Church and Crown, which Marx sought called to abolish in chapter two of *The Communist Manifesto*.

30. *Ibid*., p. 37. The increase of rent-seeking since the Second World War is taken up by Guy Standing, who argues rents generated through the ownership of assets and intellectual property rights, propped up by state subsidies, tax breaks, debt mechanisms, and privatization of public services have created a new disenfranchised class of precarious workers. While Marx proposed production to be a primal rupture within modernity ("society is more and more splitting up into two great hostile camps, into two great classes directly facing each other"), Standing argues control over scare asset classes has generated a new form of rentier capitalism. (Marx, 2019, p. 62).

31. Kornbluh (2010), p. 16.

32. Emma Short has written on the ways in which the hotel functions as an expression of modernity. See Emma Short, *Passing Through: Mobility and the Hotel in Modernity Literature* (London: Palgrave, 2019).

33. Gareth Stedman Jones, *Karl Marx: Greatness and Illusion* (London: Penguin, 2017), p.

34. See Thomas C. Jones, *Liberty's Refuge: A History of Political and Religious Asylum in Britain*, forthcoming with Harvard University Press.

35. Cumings (2016), p. 3.

36. See Kevin Anderson.

37. Annie McClanahan, *Dead Pledges: Debt, Crisis, and Twenty-First-Century Culture* (Stanford: Stanford University Press, 2017), p. 15.

38. As someone who has spent a large part of their life in rented accommodation, I await the HMO novel.

39. Columbia University, School of Arts, https://arts.columbia.edu/writing.

40. Like many contemporary novelists, including Jennifer Egan, Dana Spiotta, and Ben Lerner, Wayne teaches creative writing and novel writing workshops.

41. Teddy Wayne, *Apartment* (London: Bloomsbury, 2020), p. 7.

42. *Ibid.*, p. 7.

43. *Apartment*, p. 7.

44. *Ibid.*, p.

45. *Ibid.*, p. 7.

46. I mention Mann with some reservation due to my love of his work. The major criticisms of his novels however, particularly *The Magic Mountain* (1927) and *Dr Faustus* (1947), revolve around the essayistic tone of his narration. For Vladimir Nabokov, Mann wrote his novels to fulfil programs of ideas, in which character and psychology were made "to fit the author's teleological purpose." See Vladimir Nabokov, *Lectures on Literature* (London: Mariner Books, 1982), p. 251.

47. *Apartment*, pp. 4–5.

48. Apartment, p. 60.

49. *Ibid.*, p. 3.

50. *Apartment*, pp. 14–15

51. *Apartment*, p. 188.

52. *Ibid.*, p. 33.

53. *Ibid.*, p. 34.

54. *Ibid.*, p. 36.

55. *Ibid.*, p. 83

56. *Ibid.*, p. 192.

57. *Ibid.*, p. 194.

58. Eviction, p. 4.

59. *Ibid.*, p. 298.

60. 99 Homes, directed by Rami Bahrani (2014)

61. Rebbeca Tesfai and Matt Ruther, "Immigrant Neighborhoods and Eviction: Hidden Housing Crisis?," Cities 131 (2022), pp. 1–12.

62. Cody C. St Clair, "The Scene of Eviction: Reification and Resistance in Depression-Era Narratives of Dispossession," *American Literature* (2022) 94 (3): 497–525. / Geroge E. Kent, "Ralph Ellison and Afro-American Folk and Cultural Tradition, *CLA Journal*, 13, pp. 265–276.

63. Ellison (1952), p. 216.

64. Ellison (1952), p. 219.

65. Jameson (2013), p. 161.

66. *Ibid.*, p. 162.

67. Specifically, the papers held in the Beinecke Rare Book & Manuscript Library.

68. Matthew Desmond, *Evicted: Poverty and Profit in the American City* (London: Penguin, 2016), p. xi.

Chapter 6

1. Thomas Pynchon, *Gravity's Rainbow* (London: Vintage, 2013), p. 125.

2. Joanna Freer, "Introduction: Pynchon Studies in the Twenty-First Century" in *The New Pynchon Studies* (Cambridge: Cambridge University Press, 2019), p. 1–14.

3. *Ibid.*, p.

4. For Jameson, "only Marxism offers a philosophically coherent and ideologically compelling resolution to the dilemma of historicism [and] can give us an adequate account of the essential mystery of the cultural past." Such a totalising position (at least on the question of historicism) seems inimical to Pynchon's passion for polyvalency and is specifically critiqued in the famous section on history in *Mason & Dixon* (1997). See Jameson (2002), p. 3.

5. Tore Rye Anderson, "Mapping the World: Thomas Pynchon's Global Novels" in *Orbit: Writing Around Pynchon*, 4(1): 1, pp. 1–40, DOI: http:// dx.doi.org/10.16995/orbit.178 (January 2016), p. 2.

6. A recent catalogue search of *Orbit: Writing Around Pynchon*, a premier journal of Pynchon studies, finds no keywords, titles, or subtitles for Marx and Marxism. While this is not sufficient evidence to suggest the absence of Marxist theoretical inquiry in Pynchon scholarship, and indeed there are numerous essays engaged with the work of the Frankfurt School, for instance, it does suggest a general lack of interest in Marx's critical works.

7. Doug Haynes is an exception to this: see Doug Haynes, "Under the Beach, The Paving Stones! The Fate of Fordism in Pynchon's *Inherent Vice*," *Critique: Studies in Contemporary Fiction*, 55.1 (2014), pp. 1–17 and "'Gravity Rushes through Him': 'Volk' and Fetish in Pynchon's Rilke," *Modern Fiction Studies* 58.2 (2012), pp. 308–333.

8. GR, p. 193.

9. David McLellan, *Karl Marx: A Biography* (London: PaperMac, 1995), p. 36.

10. *GR*, p. 377.

11. *GR*, p. 377.

12. Samuel Thomas, *Pynchon and the Political* (New York & London: Routledge, 2007), p. 13.

13. Eve (2014), p. 102.

14. Freer (2014), p. 58.

15. Sean Carswell, *Occupy Pynchon: Politics After Gravity's Rainbow* (Athens: Georgia University Press, 2017), p. 12.

16. As David Harvey argues, drawing from Rosa Luxemburg, capitalism is forced to move outwards—to penetrate and enclose new regions, increase foreign trade, and export itself—renewing the conditions of further accumulation. See David Harvey, "The Geography of Capitalist Accumulation: A Reconstruction of the Marxian Theory" in *Spaces of Capital: Towards a Critical Geography* (New York: Routledge, 2001), pp. 237–66.

17. Kevin Anderson's, *Marx at the Margins: On Nationalism, Ethnicity, and Non-Western Societies* (Chicago: University of Chicago Press, 2010), presents Marx's writings on pre-capitalist and non-Western societies from the 1850s onwards, offering important tools for analyzing the evolution of his thought on matters Anderson shows to be decidedly non-peripheral to Marx's theoretical investigations and political interest.

18. See Aijaz Ahmad, *In Theory: Nations, Classes, Literatures* (London: Verso, 1992), p. 222.

19. As Marx writes, "Now, sickening as it must be to human feeling to witness those myriads of industrious patriarchal and inoffensive social organizations disorganized and dissolved into their units, thrown into a sea of woes, and their individual members losing at the same time their ancient form of civilization, and their hereditary means of subsistence, we must not forget that these idyllic village-communities, inoffensive though they may appear, had always been the solid foundation of Oriental despotism." Karl Marx, "The British Rule in India" in Karl Marx, *Surveys from Exile: Political Writings, Volume 2*, edited by David Fernbach (London: Verso, 2010), pp. 301–307, p. 306.

20. *Ibid.*, p. 307.

21. Karl Marx, "Letter to Engels in Manchester, 1858," *Marx and Engels Collected Works*, volume 40 (1983), p. 249.

22. Twelve in 1853, fifteen in 1857, and six in 1858. See Ahmad (1992), p. 231.

23. Tariq Ali "Foreword" in Marx, *Surveys from Exile: Political Writings* (2010), pp. vii–iv, p. iii. Ahmad argues Marx took little interest in India before the commissioning of this series, while also noting intertextual references such as between the work of François Bernier, the general poor state of knowledge of India prevailing in England at that time, and the web of prejudice which enveloped that knowledge, and to which Marx was not totally immune. See Amed (1992), p. 231–232.

24. Marx (2010), p. 302.

25. "Indian society," he commentated, "has no history at all, at least no known history. What we call history is but the history of the successive intruders who founded their empires on the passive basis of that unresisting and unchanging society." See Karl Marx, "The Future Results of British Rule in India" in Marx (2010), p. 319–324, p. 321.

26. *Ibid.*, p. 320.

27. Aijaz Ahmad, *In Theory: Nations, Classes, Literatures* (London: Verso, 1992), p. 231. Hardt and Negri propose Marx's analysis was limited by little knowledge of India's past and present. See Michael Hardt and Antonio Negri, *Empire* (Cambridge, Massachusetts: Harvard University Press, 2000), p. 120.

28. Thomas Pynchon, *Mason & Dixon* (London: Vintage, 1998), p. 345.

29. Carswell (2017), p. 15.

30. *Ibid.*, p. 349.

31. John A. McClure, *Late Imperial Romance* (London: Verso, 1994), p. 194.

32. *GR*, p. 556. I am here following Sam Thomas' invocation to read the novel not chronologically but in relation to setting and content. *Gravity's Rainbow* is chronologically prior, but, at the level of content, subsequent.

33. *GR*, p. 890.

34. *GR*, p. 59.

35. *GR*, p. 377–378.

36. Homi K. Bhabha, "The Other Question: The Stereotype and Colonial Discourse" in *Twentieth-Century Literary*

Theory: A Reader, second edition, edited by K.M. Newton (New York: St Martins, 1997), pp. 293–301.

37. *GR*, p. 378.

38. Marx (2010), p. 24.

39. Freer (2014), p. 12

40. Claudia Gutwirth, "Stop Making Sense: Trickster Variations in the Fiction of Louise Erdrich" in *Trickster Lives: Culture and Myth in American Fiction*, edited by Jeanne Campbell Reesman (Athens, Georgia: University of Georgia Press, 2001), pp. 148–167.

41. Roger Abrahams in *Mythical Trickster Figures: Contours, Contexts, Criticisms* (Tuscaloosa: University of Alabama Press, 1997), p. 17.

42. *Ibid.*, p. 18.

43. Carl Jung's essay positions the trickster as a product of the collective unconsciousness, a supposedly shared human structure populated by collective instincts, archetypes, and symbols. For Jung, the trickster is not only a figurative and metaphorical device expressing "a collective shadow figure" but represents a complex psychic transformation. See C. G. Jung, *Memories, Dreams, Reflections*, trans. by R.C. Wilson (London: Fontana, 1995). p. 381.

44. William J. Hynes and Will G. Doty, "Introducing the Fascinating and Perplexing Trickster Figure" in *Mythical Trickster Figures: Contours, Contexts and Criticisms* (Tuscaloosa, Alabama: University of Alabama Press, 1997), pp. 1–12, p. 3.

45. *Ibid.*, p. 13.

46. Freer (2014), p. 12.

47. Pynchon (2013), p. 377. See Gerald Vizenor, "Post Indian Comments" in *United States: Re-Viewing American Multicultural Literature*, edited by Robert J. Lee (Valencia: University of Valencia, 2009), p. 230–241, p. 236.

48. *Ibid.*, p. 377

49. *Ibid.*, p. 377.

50. *GR*, p. 378.

51. *Ibid.*, p. 378.

52. Simon Weaver and Raúl Alberto Mora, "Introduction: Tricksters, Humor and Activism" in "The Trickster Activist in Global Humor and Comedy," *International Journal of Cultural Studies*, 19.5 (2016), pp. 479–485, p. 481.

53. Jeff Baker, "Politics" in *The Cambridge Companion to Thomas Pynchon*, edited by Inger H. Dalsgaard, Luc Herman, and Brian McHale (Cambridge: Cambridge University Press, 2011) pp. 136–145.

54. Kathryn Hume, "The Religious and Political Vision of *Against the Day*" in Severs and Leise (2011), pp. 167-p. 190, 168.

55. Baker in Dalsgaard, Herman, and McHale (2011), p. 138. / *Against the Day* (London: Vintage, 2007), p. 171.

56. Hutcheon (2002) and Patricia Waugh, *Metafiction: The Theory and Practice of Self-Conscious Fiction* (London: Routledge, 1984). For Simon de Bourcier, the continued recourse to postmodernism presents Pynchon "as a sort of literary Keith Richards—still churning out riffs that were exciting and dangerous during the 70s, but [...] now just nostalgia." Simon de Bourcier, "Reading McHale Reading Pynchon or, Is Pynchon Still a Postmodernist?" in *Orbit: Writing Around Pynchon* (Oct 2014), https://www.pynchon.net/articles/10.7766/orbit.v2.2.68/.

57. *Against the Day*, p. 395.

58. *Ibid.*, p. 171.

59. Baker (2007), p. 138.

60. *Ibid.*, p. 104.

61. *Ibid.*, p. 236. Like in Steinbeck's novel, *The Grapes of Wrath* (1939), this text within a text—whether official documents, the worker's handbills and in this case a union card—are not granted a heighted authenticity by being presented visually for the reader but are read out by a character. In Steinbeck, the underscores the illusion of the document itself.

62. Marx (1990), p. 342–343.

63. *Ibid.*, p. 343.

64. *Ibid.*, p. 92.

65. Jameson (2011), p. 40.

66. *Against the Day*, p. 93.

67. *ATD*, p. 93.

68. Jameson (1974), pp. 186–187. Italics in original.

69. *Ibid.*, p. 186.

70. *ATD*, p. 88.

71. *ATD*, p. 94.

72. For an excellent history of economic and political crisis, see Philip Mirowski, *Never Let a Serious Crisis Go to Waste* (London: Verso, 2014) and two books by Gary Gerstle: *The Rise and Fall of the New Deal Order*, edited by Steve Fraser and

Gary Gerstle (Princeton, NJ: Princeton University Press, 1989) and Gary Gerstle, *The Rise and Fall of the Neoliberal Order* (Oxford: Oxford University press, 2022).

73. See Wolfang Streeck, *How Will Capitalism End? Essays on a Failing System* (London: Verso, 2016). See also Mason (2015).

74. Alison Shonkwiler, *The Financial Imaginary: Economic Mystification and the Limits of Realist Fiction* (Minneapolis: University of Minnesota Press, 2017), p. x.

75. Finance is not necessarily the highest stage of world capitalism but an attendant part of all stages within capital. As Giovanni Arrighi has demonstrated, "finance capital is not a particular stage of world capitalism, let alone its latest and highest stage. Rather it is a recurrent phenomenon which has marked the capitalist era from its earliest beginnings in late medieval and early modern Europe." See Giovanni Arrighi, *The Long Twentieth Century: Money, Power, and the Origins of our Times* (London: Verso, 2010), p. xi.

76. J.C. Chandor, *Margin Call* (2011).

77. *Ibid.*

78. Fredric Jameson, "Antmonies of the Realism-Modernism Debate," *Modern Language Quarterly* 73.3 (2012), pp. 475–85, p. 479.

79. Shane Deckard, Nicholas Lawrence, Neil Lazarus et al (2015), p. 61.

80. Nicky Marsh, Money, *Finance, and Speculation in Recent British Fiction* (London: Continuum, 2007), p. 17.

81. Cedric Watts, *Literature and Money: Financial Myth and Literary Truth* (New York: Harvester Wheatsheaf, 1990), p. 198.

82. Jennifer Hodgson and Patricia Waugh, "On the Exaggerated Reports of a Decline in British Fiction" [online] http://www.thewhitereview.org/feature/on-the-exaggerated-reports-of-a-decline-in-british-fiction/ [accessed 05/02/2018].

83. Liam McIlvanney and Ray Ryan, "Introduction" in *The Good of the Novel*, edited by Liam McIlvanney and Ray Ryan (London: Faber, 2011), p. xii.

84. As Terry Eagleton writes in his introduction to the work of the French philosopher Pierre Macherey, "The literary text is not to be thought of as an 'expression' of the human subject or as a 'reflection' of reality. It has no depth, center, unity, or singular point of origin. It is the product not of an authorial intention but of a process of production, which like the production of a shirt or a scooter operates by procedures quite independent of what the producer has in mind." Terry Eagleton, "Preface" in Pierre Macherey, A *Theory of Literary Production*, trans. by Geoffrey Wall (London & New York: Routledge, 2006), pp. vii–xiv, p. viii.

85. Terry Eagleton, "Pierre Macherey and the Theory of Literary Production," *Minnesota Review*, Number 5 (Winter 1975), pp. 134–144, p. 135.

86. Kevin McLaughlin, "The Financial Imp: Ethics and Finance in Nineteenth-Century Fiction," *Novel: A Forum on Fiction* 29.2 (Winter 1996), pp. 165–183, p. 165.

87. Kornbluh (2014), p. 16. Marx also spent hours consulting the Blue Books, drawing information, references, stories, and ideas from governmental reports on everything from factory conditions to sanitation to prostitution. See Asa Briggs and John Callow, *Marx in London* (London: Lawrence and Wishart, 1982), p. 53.

88. Marx (1990), p. 802. Paul Lafargue, Marx's son-in-law, went further: "only in England could Marx become what he has become [...] in such an economically undeveloped country as Germany was until the middle of this century, Marx could not have arrived at his critique of bourgeois economy and at a knowledge of capitalist production any more than this economically undeveloped Germany could have had the political institutions of economically developed England." See Paul Lafargue and Wilhelm Liebknecht, *Extracts from the Reminiscences of Karl Marx* (London: Lawrence and Wishart, 1942), p. 42.

89. Charles Dickens, *Great Expectations* (London: Penguin, 2006), p. 282.

90. Anna Kornbluh, *Realizing Capital: Financial and Psychic Economies in Victorian Britain* (New York: Fordham University Press, 2014), p. 1.

91. *Ibid.*, p. 3.

92. Patricia Waugh and Jennifer Hodgson, "Introduction," *The Review of Contemporary Fiction: The Future of British Fiction* 32.3 (2012), pp. 9–29, p. 10–11.

93. Paul Crosthwaite, "Framing Finance" in *Show Me the Money: The Image of Finance, 1700 to the Present*, edited by Paul Crosthwaite, Peter Knight, and Nicky Marsh (London: Manchester University Press, 2014), p. 35–61, p. 35.

94. Katy Shaw, *Crunch Lit* (London & New York: Bloomsbury, 2015), p. 8.

95. Paul Crosthwaite, "'Soon the Economic System Will Crumble': Financial Crisis and Contemporary British Avant-Garde Writing" in *Review of Contemporary Fiction: Future of British Fiction*, edited by Patricia Waugh and Jennifer Hodgson 32.3 (2012), pp. 38–48, p. 40.

96. *Ibid.*, p. 39.

97. Marx (1990), p. 143.

98. Marx (1993), p. 162–163.

99. As Hamilton Carroll and Annie McClanahan have similarly noted, while the "cultural task of adequately and accurately representing economic transformation has most often been assigned to literary-realist fiction" a raft of new novels "not typically associated with the representation of political and economic changes have [become] central to post-financial crisis culture." Hamilton Carroll and Annie McClanahan, "Fictions of Speculation: Introduction," *Journal of American Studies* 49.4 (2015), pp. 655–661, p. 657.

100. Eliot Braha in Theodore D. Kharpertian, *A Hand to Turn the Time: The Menippean Satires of Thomas Pynchon* (Rutherford: Farleigh Dickinson University Press, 1990), p. 15.

101. Crosthwaite (2012), p. 40.

102. David Witzling, "The Sensibility of Postmodern Whiteness in *V.*, or Thomas Pynchon's Identity Problem," *Contemporary Literature*, 47.3 (2006), pp. 381–415, p. 394.

103. Tony Tanner, *Thomas Pynchon* (York: Methuen Publishing, 1982), p. 60.

104. See Patrick Hurley, *Pynchon's Character Names: A Dictionary* (Jefferson, North Carolina: McFarland & Company, 2008), pp. 4–6. The relationship between characters" names and descriptive epithets is also shared with certain character within realist novels, particularly Dickens "whose freakish surplus of characters, juddering episodic plots, and teary sentiment Pynchon half imitates [...] beginning with his absurd and fantastic character names." Unlike Dickens however, Pynchon does not deploy character names in a consistent manner. See William Logan, "On the Connections between Poetry and Fiction" in *Thomas Pynchon*, edited by Harold Bloom (Philadelphia: Chelsea House, 2003), p. 136–148, p. 136.

105. Hurley (2008).

106. Marx (2010), p. 197.

107. Bottomore (1983), p. 292–293.

108. *GR*, p. 748.

109. *GR*, p. 754.

110. Thomas Pynchon, *The Crying of Lot 49* (London: Vintage, 2000), p. 86.

111. Thomas Pynchon, "Foreword" in George Orwell, *Nineteen Eighty-Four* (New York: Penguin, 2003), pp. vii–xxvi, p. xvi.

112. Thomas Pynchon, *Bleeding Edge* (London: Vintage, 2014), p. 10.

113. *Ibid.*, p. 63.

114. *Ibid.*, p. 63.

115. *Ibid.*, p. 320.

116. *Ibid.*, p. 320.

117. See Laurence Wright's *The Looming Tower: Al Qaeda's Road to 9/11* (London: Penguin, 2007).

118. In 2004, Osama Bin Laden alleged that Al-Qaeda had "repeatedly tried to convey the message of the attacks in words and deeds before September 11." See Osama Bin Laden, *Messages to the World: The Statements of Osama Bin Laden*, edited by Bruce B. Lawrence and James Howarth (New York: Verso, 2005), p. 240.

119. Undoubtedly, the primary driving force of Bin Laden's terrorism is the religious ideology of the Koran and the Hadith, see Sam Harris, *The End of Faith: Religion, Terror, and the Future of Reason* (London, The Free Press, 2005).

120. *BE*, p. 321.

121. See Pankaj Mishra, "The End of Innocence," *The Guardian* [online] https://www.theguardian.com/books/2007/may/19/fiction.martinamis [accessed 17/07/17].

122. Christopher Nealon, "Pynchon's Children" *Public Books* [online] http://www.publicbooks.org/pynchons-children/ [accessed 01/08/17].

123. Alissa G. Karl, "The zero hour of the neoliberal novel" *Textual Practice* 29.2 (2015), pp. 335–355, p. p. 335. See also Emily Johansen and Alissa Karl,

Neoliberalism, and the Novel (London: Routledge, 2016).

124. See "Bleeding Edge: Thomas Pynchon returns as prophet of the post-Snowden Era," *Wired* Magazine, available at http://www.wired.com/2013/09/pynchon-bleeding-edge-snowden/ [accessed 22/06/2016] and "The Thomas Pynchon Novel for the Edward Snowden Era: A review of *Bleeding Edge*" *The Atlantic*, http://www.theatlantic.com/magazine/archive/2013/10/losing-the-plot/309450/ [accessed 22/06/2016].

125. See for instance Nathanial Rich, "The Thomas Pynchon Novel for the Snowden Era: A Review of *Bleeding Edge*," *The Atlantic* [online] (October 2013) http://www.theatlantic.com/magazine/archive/2013/10/losing-the-plot/309450/.

126. *BE*, p. 8–9.

127. *Ibid*., p. 9.

128. *Ibid*., p. 8.

129. Judith Butler, *Precarious Life: The Powers of Mourning and Violence* (New York: Verso, 2006), pxi.

130. *BE*, p. 377.

131. Eve (2016), p. 194–195.

132. Jameson (1991), p. 51.

133. Stephen Gill, "The Global Panopticon? The Neoliberal State, Economic Life, and Democratic Surveillance," *Alternatives: Global, Local, Political 20.1(1995), pp. 1–49.*

134. *Ibid*., p. 1.

135. *BE*, p. 101

136. *Ibid*., p. 101.

137. *Ibid*., p. 104–105.

138. See Tariq Ali, *The Extreme Centre: A Warning* (London & New York: Verso, 2015).

139. *BE*, p. 406.

140. *Ibid*., p. 407.

141. *Ibid*., p. 407.

142. Mitchum Huehls, "The Great Flattening" *Contemporary Literature* 54.4 (2013), pp. 861–871, p. 866.

143. Huehls (2013), p. 866.

144. *BE*, p. 327.

145. See Haynes (2014), p. 11.

146. *BE*, p. 340.

147. *Ibid*., p. 340.

148. *Ibid*., p. 57.

149. *Ibid*., p. 54.

150. *Ibid*., p. 54.

151. *Ibid*., p. 54.

152. *Ibid*., p. 56.

153. *Ibid*., p. 56–57.

154. *Ibid*., p. 116.

155. *Ibid*., p. 37.

156. *Ibid*., p. 476.

157. *Ibid*., p. 476.

158. *Ibid*., p. 476.

Chapter 7

1. See chapter two in James Peacock, *Brooklyn Fictions: The Contemporary Urban Community in a Global Age* (London: Bloomsbury, 2016).

2. Jacqueline Woodson, *Another Brooklyn* (London: Oneworld Publications, 2017), p. 9.

3. Adam Dawson, "'We Knew We Were Being Watched': Adultification and Coming of Age in Jacqueline Woodson's *Another Brooklyn*," *Studies in American Fiction*, 49.1 (2023), pp. 99–118, p. 99.

4. *Another Brooklyn*, p. 25.

5. *Another Brooklyn*, p. 9.

6. James Peacock, "Those the Dead Left Behind: Gentrification and Haunting in Contemporary Brooklyn Fictions," *Studies in American Fiction*, 46.1 (2019), pp. 131–156, p. 149.

7. For recent accounts of the event see Randy Krehbiel, *Tulsa, 1921: Reporting a Massacre* (Norman: University of Oklahoma, 2019), Chris Messer, Thomas Shriver, and Alison Adams, "The Destruction of Black Wall Street: Tulsa's 1921 Riot and the Eradication of Accumulated Wealth," volume 77.3 *American Journal of Economics & Sociology* (May–September 2018), pp. 789–819, and Hannibal B. Johnson, "Tulsa, Then and Now: Reflections on the 1921, Tulsa Massacre," *Great Plains Quarterly* 40.3, Summer 2020, pp. 181–185.

8. Jacqueline Woodson, *Red at the Bone* (London: Weidenfeld & Nicolson, 2019), p.

9. *Ibid*., p.

10. Jacqueline Woodson, *Brown Girl Dreaming* (New York: Penguin, 2014), p. 72.

11. *Brown Girl Dreaming*, p. 72.

12. Kathryn Bond Stockton in Dawson (2023), p. 100.

13. Kathryn Bond Stockton, *The Queer Child, or Growing Sideways in the Twentieth Century* (Duke: Duke University Press, 2009), p. 1.

14. Dawson (2023), p. 101.

15. See André Jolles, *Simple Forms: Legend, Saga, Myth, Riddle, Saying, Case, Memorabile, Fairytale, Joke*, translated by Peter J. Schwartz (London: Verso, 2017).

16. Two pronouncements in particular stand out here: "like the Red Queen, capitalism runs faster and faster to stay in one place" which comes in his commentary on volume 1 of Marx's *Capital* (Jameson, 2011, p. 68); the second, his discussion of the history of emotions, and in particular ennui, which has a "narcotic indifference" equal to Alice's Caterpillar, in *The Ideologies of Theory* (Jamerson, 2008, p. 313).

17. Jameson (2015), p. 89.

18. See Leo Tolstoy, *Tolstoy on Education*, edited by Alan Pinch and Michael Armstrong (London: Athlone Press, 1982).

19. Fredric Jameson, *Jameson on Jameson: Conversations on Cultural Marxism*, edited by Ian Buchanan (Durham: Duke University Press, 2007), p. 32.

20. Chinua Achebe, *There was a Country: A Personal History of Biafra* (London: Penguin, 2012), p.

21. C.L. Innes, *Chinua Achebe* (Cambridge: Cambridge University Press, 1990), p. 2.

22. Leopold Senghor in C.L Innes (1992), p. 105.

23. Jacqueline Woodson, *Another Brooklyn* (London: OneWorld, 2017), p. 65.

24. *Ibid.*, p. 65

25. *Ibid.*, p. 65.

26. *Ibid.*, p. 66.

27. *Ibid.*, pp. 66–67.

28. *Ibid.*, p. 66.

29. *Ibid.*, p. 68.

30. *Ibid.*, p. 68.

31. Hephzibah Anderson, "Review: *Red at the Bone* by Jacqueline Woodson review—poetic and profound," *The Observer*, 27 January 2020, https://www.theguardian.com/books/2020/jan/27/red-at-bone-jacqueline-woodson-review.

32. *Red at the Bone*, p. 1.

33. *Ibid.*, p. 1.

34. *Ibid.*, p. 15.

35. *Ibid.*, p. 79.

36. *Ibid.*, p. 80–81.

37. *Ibid.*, p. 82.

38. *Ibid.*, p. 82.

39. *Ibid.*, p. 11.

40. *Ibid.*, p. 11.

41. *Ibid.*, p. 14.

42. *Ibid.*, p. 15.

43. *Ibid.*, p. 16.

44. *Ibid.*, p. 19.

Chapter 8

1. David Wallace-Wells, *The Uninhabitable Earth* (London: Penguin, 2019), p. 3.

2. David Sergeant has dedicated two chapters to Robinson in his book on literature and climate change. See David Sergeant, *The Near Future in Twenty-First-Century Fiction: Climate, Retreat and Revolution* (Cambridge Studies in Twenty-First-Century Literature and Culture) (Cambridge: Cambridge University Press, 2022).

3. Adeline Johns-Putra (2019), p. 38.

4. *Ibid.*, p. 47.

5. See my forthcoming book, *Kim Stanley Robinson: Apprenticeships in Narrative*, with Liverpool University Press.

6. Robinson followed these narratives with *The Martians* (1999), a companion to the original trilogy containing new stories, documents, maps, and images, including the Dorsa Brevia Declaration written in Green Mars, the First Hundred's initial training in Antarctica, and a volume of cultural artefacts, including Martian poetry.

7. Johns-Putra (2019), p. 150. For an excellent account see Franco Moretti, *The Way of the World* (London: Verso, 2000)

8. See "Barack Obama's favorite books of 2020 that you need to read," *The Independent* (Dec 2020): https://www.independent.co.uk/extras/indybest/books/barack-obama-favourite-book-2020-non-fiction-b1776000.html For a discussion of his successor's aversion to literature see "The President Who Doesn't Read, *The Atlantic* (Jan 2018), https://www.theatlantic.com/politics/archive/2018/01/americas-first-post-text-president/549794/

9. Alongside the incorporation of the Greimas square in many prominent works, Jameson has also written two introductions to its use. See "Foreword to A.J. Greimas" *On Meaning: Selected Writings in Semiotic Theory*" in Jameson

(2008), pp. 516–533 and "The Greimas Square" in Jameson (2019), pp. 349–360.

10. Kim Stanley Robinson, *New York: 2140* (London: Orbit, 2017), p. 206.

11. Marx (1990), p. 3.

12. Karl Marx, Manifesto, p. See chapter 3 of my *Karl Marx* for a close reading of the text.

13. Marx (1990), p. 171.

14. In 2015 authors Margaret Atwood, Helen Macdonald, and Robert MacFarlane wrote an open letter to Oxford University Press about the previous editions of the Oxford "junior" dictionary which had cut words about nature (acorn, moss, blackberry, bluebell, cauliflower, and clover) and included social media terms (chatroom, blog, and broadband). See "Oxford Junior Dictionary's replacement of 'natural' words with 21st-century terms sparks outcry," *The Guardian* (13th Jan 2015), https://www.theguardian.com/books/2015/jan/13/oxford-junior-dictionary-replacement-natural-words

15. Matthew Schneider-Mayerson, "The Influence of Climate Change: An Empirical Survey of Readers," *Environmental Humanities*, 10:2 (November 2018), pp. 474–500, p. 474.

16. Kornbluh (2019), p. 2.

17. Amitav Ghosh, "Where is the fiction about Climate Change," *The Guardian* (Friday 28th October 2016), https://www.theguardian.com/books/2016/oct/28/amitav-ghosh-where-is-the-fiction-about-climate-change- [accessed 15/02/2020].

18. Amitav Ghosh, *The Great Derangement: Climate Change and the Unthinkable* (Chicago: University of Chicago Press, 2016), p. 33.

19. *Ibid.*, p. 33.

20. Laurence Buell, *The Environmental Imagination: Thoreau, Nature Writing, and the Formation of American Culture* (Cambridge, Massachusetts: Harvard University Press, 1995), p.

21. Mark Fisher, *Capitalist Realism* (London: Zero Books, 2009), p.

22. Davis Smith-Brecheisen, "Editors' Note: Realism Reevaluated" in *Mediations* 33.1–2, Fall 2019–Spring 2020, p. 1.

23. Jameson (2005), p. 187.

24. *Ibid.*, p. 396.

25. Siân Adiseshiah, "The Revolution will not be Dramatized: The Problem of Mediation in Carol Churchill's Revolution Plays," *Hungarian Journal of English and American Studies* 19.2 (2013), pp. 377–393, p. 377.

26. As Robinson defines it, "For Marxism, '*Werteswandel*' is in dialectical relation with changes in material circumstances and systems, not just modes of production, but also modes of exchange, or modes of valuation. The mode of production isn't really the whole story anymore." See Kim Stanley Robinson in Helena Feder, "The Realism of our Time: Interview with Kim Stanley Robinson," *Radical Philosophy* [online] https://www.radicalphilosophy.com/wp-content/uploads/2018/01/rp201_robinson.pdf [accessed 07/02/18].

27. Magdalena Mączyńska, "Welcome to the Post-Anthropolis: Urban Space and Climate Change" in Nathaniel Rich's *Odds Against Tomorrow*, Lev Rosen's *Depth*, and Kim Stanley Robinson's *New York 2140*," *Journal of Modern Literature* Vol. 43, No.2 (Winter 2020, pp. 165–181), p. 165.

28. Anna Kornbluh, "Climate Realism, Capitalist and Otherwise" in *Mediations*, 33, 1–2 (2019–2020), pp. 99–118, p. 103.

29. Anna Kornbluh, "Climate Realism, Capitalist and Otherwise," *Mediations* 33.1–2 (Fall 2019), pp. 99–118.

30. *Ibid.*, p. 111.

31. Robinson (2018), p. 7.

32. James Joyce, *Finnegan's Wake* (London: Penguin, 2000), p. 3.

33. Adeline Johns-Putra, *Climate Change and the Contemporary Novel* (Cambridge: Cambridge University Press, 2019), p. 165

34. See Stuart Sim, *Manifesto for Silence: Confronting the Politics and Culture of Noise* (Edinburgh: Edinburgh University Press, 2007).

35. Frank Kermode, *The Sense of an Ending: Studies in the Theory of Fiction with a New Epilogue* (Oxford: Oxford University Press, 2000), p. 45.

36. I must mention an anecdote from one of my undergraduate seminars: a student had a reaction so visceral it resulted in a post-seminar call home to her mother in which she triumphantly informed her that there was no such thing as time.

37. Claeys (2018), p. 461.

Epilogue

1. From *Marxism and Form* (1973) to *The Benjamin Files* (2020). See Robert Tally, *Fredric Jameson: The Project of Dialectical Criticism* (London: Pluto Press, 2014) for an excellent introduction to Jameson's work.

2. Peter Osborne, *How to Read Marx* (London: Granta, 2005), p. 3.

3. *Ibid.*, p. 3–4.

Appendix

1. See *The Idea of Communism*, edited by Slavoj Žižek and Costas Douzinas (London: Verso, 2010), *The Idea of Communism 2: The New York Conference*, edited by Slavoj Žižek (London: Verso, 2013), and *The Idea of Communism 3: The Seoul Conference*, edited by Slavoj Žižek and Alex Taek-Gwang Lee (London: Verso, 2016).

2. Žižek and Douzinas (2010), p. ix.

3. See Raphael Samuel, *The Lost World of British Communism* (London: Verso, 2017) and *Communism in the 21st Century*, 3 volumes, edited by Shannon Brincat (Oxford: Praeger, 2014).

4. Alan Johnson, "The New Communism: Resurrecting the Utopian Delusion," *World Affairs*, May–June 2012 [online] http://www.worldaffairsjournal.org/article/newcommunism-resurrecting-utopian-delusion [accessed 19/09/2018].

5. Ray Pahl, "Is the Emperor Naked? Some Comments on the Adequacy of Sociological Theory in Urban and Regional Research," *International Journal of Urban and Rural Research* 13 (1989), pp. 127–129, p. 127. See Jan Pakulski and Malcolm Waters, *The Death of Class* (London: Sage, 2009).

6. See Terry Eagleton, *The Illusions of Postmodernism* (Oxford: Blackwell Publishers, 1996) and Alex Callinicos, *Against Postmodernism: A Marxist Critique* (Cambridge: Polity, 1989).

7. Doug Henwood, *After the New Economy: The Binge and the Hangover That Won't Go Away* (New York: New York Press, 2003), p. 28.

8. See David Harvey, *A Brief History of Neoliberalism* (Oxford: Oxford University Press, 2005).

9. Alison Shonkwiler, *The Financial Imaginary: Economic Mystification and the Limits of Realist Fiction* (London: University of Minnesota Press, 2017), p. 74.

10. Benjamin Kunkel, "Into the Big Tent," *London Review of Books*, 32.8 (April 2010), pp12–16, p. 12.

11. See Erik Olin Wright, *Class Counts* (Cambridge: Cambridge University Press, 2010) and Erik Olin Wright, *Understanding Class* (London: Verso, 2015). For a useful overview of class contexts see Siân Adiseshiah, "Chavs, Gyppos, and Scum? Class in *Twenty-First Century Drama*" in *Twenty-first Century Drama: What Happens Now*, edited by Siân Adiseshiah and Louise LePage (London: Palgrave Macmillan, 2016), pp. 149–173.

12. Domenico Losurdo, *Class Struggle: A Political and Philosophical History*, trans. by Gregory Elliot (New York: Palgrave, 2016).

13. See for instance, David Roediger, *Class, Race, and Marxism* (London: Verso, 2017).

14. Chantal Mouffe, *For a Left Populism* (London: Verso, 2018), p. 1.

15. Andrew Hindmoor has argued that these electoral defeats are in part connected to a "self-harming" vision held by left political movements, which have failed to adequately account for the success of progressive movements and the benefits of neoliberalism. See Andrew Hindmoor, *What's Left Now? The History and Future of Social Democracy* (Oxford: Oxford University Press, 2018).

16. A more detailed editorial history can be found in Andrew Rowcroft, *Karl Marx* (London: Routledge, 2020).

17. See Ashley J. Bohrer, *Marxism and Intersectionality: Race, Gender, Class and Sexuality under Contemporary Capitalism* (New York: Columbia University Press, 2019).

18. Gareth Stedman Jones, "'Pressure from Without': Karl Marx and 1867," *Parliamentary History* (2017), 36.1, pp. 117–130, p. 118.

19. In an 1882 letter to Edward Bernstein, Marx responded to the political programme of the French worker's party, writing, "Ce qu'il y a de certain c'est que moi, je ne suis pas Marxiste" [What is

certain is that I am not a Marxist]. See Karl Marx, *Marx Engels Collected Works* (London: Lawrence & Wishart,1996), p. 388.

20. See Rowcroft (2020).

21. Mathias Nilges and Emilio Sauri, "Editor's Note," *Mediations: Journal of the Marxist Literary Group*, 24.2 (2009), pp. 1–11, p. 2.

22. *Ibid.*, p. 2–3.

23. For a recent collection of essays on Marx and aesthetic criticism see *Aesthetic Marx*, edited by Samir Gandesha and Johan F. Hartle (London: Bloomsbury, 2017).

24. Carey Nelson and Lawrence Grossberg, "Introduction: The Territory of Marxism" in *Marxism and the Interpretation of Culture*, edited by Lawrence Grossberg and Carey Nelson (Illinois: University of Illinois Press, 1988), p. 2.

25. John Berger, *Landscapes: John Berger on Art*, edited by Tom Overton (London: Verso, 2016), p. 47.

26. *Ibid.*, p. 47.

27. Edmund Wilson, "Marxism and Literature" in Edmund Wilson, *Literary Essays and Reviews of the 1930s & 40s: The Triple Thinkers, The Wound and the Bow, Classics and Commercials, Uncollected Reviews* (New York: Library of America, 2007), pp. 197–212, p. 197. For an account of Marx's engagement with literature see S.S. Prawer, *Karl Marx and World Literature*, second edition (London: Verso, 2011). The aesthetic has furnished a powerful pull on generations of scholars and critics from the Second World War onwards. Perry Anderson has characterised Western Marxism as primarily concerned with superstructures, while Julian Bourg has noted, in his study of the French national situation, a shift from revolution to ethics fostered a concern with cultural questions. See Perry Anderson, *Considerations on Western Marxism* (London: Verso, 1979) and Julian Bourg, *From Revolution to Ethics: May 1968 and Contemporary French Thought*, second edition (Montreal: McGill University Press, 2017).

28. Imre Szeman, "Marxist Literary Theory, Then and Now" in *Contemporary Marxist Theory*, edited by Pendakis, Andrew, Jeff Diamanit, Nicholas Brown, Josh Robinson, and Imre Szeman (London & New York: Bloomsbury Academic, 2014), pp. 379–388, p. 381. Italics in original.

29. *Ibid.*, p. 380.

30. *Ibid.*, p. 381.

31. *Ibid.*, p. 387.

32. *Ibid.*, p. 388.

33. *Ibid.*, p. 388.

34. Mathias Nilges and Emilio Sauri have likewise identified "the crisis of futurity that underlies contemporary literary studies" in general and critical materialism in particular, "asking what a third option for a future literary criticism might look like." See Mathias Nilges and Emilio Sauri, "Introduction: Literature and Materialism Revisited" in *Literary Materialisms*, edited Mathias Nilges and Emilio Sauri (New York: Palgrave Macmillan, 2013), pp. 1–16, p. 4.

Bibliography

Abbas, Niran, ed. *Thomas Pynchon: Reading from the Margins* (Madison: Fairleigh Dickinson University Press, 2003).
Abrahams, Roger. *Mythical Trickster Figures: Contours, Contexts, Criticisms* (Tuscaloosa: University of Alabama Press, 1997).
Achebe, Chinua. *There Was a Country: A Personal History of Biafra* (London: Penguin, 2012).
Adams, Mark B. "*Red Star*: Another Look at Aleksandr Bogdanov," *Slavic Review* 48.1 (1989), pp. 1–15.
Adiseshiah, Siân. "Revolution and the End of History: Caryl Churchill's *Mad Forest* in *Modern Drama*" 52:3 (Fall 2009), Pp. 283–299.
______. "The Revolution Will Not Be Dramatized: The Problem of Mediation in Caryl Churchill's Revolution Plays," *Hungarian Journal of English and American Studies* 19.2 (2013), pp. 377–393.
______, and Louise LePage. "*Twenty-First Century Drama" in Twenty-first Century Drama: What Happens Now* (London: Palgrave Macmillan, 2016).
______, and Rupert Hildyard. *Twenty-First Century Fiction: What Happens Now* (Basingstoke: Palgrave Macmillan, 2013).
Adorno, Theodor W. *Hegel: Three Studies*, trans. by Shierry Weber Nicholson (Cambridge, Massachusetts: MIT Press, 1993).
Agamben, Giorgio. *What Is an Apparatus? and Other Essays*, trans. by David Kishik and Stefan Pedatella (California: Stanford University Press, 2009).
Aksikas, Jaafar. "Cultural Studies and Marxism," *Rowman and Littlefield* [online] https://www.rowmaninternational.com/our-publishing/series/cultural-studies-and-marxism/ [accessed 01/06/2017].
Ali, Tariq. *The Extreme Centre: A Warning* (London & New York: Verso, 2015).
Alighieri, Dante. *The Divine Comedy: Hell* (London: Penguin Classics, 1977).
______. *The Divine Comedy, Volume 1: Inferno*, trans. by Mark Musa (London: Penguin, 1984).
Allen, Kieran. *Marxism and the Alternative to Capitalism* (London: Pluto Press, 2011).
Althusser, Louis. *For Marx* (London: Vintage: 2005).
______, and Étienne Balibar. *Reading Capital*, trans. by Ben Brewster (London & New York: Verso, 2009).
Amin, Samir. *Specters of Capitalism: A Critique of Current Intellectual Fashions*; trans. by Shane Henry Mage (New York: Monthly Review Press, 1998).
Anderson, Perry. *Considerations on Western Marxism* (London: Western Printing, 1976).
______. *In the Tracks of Historical Materialism* (London: Verso, 1983).
______. *Spectrum: From Right to Left in the World of Ideas* (London: Verso, 2007).
Anthony Johnson, Mark, and Abdullah Mamun. "The Failure of Lehman Brothers and Its Impact on Other Financial Institutions," *Financial Economics* 22.5 (2012), pp. 375–385.
Apter, Emily, and Elaine Freedgood. "Afterword" in "The Way We Read Now," *Representations* 108.1 (2009), pp. 139–146.
Aristotle. *Poetics* (Oxford: Oxford University Press, 2013).

Armitt, Lucie. *Twentieth-century Gothic* (Cardiff: University of Wales Press, 2011).
Aronowitz, Stanley. *The Crisis in Historical Materialism: Class, Politics and Culture in Marxist Theory* (Basingstoke: Macmillan 1990).
Aronson, Ronald. *After Marxism* (New York: Guilford Press, 1988).
Arthur, Christopher J. "Contradiction and Abstraction: A Reply to Finelli," *Historical Materialism* 17 (2009), pp. 170–182.
______. *The New Dialectic and Marx's Capital* (Cambridge, Massachusetts: MIT Press, 2000).
______. *The New Dialectic in Marx's Capital* (Boston: Brill, 2004).
Badiou, Alain. *The Communist Hypothesis* (London & New York: Verso, 2015).
______. *Theory of the Subject* (London: Continuum, 1999).
______, and Slavoj Žižek "Have Michael Hardt and Antonio Negri Rewritten the Communist Manifesto for the Twenty-First Century?" *Rethinking Marxism* 13.3 (2001), pp. 190–198.
Baudrillard, Jean. *For a Critique of the Political Economy of the Sign*, trans. by Charles Levin (St Louis, Missouri: Telos Press Publishing, 1981).
______. *The Mirror of Production*; trans. and introduced by Mark Poster (St Louis: Telos Press, 1975).
Beck, John, and Ryan Bishop, ed. *Cold War Legacies: Systems, Theory, Aesthetics* (Edinburgh: Edinburgh University Press, 2016).
Bellamy Foster, John Brett Clark, and Richard York, ed. *The Ecological Rift: Capitalism's War on the Earth* (New York: Monthly Review Press, 2011).
Benjamin, Walter. *Charles Baudelaire: A Lyric Poet in the Era of High Capitalism*, trans. by Harry Zohn (London: Verso, 1997).
______. *Illuminations*, edited and introduced by Hannah Arendt, trans. by Harry Zohn (London: Fontana, 1992).
______. "Left-Wing Melancholy (On Erich Kästner's New Book of Poems)," *Screen* 15.2 (1974), pp. 28–32.
______. *Understanding Brecht*, trans. by Anna Bostock (London: Verso, 1998).
Bentley, Nick, Nick Hubble, and Leigh Wilson. *The 2000s: A Decade of Contemporary British Fiction* (London & New York: Bloomsbury, 2015).
Berger, James. *After the End: Representations of Post-Apocalypse* (Minneapolis: University of Minnesota Press).
Berger, John. *Landscapes: John Berger on Art*, edited by Tom Overton (London: Verso, 2016).
Berlant, Lauren. "Cruel Optimism: On Marx, Loss, and the Senses," *New Formations* 63 (Winter 2007), pp. 33–51.
Berman, Marshal. *The Adventures of Marxism* (London: Verso, 2002).
Berressem, Hanjo. *Pynchon's Poetics: Interfacing Theory and Text* (Urbana: University of Illinois Press, 1993).
Best, Stephen, and Sharon Marcus. "Surface Reading: An Introduction," *Representations* 108.1 (2009), pp. 1–21.
Bhaskar, Roy. *Dialectic: The Pulse of Freedom* (London & New York: Routledge, 2008).
Birns, Nicholas. *Theory After Theory. an Intellectual History of Literary Theory from 1950 to the Early 21st Century* (New York: Broadview Press, 2010).
Blanchot, Maurice. *The Writing of Disaster*; trans. by Ann Smock (Lincoln: University of Nebraska Press, 1995).
Blyth, Mark. *Austerity: The History of a Dangerous Idea* (New York & Oxford: Oxford University Press, 2013).
Bogdanov, Alexander. *Red Star: The First Bolshevik Utopia*, edited by Loren R. Graham and Richard Stites, trans. by Charles Rougle (Indiana: Indiana University Press, 1984).
Boheemen-Saaf, Christine. *Derrida, Lacan, and the Trauma of History: Reading, Narrative, and Postcolonialism* (Cambridge: Cambridge University Press, 1999).
Bottomore, Tom, ed. *A Dictionary of Marxist Thought*. (Oxford: Blackwell, 1987).
Bould, Mark, and China Miéville, eds. *Red Planets: Marxism and Science Fiction* (London: Pluto Press, 2009).

______, and Sheryl Vint. *The Routledge Concise History of Science Fiction* (London: Routledge, 2011).
______, Andrew M. Butler, Adam Roberts, and Sherryl Vint, eds. *The Routledge Companion to Science Fiction* (London: Routledge, 2011).
Bourdieu, Pierre. *Bourdieu: A Critical Reader*, edited by Richard Shusterman (Oxford: Blackwell, 1999).
Bourg, Julian. *From Revolution to Ethics: May 1968 and Contemporary French Thought* (Montreal & Kingston: McGill-Queens University Press, 2007).
______. *From Revolution to Ethics: May 1968 and Contemporary French Thought* (London: McGill-Queen's University Press, 2007).
Bowman, Paul. *Post-Marxism Versus Cultural Studies: Theory, Politics and Intervention* (Edinburgh: Edinburgh University Press, 2005).
Boxall, Peter. *The Value of the Novel* (New York: Cambridge University Press, 2015).
Breckman, Warren. *Adventures of the Symbolic: Post-Marxism and Radical Democracy* (New York: Columbia University Press, 2013).
______. "Times of Theory: On Writing the History of French Theory," *Journal of the History of Ideas* 71.3 (2010), pp. 339–361.
Breton, André. *Communicating Vessels*, trans. by Mary Ann Caws & Geoffrey T. Harris (Lincoln: University of Nebraska Press, 1990).
Brooker, William. *The Blade Runner Experience: The Legacy of a Science Fiction Classic* (London: Wallflower Press, 2005).
Brooks, Neil, and Josh Tosh, eds. *The Mourning After: Attending the Wake of Postmodernism* (New York: Rodopi, 2007).
Brown, Wendy. "Resisting Left Melancholia," *Boundary 2* 26.3 (1999), pp. 19–27.
Buck-Morss, Susan. *Dreamworld and Catastrophe: The Passing of Mass Utopia in the West* (Cambridge, MA: MIT press, 2002).
Budgen, Sebastian, Stathis Kouvelakis, and Slavoj Žižek, eds. *Lenin Reloaded: Toward a Politics of Truth* (Durham: Duke University Press, 2007).
Buhle, Paul. *Marxism in the United States* (London: Verso, 2013).
Burling, William. "The Theoretical Foundation of Utopian Radical Democracy in Kim Stanley Robinson's Blue Mars," *Utopian Studies* 16.1 (2005), pp. 75–96.
______, ed. *Kim Stanley Robinson Maps the Unimaginable: Critical Essays* (Jefferson, NC: McFarland, 2009).
Burrough, Bryan. *Days of Rage: America's Radical Underground, the FBI, and the Forgotten Age of Revolutionary Violence* (New York: Penguin, 2015).
Butler, Judith, Ernesto Laclau, and Slavoj Žižek. *Contingency, Hegemony and Universality: Contemporary Dialogues on the Left* (London: Verso, 2011).
Byron, Glennis, and David Punter, eds. *Spectral Readings: Towards a Gothic Geography* (Basingstoke: Macmillan, 1999), pp. 1–8, p. 2.
Callinicos, Alex. *Against Postmodernism: A Marxist Critique* (Cambridge: Polity, 1989).
______. *Deciphering Capital: Marx's Capital and Its Destiny* (London: Bookmarks, 2014).
______. *The Revenge of History: Marxism and the East European Revolutions* (Pennsylvania: Penn State University Press, 1991).
______. *The Revolutionary Ideas of Karl Marx* (Chicago: Haymarket, 2010).
Campbell Reesman, Jeanne, ed. *Trickster Lives: Culture and Myth in American Fiction* (Athens: University of Georgia Press, 2001).
Carroll, Hamilton, and Annie McClanahan. "Fictions of Speculation: Introduction," *Journal of American Studies* 49.4 (2015), pp. 655–661.
Carswell, Sean. *Occupy Pynchon: Politics After Gravity's Rainbow* (Athens: Georgia University Press, 2017), p. 12.
Cassidy, John. "What Has Changed Since Lehman Failed?" *The New Yorker* http://www.newyorker.com/online/blogs/johncassidy/2013/08/mr-paulson-and-the-banksters-whats-happening-now-hank.html [accessed 1st July 2014].
Chetwynd, Ali. "Review of Dalsgaard, Herman and McHale" in *College Literature* 39.4 (2012), pp. 142–145.

Cho, Daniel K. "Tumults of Utopia: Repetition and Revolution in Kim Stanley Robinson's Mars Trilogy," *Cultural Critique*, 75 (2010), pp. 65–81.
Claeys, Gregory, edited. *The Cambridge Companion to Utopian Literature* (Cambridge: Cambridge University Press, 2010).
Clark, Terry Nichols, and Seymour Martin Lipset, eds. *The Breakdown of Class Politics: A Debate on Post-Industrial Stratification* (Baltimore: John Hopkins University Press, 2001).
Cohen, Emily Jane. "Museums of the Mind: The Gothic and the Art of Memory," *ELH* 62.4 (1995), pp. 883–905.
Cohen, Margaret. *Profane Illumination: Walter Benjamin and the Paris of Surrealist Revolution* (Berkley: California Press, 1993).
Coole, Diana, and Samantha Frost eds. *New Materialisms: Ontology, Agency, and Politics*, edited by Coole and Frost (Durham & London: Duke University Press, 2010).
Cooper, Luke, and Simon Hardy. *Beyond Capitalism? the Future of Radical Politics* (London: Zero Books, 2012).
Cooper, Peter. *Signs and Symptoms: Thomas Pynchon and the Contemporary World* (Berkley: University of California Press, 1983).
Cowart, David. *Thomas Pynchon & the Dark Passages of History* (Athens & London: University of Georgia Press, 2011).
Cox, Laurence, and Alf Gunvald Nilsen. *We Make Our Own History: Marxism and Social Movements in the Twilight of Neoliberalism* (London: Pluto Press, 2014).
Craps, Stef, and Stijn Vanheule. "*Nachträglichkeit*: A Freudian Perspective on Delayed Traumatic Reactions," *Theory & Psychology*, 24.5 (2014), pp. 668–687.
Crossley, Robert. *Imagining Mars: A Literary History* (Connecticut: Wesleyan University Press, 2011).
Crosthwaite, Paul. "Soon the Economic System Will Crumble": Financial Crisis and Contemporary British Avant-Garde Writing," *Review of Contemporary Fiction: Future of British Fiction* 32.3 (2012), pp. 38–48.
______. *The Markey Logics of Contemporary Fiction* (Cambridge: Cambridge University Press, 2019).
______. *Trauma, Postmodernism, and the Aftermath of World War II* (Basingstoke: Palgrave Macmillan 2009).
______, Peter Knight, and Nicky Marsh. *Show Me the Money: The Image of Finance, 1700 to the Present* (London: Manchester University Press, 2014).
Crouch, Colin. *Post-Democracy* (Cambridge: Polity Press, 2004).
Dalsgaard, Inger H., Luc Herman, Brian McHale, eds. *The Cambridge Companion to Thomas Pynchon* (Cambridge: Cambridge University Press, 2014).
Davies, Paul. *The Cosmic Blueprint: Order and Complexity at the Edge of Chaos* (London Heinemann, 1987).
Davies, William. *The Limits to Neoliberalism: Authority, Sovereignty and the Logic of Competition* (London: Sage Publications, 2014).
______. "The New Neoliberalism." *New Left Review*, 101, September-October 2016 [online] https://newleftreview.org/II/101/william-davies-the-new-neoliberalism [accessed 20/02/2018].
Dean, Jodi. *Crowds and Party* (London & New York: Verso, 2016).
______. "The Question of Organization," *The South Atlantic Quarterly* 113.4 (2014), pp. 821–835.
______. *The Communist Horizon* (London: Verso, 2012).
Deckard, Shane, Nicholas Lawrence, Neil Lazarus, Graeme McDonald, Upamanyu Pablo Mukherjee, Benita Perry, and Stephen Shapiro. *Combined and Uneven Development: Towards a New Theory of World Literature (Warwick Research Collective)* (Liverpool: Liverpool University Press, 2015).
Deleuze, Giles. *Foucault*, trans. and edited by Sean Hand (London: Continuum, 1999).
______, and Felix Guattari. *A Thousand Plateaus: Capitalism and Schizophrenia* (London: Bloomsbury, 1988).
Dellamora, Richard, ed. *Postmodern Apocalypse: Theory and Cultural Practice at the End* (Philadelphia: University of Pennsylvania Press, 1995).

Demetz, Peter. *Marx, Engels and the Poets: Origins of Marxist Literary Criticism*, trans. by Jeffrey L. Sammons (Chicago: University of Chicago Press, 1967).
Derrida, Jacques. *Spectres of Marx: The State of Debt, the Work of Mourning, and the New International* (London: Routledge, 2006).
______. *Writing and Difference* (London: Routledge, 2001).
Dickens, Charles. *Great Expectations* (London: Penguin, 2006).
Douzinas, Costas, and Slavoj Žižek. *The Idea of Communism* (London & New York: Verso, 2010).
Drucker, Peter F. *The Unseen Revolution: How Pension Fund Socialism Came to America* (New York: Harper & Row, 1976).
Eagelton, Terry. *After Theory* (London: Penguin, 2004).
______. *Culture and the Death of God* (New Haven & London: Yale University Press, 2014).
______. *Marxism and Literary Criticism* (Routledge: London & New York, 2010).
______. *Reason, Faith, and Revolution: Reflections on the God Debate* (New Haven & London: Yale University Press, 2009).
______. *The Event of Literature* (London: Yale University Press, 2012).
______. *The Ideology of the Aesthetic* (Oxford: Blackwell, 1990).
______. *The Illusions of Postmodernism* (Oxford: Blackwell, 1996).
______. *Why Marx Was Right* (New Haven & London: Yale University Press, 2011).
Eggers, Dave. *A Hologram for the King* (London: Penguin, 2014).
Elliott, Gregory. *Ends in Sight: Marx/Fukuyama/Hobsbawn/Anderson* (London: Pluto, 2008).
Emrys, John Eller. "A Conversation with Dana Spiotta," *12th Street: The Journal of Writing and Democracy* (2012), available at http://www.12thstreetonline.com/2012/11/27/a-talk-with-dana-spiotta/ [accessed 21/02/17].
Eng, David L., and David Kazanjian. In *Loss: The Politics of Mourning* (Berkeley: University of California Press, 2003).
Eve, Martin. *Literature Against Criticism: University English and Contemporary Fiction in Conflict* (Cambridge: Open Book Publishers, 2016).
______. *Pynchon and Philosophy: Wittgenstein, Foucault and Adorno* (Basingstoke: Palgrave Macmillan, 2014).
Felski, Rita. *The Limits of Critique* (Chicago: The University of Chicago Press, 2015).
Ferguson, Iain. *Politics of the Mind: Marxism and Mental Distress* (London: Bookmarks Publications, 2017).
Fisher, Mark. *Capitalist Realism: Is There No Alternative*? (Ropley: Zero Books, 2009).
______. *The Weird and the Eerie* (London: Repeater Books, 2016).
Fogg, Martyn J. *Terraforming: Engineering Planetary Environments* (Warrendale, PA: Society for Automotive Engineers, 1995).
Forna, Aminatta. "The Nickel Boys by Colson Whitehead Review—Essential Follow-up to the Underground Railroad." *The Guardian*, 26 Jul. 2019. Web.
Foucault, Michel. *Discipline and Punish: The Birth of the Prison*, trans. by Alan Sheridan (New York: Vintage, 1995).
______. *The Archaeology of Knowledge & the Discourse of Language*, trans. by A.M. Sheridan Smith (New York: Pantheon, 1972).
Freer, Joanna. *Thomas Pynchon and American Counterculture* (New York: Cambridge University Press, 2014).
Freud, Sigmund. *The Interpretation of Dreams*; trans. by James Strachey (New York: Avon Books, 1965).
______. *The Penguin Freud Reader*, edited by Adam Philips (London: Penguin Classics, 2006).
______. *The Standard Edition of the Complete Psychological Works*; edited and trans. by James Strachey, Volume XIV, 1914–1916 (London: Hogarth Press, 1957).
Fromm, Erich, and Karl Marx. *Marx's Concept of Man, Including Economic and Philosophical Manuscripts* (London: Bloomsbury, 2015).
Fukuyama, Francis. "The End of History?" *National Interest* 16 (Summer 1989), pp. 3–18.
______. *The End of History and the Last Man* (London: Penguin, 1992).

Fulbrook, Mary. *Anatomy of a Dictatorship: Inside the GDR 1949–1989* (New York: Oxford University Press, 1995).
Furet, François. *In the Workshop of History*, trans. by Jonathan Mandelbaum (Chicago: University of Chicago Press, 1985), p. 30.
Geras, Norman. "Ex-Marxism Without Substance: Being a Reply to Laclau and Mouffe," *New Left Review* 1.169 (May-June 1988), pp. 34–61.
______. *Marx and Human Nature* (London: New Left Books, 1983).
Gibson, William, and Bruce Sterling. *The Difference Engine* (London: Vista, 1991).
Gibson-Graham, J.K. *A Postcapitalist Politics* (Minneapolis: University of Minnesota Press, 2006).
Gill, Stephen. "The Global Panopticon? the Neoliberal State, Economic Life, and Democratic Surveillance," *Alternatives: Global, Local, Political* 20.1(1995), pp. 1–49.
Glocer, Fiorini, Leticia Thierry Bokanowski, and Sergio Lewkowicz, eds. *On Freud's "Mourning and Melancholia"* (London: Routledge Books, 2009).
Goldstein, Philip. *Post-Marxist Theory: An Introduction* (Albany: University of New York Press, 2005).
Gottfried, Paul E. *The Strange Death of Marxism: The European Left in the New Millennium* (Columbia; Missouri: University of Missouri Press, 2005).
Gorz, Andre. *Farwell to the Working Class: An Essay on Post-Industrial Socialism*, trans. by Mike Sonenscher (London, Pluto Press, 1982).
Graham, Hugh, and Ted Robert Gurr, eds. *The History of Violence in America: Violence in America: Historical and Comparative Perspectives* (New York: Prager, 1969).
Gramsci, Antonio. *Selections from the Prison Notebooks*, edited and trans. by Quintin Hoare and Geoffrey Nowell-Smith (London: Lawrence and Wishart, 1971).
Green, Jeremy. *Late Postmodernism: American Fiction at the Millennium* (London: Palgrave MacMillan, 2005).
Green, Sam, and Bill Siegel, dir. *The Weather Underground* (2002).
Habermas, Jürgen. "Modernity: An Unfinished Project" in *Habermas and the Unfinished Project of Modernity: Critical Essays on the Philosophical Discourse of Modernity*, edited by Maurizio Passerin D'Entreves and Seyla Benhabib (Cambridge; MA: MIT Press, 1997), pp. 38–58.
______. *The Philosophical Discourse of Modernity: Twelve Lectures*, trans. and edited by Fredrick Lawrence (Cambridge; Massachusetts, MIT Press, 1990).
Hale, Thomas N., and Anne-Marie Slaughter. "Hardt and Negri's Multitude: The Worst of Both Worlds," *OpenDemocracy* (2005), http://www.opendemocracy.net/globalization-vision_reflections/marx_2549.jsp [accessed 9th July 2014].
Hall, Stuart, and Martin Jacques, ed. *The Hard Road to Renewal: Thatcherism and the Crisis of the Left* (London: Verso, 1988).
______. *The Politics of Thatcherism* (London; Lawrence and Wishart, 1983).
______. *The Politics of Thatcherism* (London; Lawrence and Wishart, 1983).
Hardt, Michael, and Antonio Negri. *Commonwealth* (Cambridge, MA: Harvard University Press, 2009).
______. *Multitude: War and Democracy in the Age of Empire* (London & New York: Penguin, 2006).
Harvey, David. *A Brief History of Neoliberalism* (Oxford: Oxford University Press, 2007).
______. *A Companion to Marx's Capital* (London & New York: Verso, 2010).
______. *Seventeen Contradictions and the End of Capitalism* (London: Profile Books, 2014).
______. *The Enigma of Capital and the Crisis of Capitalism* (London: Profile Books, 2011).
Haynes, Doug. "Under the Beach, the Paving-Stones! the Fate of Fordism in Pynchon's *Inherent Vice*," *Studies in Contemporary Fiction* 55.1 (2014), pp. 1–16.
Hegel, Georg Wilhelm Fredrich. *Phenomenology of Spirit*, trans. by A.V. Miller (New York: Oxford University Press, 1977).
______. *The Science of Logic*, trans. and edited by George Di Giovanni (Cambridge: Cambridge University Press, 2015).
Hindess, Barry. *Pre-Capitalist Modes of Production* (London: Routledge & Kegan Paul, 1975).

______. *Politics and Class Analysis* (Oxford: Blackwell, 1987).
______. *The Decline of Working Class Politics* (London: Granda, 1971).
______, and Paul Q. Hirst. *Mode of Production and Social Formation* (London: Macmillan, 1977).
Hitchens, Christopher. *A Long Short War: The Postponed Liberation of Iraq* (London: Plume, 2003).
______. "The Revenge of Karl Marx: What the Author of *Das Kapital* Reveals About the Current Economic Crisis," *The Atlantic* [online] https://www.theatlantic.com/magazine/archive/2009/04/the-revenge-of-karl-marx/307317/ [accessed 02/06/2017].
Hobsbawn, Eric. *Age of Extremes: The Short Twentieth Century*, 1914–91 (London: Abacus, 1995).
Hodgson, Jennifer, and Patricia Waugh. "On the Exaggerated Reports of a Decline in British Fiction," *The White Review*, [online] http://www.thewhitereview.org/features/on-the-exaggerated-reports-of-a-decline-in-british-fiction/ [accessed 08/05/2017].
Holloway, David. "The War on Terror Espionage Thriller, and the Imperialism of Human Rights." *Comparative Literature Studies* 46.1 (2009), pp. 20–44.
______. *9/11 and the War on Terror* (Edinburgh: Edinburgh University Press, 2008).
Hudis, Peter. *Marx's Concept of the Alternative to Capitalism* (Chicago: Haymarket Books, 2012).
Huehls, Mitchum. "The Great Flattening" *Contemporary Literature* 54.4 (2013), pp. 861–871.
Hunt, Elle. "Paris Climate Agreement: Trump Pulls Out of Global Accord," *The Guardian* [online] https://www.theguardian.com/environment/live/2017/jun/01/donald-trump-paris-climate-agreement-live-news [accessed 20/02/2018].
Hutcheon, Linda. *The Politics of Postmodernism*, second edition (London & New York: Routledge, 2002).
Huyssen, Andreas. *Twilight Memories: Marking Time in a Culture of Amnesia* (London & New York: Routledge, 1995).
Irwin, Neil. *The Alchemists: Three Central Bankers and a World on Fire* (New York: Penguin, 2013).
Jacques Bidet, and Stathis Kouvelakis, eds. *Critical Companion to Contemporary Marxism*, Historical Materialism Book Series, volume 16 (Boston: Brill, 2008).
James, David. *Modernist Futures: Innovation and Inheritance in the Contemporary Novel* (New York: Cambridge University Press, 2012).
Jameson, Fredric. *A Singular Modernity: Essay on the Ontology of the Present* (London & New York: Verso, 2002).
______. "Antimonies of the Realism-Modernism Debate," *Modern Language Quarterly* 73.3, pp. 475–85.
______. *Archaeologies of the Future: The Desire Called Utopia and Other Science Fictions* (London: Verso, 2005).
______. "Culture and Finance Capital," *Critical Inquiry*, 24.1(1997), pp. 246–265.
______. "Future City," *New Left Review* 21 (May-June 2003), pp. 65–79.
______. *Jameson on Jameson: Conversations on Cultural Marxism*, edited by Ian Buchanan (Durham: Duke University Press, 2007).
______. *Late Marxism: Adorno, or the Persistence of the Dialectic* (London: Verso, 2007).
______. "Marxism After Postmodernism," *New Left Review* 1.176 (1989), pp. 31–45.
______. *Marxism and Form: Twentieth- Century Dialectical Theories of Literature* (Princeton: Princeton University Press, 1971).
______. *Postmodernism Or, the Cultural Logic of Late Capitalism* (London & New York: Verso, 2009).
______. "Radical Fantasy," *Historical Materialism*, 10:4 (2002), pp. 273–280.
______. *Raymond Chandler: The Detections of Totality* (London: Verso 2016).
______. *Representing Capital: A Reading of Volume 1* (London: Verso, 2014).
______. *The Antinomies of Realism* (London: Verso, 2013).
______. *The Ideologies of Theory, Essays 1971–1986, Volume 2* (Minneapolis: University of Minnesota Press, 1988).

______. *The Political Unconscious: Narrative as a Socially Symbolic Act* (London: Routledge, 1989).
______. *The Seeds of Time* (New York: Columbia University Press, 1994).
______. *Valences of the Dialectic* (London & New York: Verso, 2009).
Janzen, David "Void of Debt: Crisis and the Remaking of Indebtedness," *Meditations: Journal of the Marxist Literary Group* 26.1 (2012), pp. 187–193, p. 187.
Jay, Martin. *The Dialectical Imagination: A History of the Frankfurt School and the Institute of Social Research, 1923–1950* (Berkeley: University of California Press, 1996).
Jennings, Michael W., Brigid Doherty, and Thomas Y. Levin, eds. *Walter Benjamin's The Work of Art in the Age of Its Technological Reproducibility* (Cambridge: Harvard University Press, 2008).
Johansen, Emily, and Alissa G. Karl. "Introduction: Reading and Writing the Economic Present" in "Neoliberalism and the Novel," *Textual Practice* 29.2 (2015), pp. 201–214, p. 201.
Jones, Owen. *Chavs: The Demonization of the Working Class* (London: Verso, 2012).
Jung, Carl. *Memories, Dreams, Reflections*, trans. by R.C. Wilson (London: Fontana, 1995).
Kakutani, Michiko. "A Pynchonesque Turn by Pynchon," *New York Times*, 20th November 2006, p. 21.
Kalestky, Anatole. *Capitalism 4.0: The Birth of a New Economy* (London: Bloomsbury, 2011).
______. "The Case Against a Chinese Financial Crisis" *Reuters* (24th February 2014), http://blogs.reuters.com/anatole-kaletsky/2014/02/24/the-case-against-a-chinese-financial-crisis/ [accessed 2nd July 2014].
Kay, Sarah. "Surface Reading and the Symptom That Is Only Skin Deep," *Paragraph* 35.3 (2012), pp. 451–459. nc.
Keeble, Arin. *The 9/11 Novel: Trauma, Politics, Identity* (Jefferson, : McFarland, 2014).
Keucheyan, Razmig. *The Left Hemisphere: Mapping Critical Theory Today*; trans. by Greggory Elliot (London & New York: Verso, 2014).
Klein, Naomi. *The Shock Doctrine: The Rise of Disaster Capitalism* (London: Penguin, 2008).
Kojève, Alexandre. *Introduction to the Reading of Hegel: Lectures on the Phenomenology of Spirit*, edited by Allan Bloom, trans. by James H. Nichols, Jr. (Ithaca, NY: Cornell University Press; 1980).
Konstantinou, Lee. *Cool Characters: Irony and American Fiction* (Cambridge, MA: Harvard University Press, 2016).
Koolhaus, Rem, Judy Chung, Jeffrey Inaba, and Sze Tsung Leong. *Guide to Shopping, Harvard Design School Project on the City* (Cambridge: Taschen, 2001).
______, Stefano Boeri, Sanford Kwinter, Nadia Tazi, Hans-Ulrich Obrist eds. *Mutations* (Barcelona: Actar, 2001).
Kornbluh, Anna. *Realizing Capital: Financial and Psychic Economies in Victorian Britain* (New York: Fordham University Press, 2014).
Kritzman, Lawrence D. *The Columbia History of Twentieth-century French Thought* (New York: Columbia University Press, 2006).
Kushner, Rachel. *The Flamethrowers* (London: Vintage, 2014).
Laclau, Ernesto, and Chantal Mouffe. *Hegemony and Socialist Strategy: Towards a Radical Democratic Politics*, second edition (London: Verso, 2014).
______. *New Reflections on the Revolution of Our Time* (New York: Verso, 1990).
______. *Politics and Ideology in Marxist Theory: Capitalism, Fascism, Populism* (London: Verso, 2011).
Laity, Paul. "Jonathan Lethem: I've always thought of myself as a dark writer, but this is utterly different," *The Guardian* [online] https://www.theguardian.com/books/2017/feb/10/jonathan-lethem-interview-the-blot [accessed 05/06/17].
Laplanche, J., and J.B. Pontalis. *The Language of Psychoanalysis*, trans. by Donald Nicholson-Smith (London: Karnac Books, 1988).
Lethem, Jonathan. *Dissident Gardens* (London: Vintage, 2014).
Levitas, Ruth. *Utopia as Method: The Imaginary Reconstitution of Society* (London: Palgrave Macmillan, 2013).

Link, Alex. "The Mysteries of *Postmodernism*, Or, Fredric Jameson's Gothic Plots," *Gothic Studies* 11.1 (2009).
Lipset, Seymour Martin. *Consensus and Conflict: Essays in Political Sociology* (New Brunswick: Transaction Publishers, 1990).
______. "Marx Engels, and America's Political Parties," *The Wilson Quarterly* 2.1 (1978), pp. 90–104.
______. and Gary Marks. *It Didn't Happen Here: Why Socialism Failed in the United States* (New York: W.W. Norton & Company, 2000).
Lo, Andrew W. "Reading About the Financial Crisis: A 21-Book Review." *Journal of Economic Literature* 50.1 (2012), pp. 151–178.
Lordon, Frédéric. *Willing Slaves of Capital: Spinoza and Marx on Desire* (London: Verso, 2014).
Lowy, Michael. "Marx's Dialectic of Progress: Closed or Open?" *Socialism and Democracy*, 14:1 (2007), pp. 35–44, p. 35.
______. *Morning Star: Surrealism, Marxism, Anarchism, Situationism, Utopia* (Austin: University of Texas Press, 2009).
Lukács, Georg. *History and Class Consciousness: Studies in Marxist Dialectics* (Pontypool, Wales: Merlin Press, 2010).
______. *The Theory of the Novel* (London: Merlin Press, 1971).
Luxemburg, Rosa. *Socialism or Barbarism: Selected Writings*, edited by Paul Le Blanc and Helen C. Scott (London: Pluto Press, 2010).
______. *The Complete Works of Rosa Luxemburg, Volume I: Economic Writings*, edited by Peter Hudis, trans. by David Fernbach, Joseph Fracchia, and George Shriver (London & New York: Verso, 2013).
Lyotard, Jean-François. *Libidinal Economy*, trans. by Iain Hamilton Grant (London: Athlone Press, 1993).
MacEwan, Arthur. "Why Are We Still Socialists and Marxists After All This?" *Socialist Register* (1990), pp. 311–327.
MacGregor, David. *The Communist Ideal in Hegel and Marx* (London & New York: Routledge, 2015).
Macherey, Pierre. *A Theory of Literary Production*, trans. by Geoffrey Wall (London: Routledge, 1978).
Mack, Michael. *Contamination: Beyond Dialectics in Modern Literature, Science and Film* (Edinburgh: Edinburgh University Press, 2016), p. 2.
Macmillan, Chris. *Žižek and Communist Strategy: On the Disavowed Foundations of Global Capitalism* (Edinburgh: Edinburgh University Press, 2012).
Makdisi, Saree, Cesare Casarino, and Rebecca E. Karl, eds. *Marxism Beyond Marxism* (New York & London: Routledge, 1996).
Manaugh, Geoff. "Unsolving the City: An Interview with China Miéville" [online] http://www.bldgblog.com/2011/03/unsolving-the-city-an-interview-with-china-mieville/ [accessed 10/04/2017].
Marcuse, Herbert. *Reason and Revolution* (London: Routledge, 1986).
Marsh, Nicky. *Money. Finance, and Speculation in Recent British Fiction* (London: Continuum, 2007).
Martelle, Scott. *Blood Passion: The Ludlow Massacre and Class War in the American West* (New Brunswick, NJ: London: Rutgers University Press, 2008).
Martin, Randy. *The Financialization of Daily Life* (Philadelphia, Temple University Press, 2002).
Marx, Karl. *Capital: A Critique of Political Economy*, volume 1, trans. by Ben Fowkes (London: Penguin, 1990).
______. *Grundrisse: Foundations of the Critique of Political Economy (Rough Draft)*; trans. by Martin Nicolaus (London: Penguin, 1993).
______. *Surveys from Exile: Political Writings Volume 2*, introduced by David Fernbach (London & New York: Verso, 2010).
______. *The Communist Manifesto* (Oxford: Oxford University Press, 1992).
______. *The German Ideology* edited and with an introduction by Christopher John Arthur (London: Lawrence & Wishart, 1970).

______. *The German Ideology: Including Theses on Feuerbach and an Introduction to the Critique of Political Economy* (New York: Prometheus Books, 1998).
______, and Erich Fromm. *Marx's Concept of Man: Including Economic and Philosophical Manuscripts* (London: Bloomsbury, 2013).
______, and Friedrich Engels. *Marx and Engels Collected Works*, volume 40, Letters 1856–1859 (London: Lawrence & Wishart, 2010).
Mason, Paul. *Post-Capitalism: A Guide to Our Future* (London: Penguin, 2015).
Mazower, Mark. *Dark Continent: Europe's Twentieth Century* (London Penguin 1999).
McClure, John A. *Late Imperial Romance* (London: Verso, 1994).
McInerney, Jay. "The Uses of Invention," *The Guardian* [online] (17th September 2015) https://www.theguardian.com/books/2005/sep/17/fiction.vsnaipaul [accessed 28/11/16].
Mckinley, Vern P. *Financing Failure: A History of Bailouts* (California: Independent Institute, 2012).
McLaughlin, Kevin. "The Financial Imp: Ethics and Finance in Nineteenth-Century Fiction," *Novel: A Forum on Fiction* 29.2 (Winter 1996), pp. 165–183.
McLaughlin, Robert L. "Unreadable Stares: Imperial Narratives and the Colonial Gaze in *Gravity's Rainbow*" in *Pynchon Notes* 50–51 (2002).
McLellan, David, ed. *Karl Marx: Selected Writings* (Oxford: Oxford University Press, 2000).
McNally, David. *Monsters of the Market: Zombies, Vampires, and Global Capitalism* (Chicago, Illinois: Haymarket Books, 2012).
Medhurst, John. *That Option No Longer Exists: Britain 1974–76* (London: Zero Books, 2014).
Medovoi, Leerom. "The Biopolitical Unconscious: Toward an Eco-Marxist Literary Theory," *Mediations* 24.2 (2009), pp. 122–139, p. 122.
Meiksins Wood, Ellen. *The Retreat from Class: The New True Socialism* (London: Verso, 1986).
Merleau-Ponty, Maurice. *Adventures of the Dialectic* translated by Joseph Bien (London: Heinemann Educational 1974).
Miéville, China. "China Miéville's Top 10 Weird Fiction Books" *The Guardian* [online] Thursday 16th May 2002 [accessed 25/04/17].
______. "Marxism and Fantasy: Editorial Introduction," *Historical Materialism* 10.4 (2002), pp. 39–49.
______. "Marxism and Halloween. Socialism 2013" [podcast] 30th October 2013 https://www.youtube.com/watch?v=paCqiY1jwqc [accessed 11/04/2017].
______. *The City & the City* (London: Macmillan, 2009).
Miliband, Ralph. *Class War Conservatism and Other Essays*, introduced by Tariq Ali (London: Verso, 2015).
Miller, Keith. "Capital by John Lanchester: Review," 23rd February 2012, available at http://www.telegraph.co.uk/culture/books/bookreviews/9100944/Capital-by-John-Lanchester-review.html [accessed 04/08/2015].
Mirowski, Philip. *Never Let a Serious Crisis Go to Waste: How Neoliberalism Survived the Financial Meltdown* (London & New York: Verso, 2013).
Moseley, Fred. *Marx's Method in Capital: A Re-Examination*, edited by Fred Moseley (London: Prometheus, 1993).
Mouffe, Chantal. *The Return of the Political* (London & New York: Verso, 1993).
Moylan, Tom. *Demand the Impossible: Science Fiction and the Utopian Imagination*, edited by Raffaella Baccolini (Bern: Peter Lang, 2014).
Nealon, Christopher. "Reading on the Left," *Representations* 108.1 (2009), pp. 225–50.
Nealon, Jeffrey T. *Post-Postmodernism Or, the Cultural Logic of Just in Time Capitalism* (Stanford: Stanford University Press, 2012).
______, and Caren Irr, eds. *Rethinking the Frankfurt School* (Albany: SUNY Press, 2002).
Negri, Antonio. "Is It Possible to Be Communist Without Marx?" *Critical Horizons* 12.1 (2011), pp. 5–14.
Nelson, Carey, and Lawrence Grossberg, eds. *Marxism and the Interpretation of Culture* (Illinois: University of Illinois Press, 1988).

Newsinger, John. "Fantasy and Revolution: An Interview with China Miéville," *International Socialism* 88 (2000), pp. 153–63.
North, Joseph. *Literary Criticism: A Concise Political History* (Cambridge, Massachusetts: Harvard University Press, 2017).
O'Gormon, Daniel, and Robert Eaglestone, ed. *The Routledge Companion to Twenty-First Century Literary Fiction* (London: Routledge, 2018).
Ojeili, Chamsy. "Post-Marxism with Substance: Castoridiais and the Autonomy Project," *New Political Science* 23:2 (2001), pp. 225–239.
Ollman, Bertell. *Dance of the Dialectic: Steps in Marx's Method* (Urbana: University of Illinois Press, 2003).
Osborne, Peter. *How to Read Marx* (London: Granta, 2005).
Pahl, Ray. "Is the Emperor Naked? Some Comments on the Adequacy of Sociological Theory in Urban and Regional Research," *International Journal of Urban and Rural Research* 13 (1989), pp. 127–129.
Pak, Chris. *Terraforming: Ecopolitical Transformations and Environmentalism in Science Fiction* (Liverpool: Liverpool University Press, 2016).
Pakulski, Jan, and Malcolm Waters. *The Death of Class* (London: Sage, 2009).
Pendakis, Andrew, Jeff Diamanit, Nicholas Brown, Josh Robinson, and Imre Szeman. *Contemporary Marxist Theory: A Reader* (London & New York: Bloomsbury Academic, 2014).
Piketty, Thomas. *Capital in the Twenty-First Century*; trans. by Arthur Goldhammer (Harvard: Harvard University Press, 2014).
Poe, Edgar Allan. *Tales of Mystery and Imagination* (Herefordshire: Wordsworth Classics, 1993).
Prager, Jonas. "The Financial Crisis of 2007/8: Misaligned Incentives, Bank Mismanagement, and Troubling Policy Implications," *Economics, Management & Financial Markets* 8.2 (2013), pp. 11–56.
Procter, James. *Stuart Hall* (London & New York: Routledge, 2004), p. 1.
Pynchon, Thomas. *Against the Day* (London: Vintage, 2006).
______. *Bleeding Edge* (London: Vintage, 2014).
______. *Gravity's Rainbow* (London: Vintage, 2013).
______. "Journey Into the Mind of Watts," *The New York Times*, June 12th, 1966, available at https://www.nytimes.com/books/97/05/18/reviews/pynchon-watts.html [accessed 17/08/2015].
______. *Mason & Dixon* (London: Vintage, 1998).
Radstone, Susannah, and Bill Schwarz, eds. *Memory: Histories, Theories, Debates* (New York: Fordham University Press, 2010).
Ricciardi, Alessia. *The Ends of Mourning: Psychoanalysis, Literature, Film* (California: Stanford University Press, 2003).
Rich, Nathaniel. "The Thomas Pynchon Novel for the Snowden Era: A Review of Bleeding Edge," *The Atlantic* [online] (October 2013) http://www.theatlantic.com/magazine/archive/2013/10/losing-the-plot/309450/ [accessed 15/12/2016].
Rimmon-Kenan, Shlomith. *A Glance Beyond Doubt: Narration, Representation, Subjectivity* (Athens: Ohio University Press, 2015).
Robertson, Gillian, and John Rundell ed. *Rethinking Imagination: Culture and Creativity* (New York: Routledge, 1994).
Robinson, Kim Stanley. *Blue Mars* (London: HarperVoyager, 2009).
______. *Green Mars* (London: HarperVoyager, 2009).
______. *Red Mars* (London: HarperVoyager, 2009).
______. *The Martians* (London: HarperCollins, 1999).
Rupert, Mark, and Hazel Smith, eds. *Historical Materialism and Globalisation: Essays on Continuity and Change* (London: Routledge, 2016).
Russo, John, and Sherry Lee Linkon, eds. *New Working Class Studies* (Ithaca, NY: Cornell University Press, 2005).
Sanghera, Sathnam. "Confessions of the Man Who Caused the Credit Crunch: There's a New Kid on the Crunch-Lit Block—but the Books Don't Get Any Better," *The Times*, 20th April 2000, p. 8.

Sartre, Jean-Paul. *Critique of Dialectical Reason*; trans. by Alan Sheridan Smith and edited by Jonathan Ree (London: Verso, 1982).

______. *Search for a Method*, trans. by Hazel Barnes (London: Vintage, 1963).

______. *What Is Literature?* trans. by Benard Frechtman (New York: Routledge, 2001).

Scorsese, Martin, dir. *The Wolf of Wall Street* (Paramount Pictures, 2014).

Sedgwick, Eve Kosofsky. *The Coherence of Gothic Conventions* (London: Methuen, 1986).

Seed, David. *The Fictional Labyrinths of Thomas Pynchon* (Iowa City: University of Iowa Press, 1988).

Sees, David, ed. *A Companion to Science Fiction* (Oxford: Blackwell, 2005).

Severs, Jeffrey, and Christopher Leise. *Pynchon's Against the Day: A Corrupted Pilgrims Guide* (Newark: University of Delaware Press, 2011).

Shaw, Katy. *Crunch Lit* (London & New York: Bloomsbury, 2015).

Sheridan, Alan. *Michel Foucault: The Will to Truth* (London & New York: Tavistock, 1980).

Sherpe, Klaus, and James Gussen. "Reading the Aesthetics of Resistance: Ten Working Theses," *New German Critique* 30 (1983), pp. 97–105.

Sherry, Michael. *In the Shadow of War: The US Since the 1930s* (London: Yale University Press, 1995).

Sim, Stuart, ed. *Post-Marxism: A Reader* (London: Edinburgh University Press).

______. *Post-Marxism: An Intellectual History* (London & New York: Routledge, 2013).

Singer, Brian. "The Early Castoriadis: Socialism, Barbarism, and the Bureaucratic Thread," *Canadian Journal of Political and Social Theory*, 3 (1979), pp. 35–56.

______. "The Later Castoriadis: Institutions Under Interrogation," *Canadian Journal of Political and Social Theory* (1980), pp. 75–101.

Smith, Allan Lloyd. *American Gothic Fiction* (London: Continuum, 2004).

Smith, Murray E.G. *Global Capitalism in Crisis: Karl Marx and the Decay of the Profit System* (London: Fernwood Press, 2012).

Sokal, Alan, and Jean Bricmont. *Fashionable Nonsense: Postmodern Intellectuals' Abuse of Science* (New York: Picador, 1998).

______. *Intellectual Impostures* (London: Profile Books, 2003).

Sombart, Werner. *Why Is There No Socialism in the United States?* trans. by C.T. Husbands and Patricia M. Hocking (London: Palgrave, 1976).

Spiotta, Dana. *Eat the Document* (London: Scribner's, 2006).

______. *Lightning Field* (New York: Scribner's, 2002).

______. *Stone Arabia* (Edinburgh: Canongate, 2011).

Stedman Jones, Gareth. *Karl Marx: Greatness and Illusion* (London: Penguin Books, 2017).

Stern, Robert. "Hegel, British Idealism, and the Curious Case of the Concrete Universal," *British Journal for the History of Philosophy* 15.1 (2007), pp. 115–153.

Stiglitz, Joseph. *Globalization and Its Discontents* (London: Penguin, 2003).

Stockman, David. *The Great Deformation: The Corruption of Capitalism in America* (Philadelphia: Perseus, 2013).

Storey, John. *Cultural Theory and Popular Culture: An Introduction*, 3rd edition (Harlow: Prentice Hall, 2001).

Strange, Gerard. "Understanding the Fundamentals of Capital, the Crisis and the Alternatives: Marx's Legacy Beyond Revolutionary Marxism," *British Journal of Politics and International Relations* 15.1 (2013), pp. 107–124.

Strange, Susan. *Casino Capitalism* (Manchester: Manchester University Press, 2016).

Streck, Wolfgang. "How Will Capitalism End," *New Left Review* (May-June 2014), pp. 35–64.

______. *How Will Capitalism End? Essays on a Failing System* (London: Verso, 2016).

Stuckler, David, and Sanjay Basu. *The Body Economic: Why Austerity Kills* (New York: Basic Books, 2013).

Suvin, Darko. *Metamorphoses of Science Fiction: On the Poetics and History of a Literary Genre* (New Haven: Yale University Press, 1979).

Swiffen, Amy, and Joshua Nichols, eds. *The Ends of History: Questioning the Stakes of Historical Reason* (London: Routledge, 2014).

Swyngedouw, Erik. "The Communist Hypothesis and Revolutionary Capitalisms:

Exploring the Idea of Communist Geographies for the Twenty-first Century," *Antipode* 41.1 (2009), pp. 298–319.
Szeman, Imre. "Marxism After Marxism" in *Meditations* 24.1 (2008), pp. 190–197.
______, and Maria Whiteman. "Future Politics: An Interview with Kim Stanley Robinson," *Fiction Studies* 3.2 (2004), pp. 177–188.
Taylor, Fredrick. *The Berlin Wall, 13th August 1961–9th November 1989* (London: Bloomsbury, 2006).
Terdiman, Richard. *Present Past: Modernity and the Memory Crisis* (Ithaca & London: Cornell University Press, 2000).
Thacker, Eugene. *In the Dust of This Planet: Horror of Philosophy*, volume 1 (London: Zero Books, 2011).
Therborn, Goran. *From Marxism to Post-Marxism* (London: Verso, 2010).
Thoburn, Nicholas. "Do Not Be Afraid, Join Us, Come Back? on the 'Idea of Communism' in Our Time," *Cultural Critique* 84.1 (2013), pp. 1–34.
Thomas, Peter D. "The Communist Hypothesis and the Question of Organization," *Theory & Event*, 16.4 (2013).
Thomas, Samuel. *Pynchon and the Political* (New York & London: Routledge, 2007).
Tiffany, Daniel. "Cheap Signalling: Class Conflict and Diction in Avant-Garde Poetry" *Boston Review*, [online] http://www.bostonreview.net/poetry/daniel-tiffany-cheap-signaling-class-conflict-and-diction-avant-garde-poetry [accessed 15/07/16].
Tomalin, Claire. "Capital by John Lanchester—review" in *The Observer*, Sunday 4th March 2012, available at http://www.theguardian.com/books/2012/mar/04/capital-john-lanchester-review [accessed 08/06/17].
Tormey, Simon, and Jules Townshend. *Key Thinkers from Critical Theory to Post-Marxism* (London: SAGE Publications, 2006).
Torry, Harriet. "Germany Celebrates 25th Anniversary of Fall of the Berlin Wall: Merkel Hails Fall of Berlin Wall as Proof Dreams Can Come True," *The Wall Street Journal* 9th November 2014 [accessed 24/07/16].
Traverso, Enzo. *Left-Wing Melancholia: Marxism, History, and Memory* (New York: Columbia University Press, 2016).
Trimmer, Nicoline. *Do You Feel It Too? the Post-postmodern Syndrome in American Fiction at the Turn of Millennium* (Amsterdam: Rodopi, 2010).
Trotsky, Leon. *History of the Russian Revolution*, trans. by Max Eastman (London: Penguin Books, 1967).
Tucker, Robert C., ed. *The Lenin Anthology* (London & New York: W.W. Norton & Company, 1975).
Turl, Adam. "A Thousand Lost Worlds: Notes on Gothic Marxism" *Red Wedge* [online] http://www.redwedgemagazine.com/evicted-art-blog/a-thousand-lost-worlds-notes-on-Gothic-marxism [accessed 08/06/2017].
Varoufakis, Yanis. *And the Weak Suffer What They Must? Europe, Austerity, and the Threat to Global Stability* (New York: Nation Press, 2016).
Varsava, Jerry. "Thomas Pynchon and Postmodern Liberalism," *Canadian Review of American Studies* 25.3 (1995), pp. 63–101.
Varvogli, Aliki. "Radical Motherhood: Narcissism and Empathy in Russell Banks's *The Darling* and Dana Spiotta's *Eat the Document*," *Journal of American Studies*, 44 (2010), pp. 657–673.
Veggian, Henry. "Thomas Pynchon's *Against the Day*," in *Boundary* 35:1 (2008), pp. 197–215.
Vice, Sue, ed. *Psychoanalytic Criticism: A Reader* (Cambridge: Polity Press, 1996).
Walker, Gavin. "On Marxism's Field of Operation: Badiou and the Critique of Political Economy," *Historical Materialism* 20.2 (2012), pp. 39–74, p. 40.
Wark, Mckenzie. "A Functional Form Has Its Own Beauty: An Interview with Kim Stanley Robinson," *Los Angles Review of Books* [online] https://lareviewofbooks.org/article/a-functional-form-has-its-own-beauty-an-interview-with-kim-stanley-robinson/ [accessed 09/08/2017].
Watts, Cederic. *Literature and Money: Financial Myth and Literary Truth* (New York: Harvester Wheatsheaf, 1990).

Waugh, Patricia, and Jennifer Hodgson eds. *The Review of Contemporary Fiction: The Future of British Fiction* 32.3 (2012).
______. *Metafiction: The Theory and Practice of Self-Conscious Fiction* (London: Methuen, 1984).
Wayne, Teddy. *Apartment* (London: Bloomsbury, 2020).
Weiss, Peter. *The Aesthetics of Resistance*, volume 1, trans. by Joachim Neugroschel (Durham: Duke University Press, 2005).
Whitehead, Andreas. *Memory* (London & New York: Routledge, 2009).
Whitehead, Colson. *The Nickel Boys* (London: Fleet, 2019).
Williams, Raymond. "Base and Superstructure in Marxist Cultural Theory," *New Left Review* 1.82 (1973).
______. *Raymond Williams on Culture and Society: Essential Writings*, edited by Jim McGuigan (London: Sage, 2014).
______. *Towards 2000* (London: Hogarth Press, 1983).
Wilson, Japhy, and Erik Swyngedouw. *The Post-Political and Its Discontents: Spaces of Depoliticisation, Spectres of Radical Politics* (Edinburgh: Edinburgh University Press, 2015).
Winders, James A. "Poststructuralist Theory, Praxis and the Intellectual," *Contemporary Literature* 27.1 (1986), pp. 73–84, p. 74.
Witham, Nick. *The Cultural Left and the Reagan Era: US Protest and Central American Revolution* (London: I.B. Tauris, 2015).
Wolff, Robert Paul. *In Defense of Anarchism* (Berkeley: University of California Press, 1998).
______. "On Being an Anarchist and a Marxist," *Science & Society* 79.2 (2015), pp. 314–317.
Wolin, Richard. *Walter Benjamin: An Aesthetic of Redemption* (New York: Columbia University Press, 1982).
Woodson, Jacquleine. *Another Brooklyn* (London: Oneworld Publications, 2017).
______. *Brown Girl Dreaming* (New York: Penguin, 2014).
______. *Red at the Bone* (London: Weidenfeld & Nicolson, 2019).
Wright, Erik Olin. *Class Counts* (Cambridge: Cambridge University Press, 2010).
______. *Understanding Class* (London: Verso, 2015).
Zinn, Howard. *A Peoples History of the United States: Present* (London: Longman, 2003).
Žižek, Slavoj. "A Plea for Leninist Intolerance," *Critical Enquiry*, 28.2 (2002), pp. 542–566.
______. *Did Someone Say Totalitarianism? Five Interventions in the (Mis)use of a Notion* (London: Verso, 2001).
______. *First as Tragedy Then as Farce* (London & New York: Verso, 2009).
______. *Revolution at the Gates: Selected Writings on Lenin from 1917* (London & New York: Verso, 2002).
______. *The Sublime Object of Ideology* (London: Verso, 2008).
______. "Melancholy and the Act," *Critical Enquiry*, 26.4 (2000), pp. 657–681.
______, edited. *The Idea of Communism 2: The New York Conference* (London: Verso, 2013).
______, Frank Ruda, and Agon Hamza. *Reading Marx* (London: Polity Press, 2018).
______. and Taek-Gwang Lee edited *The Idea of Communism 3: The Seoul Conference* (London & New York: Verso, 2016).

Index

Milton Keynes UK
Ingram Content Group UK Ltd.
UKHW011627200224
438156UK00005B/197

9 781476 692265